# MUNCHAUSEN BY PROXY SYNDROME

## Misunderstood Child Abuse

Edited by

## Teresa F. Parnell
## Deborah O. Day

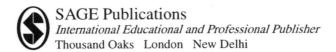

SAGE Publications
*International Educational and Professional Publisher*
Thousand Oaks  London  New Delhi

*For information:*

SAGE Publications, Inc.
2455 Teller Road
Thousand Oaks, California 91320
E-mail: order@sagepub.com

SAGE Publications Ltd.
6 Bonhill Street
London EC2A 4PU
United Kingdom

SAGE Publications India Pvt. Ltd.
M-32 Market
Greater Kailash I
New Delhi 110 048 India

Printed in the United States of America

*Library of Congress Cataloging-in-Publication Data*

Main entry under title:

Munchausen by proxy syndrome: misunderstood child abuse / edited by
 Teresa F. Parnell, Deborah O. Day.
  p. cm.
 Includes bibliographical references and index.
 ISBN 0-8039-5811-0 (cloth). — ISBN 0-8039-5812-9 (pbk.)
 1. Munchausen syndrome by proxy. I. Parnell, Teresa F. II. Day,
Deborah O.
RC569.5.M83M87 1997
616.85'822—dc21           97-4838

98 99 00 01 02 03 04 10 9 8 7 6 5 4 3 2

| | |
|---|---|
| *Acquiring Editor:* | C. Terry Hendrix |
| *Editorial Assistant:* | Dale Mary Grenfell |
| *Production Editor:* | Michèle Lingre |
| *Production Assistant:* | Denise Santoyo |
| *Typesetter/Designer:* | Christina Hill |
| *Indexer:* | Teri Greenberg |
| *Cover Designer:* | Candice Harman |
| *Print Buyer:* | Anna Chin |

# MUNCHAUSEN
# BY PROXY
# SYNDROME

*To Edward,*
*whose love and unwavering support*
*are an inspiration;*
*and to the other special people in my life—*
*Carol, Cam, Tiffany, Lulu, Cleo, and especially Nicholas*

*—Teresa Parnell*

*To Calvin, Ryan, and Lauren,*
*without whose love, patience, and support*
*this book would not have been written*

*—Deborah Day*

# Contents

# Foreword

Our own journey into the world of Munchausen by proxy syndrome and the unusual mix of patients, victims, therapists, attorneys, pediatricians, and social workers who inhabit this world began unexpectedly some 12 years ago. Encountering a surprising number of what at the time appeared to be a series of bizarre cases of factitious illness at our pediatric hospital started us on our own search to learn more about the nature of the disorder and how we could work therapeutically with these cases. A process of researching the mental health literature, encountering more cases, writing some journal papers, and consulting on patients with our colleagues around the United States revealed the unfortunate dearth of literature and clinical knowledge available to those working with these challenging cases; it also began a long and fruitful process that evolved into our own long commitment to the study and treatment of this disorder.

One of the most rewarding outcomes of this process was the bonus of developing long-distance collegial relationships with fellow professionals who were also crossing this uncharted terrain, equally eager to share observations, data, and clinical experiences. Drs. Parnell and Day are among the mental health professionals we have discovered as colleagues and have had the pleasure of collaborating with in professional presentations, informal cross-country consultations, and brainstorming sessions aimed at developing research ideas. Thus it is an honor for us to share some remarks on this contribution to the small but growing Munchausen by proxy syndrome literature—this edited book about the disorder.

The first series of chapters in this book thoroughly reviews the past and current literature on the basics of Munchausen by proxy syndrome, explicating the latest thinking on how these cases present in the pediatric setting, what we know about these families, and the process of making the diagnosis. But the major contribution of this particular volume comes in Part II, which addresses the psychotherapeutic treatment of the parent with the disorder as well as the child-victim, as up until now there has been little in the way of useful theory development or data available on successful treatment approaches. Much thought and practice have obviously gone into the chapters in this book that conceptualize the treatment process. The contributors offer many useful guidelines outlining the steps necessary for practitioners to develop trusting, supportive therapeutic relationships with perpetrator-parents in which those parents can begin to acknowledge their abuse of their children and their own dangerous deceptions, along with the parents' own histories of neglect, abuse, or other family secrets.

Many of us who work primarily in the pediatric, child abuse, and victim treatment arenas approach our work from a child-centered perspective, which sometimes leads us to have blind spots when it comes to taking the perspective of the parent or backing up to look more evenly at the family systems view of the problem. As adult therapists in a private practice independent of the world of children's hospitals, social services, or the courtroom, Drs. Parnell and Day have been able to immerse themselves in the world of the perpetrator-parent and the Munchausen by proxy family system with a level of empathy and openness that allows for new insights and productive working relationships. This is a very important contribution to the growing literature on this disorder.

The bizarre presentation of Munchausen by proxy syndrome, coupled with the sensationalism of the mass media treatment of this disorder (in no small part fostered by both the perpetrators and members of the legal profession who often enter unwittingly into their spheres), makes this work frequently difficult, and at times harrowing. Successful outcomes in these cases require not only treating the patients, but moving beyond that treatment to engage the social realm in a "therapeutic" manner, which many of us are untrained or ill equipped to do. For those who find themselves in this predicament, this book, with its attention to the details of every aspect of the process, will afford a welcome set of guideposts.

Judith A. Libow
Herbert A. Schreier
*Children's Hospital, Oakland*

# Preface

In 1989, a local child protection agency selected Dr. Deborah Day to evaluate a woman suspected of having perpetrated Munchausen by proxy syndrome abuse. This request came because of Dr. Day's years of experience with abuse perpetrators and victims, not because of any expertise she was thought to have in Munchausen by proxy syndrome. As awareness of the disorder slowly began to emerge in a local research/teaching hospital, more cases were suspected. Out of necessity, Dr. Day's experience with one case made her the local "expert" psychologist, as more requests came for evaluation and then treatment of these women and their child victims.

Of course, a single case does not make one an expert, especially where the stakes are as high as a child's life or the dissolution of a family. However, when we searched the literature in hopes of finding guidance from other professionals' experiences, we were disappointed. Excellent work had been done toward clarifying the diagnosis of Munchausen by proxy syndrome, or MBPS, and toward providing guidelines for identifying cases, by writers such as Drs. Roy Meadow, Herbert Schreier, Judith Libow, and Donna Rosenberg. Unfortunately, there was virtually no information for mental health professionals on psychological evaluation of and psychotherapy with perpetrators or victims. Therefore, we continued to learn by experience with these families, while watching knowledge of the syndrome grow in the research literature.

We have now been consulted in more than 30 suspected cases of Munchausen by proxy syndrome nationwide. We have also been contacted regarding approximately 10 additional suspected cases in which the professionals involved have been unable to arrange the comprehensive evaluations recommended. MBPS cases are extraordinarily overwhelming, and it is only through a team approach that we have been able to endure and learn so much.

Like other forms of child abuse, Munchausen by proxy syndrome raises many troubling issues, such as believability of the accusations, how to balance victim and perpetrator needs, and potential destruction of a family unit. So persuasive are the perpetrators, and so incomprehensible are some of the allegations, that at times we have had our own struggle with the veracity of allegations. We have also struggled with finding a needed balance in situations where one human being purposely victimizes another: recognizing the horror of some victims' experiences while acknowledging the pain that would lead perpetrators to be so severely detached from their children. We have also struggled with the issue of the safety of the child versus the loss associated with removal from family, recognizing that there is always potential for misidentification of cases.

The "one-case phenomenon" continues to confront us as we consult with other mental health professionals. MBPS is still so recently recognized that our psychologist colleagues are finding few communities in which there are "experts" in this diagnosis. Thus a clinician may find him- or herself handling a single case in the course of an entire career, and must scramble for ideas on the long-term management of the Munchausen by proxy family, especially for therapy models for treating the perpetrator.

Whereas these struggles regarding psychological evaluation and psychotherapy occur within the scope of our discipline, it is rarely within the mental health field that this syndrome first affects a community. The fields of medicine, child protection, social work, and the law are often already grappling with the impact of a case before mental health professionals are consulted. The broad community influence of the MBPS case demands multidisciplinary communication and cooperation for effective management. Such collaboration has been achieved by many of the contributors to this book through the development of a protocol for action in their community. Perhaps because of this protocol, a relatively large number of case investigations have resulted in acknowledgment by perpetrators of their actions. This in turn has opened the way for meaningful treatment of the perpetrators.

As our work continued with this fascinating population, we considered writing a book in the fall of 1992 to share the exciting advances being made in perpetrator therapy. In the meantime, Schreier and Libow published *Hurting for Love: Munchausen by Proxy Syndrome* (1993a), which provides a wonderful review of the literature and immensely interesting dynamic formulations of the MBPS perpetrator. We intend this book to be an extension of their work, with more insights into therapy and the multidisciplinary impacts of these cases.

The purposes of this volume are threefold: (a) to provide an overview of Munchausen by proxy syndrome; (b) to present an intensive, long-term psychotherapy model that has developed out of our work with acknowledged perpetrators; and (c) to increase understanding of the impact of MBPS cases on various disciplines, clarifying each discipline's role in case management and presenting techniques for handling cases from each perspective. In order to accomplish the third purpose, we have called upon the expertise of our colleagues in the fields of medicine, education, social work, law, and hospital administration. Without the contributions of Matthew Seibel, Robin Wilkinson, Toni Baker, Sue Whelan-Williams, Karen Palladino, and Ralph "Terry" Hadley, this book would lack a vital multidisciplinary focus.

There are, unfortunately, some perspectives that are not covered in this volume. We solicited chapters from such professionals as nurses, child protective service attorneys, gastroenterologists, and defense attorneys, but we found that many professionals who are experienced with MBPS cases were uncomfortable as first-time authors, and that those with more writing experience had limited exposure to the disorder.

Inasmuch as research into Munchausen by proxy syndrome represents a rapidly changing field of study, we hope to hear from our colleagues worldwide about their reactions to this book, so that we may add to and refine our perspective. We should note that, although many of our own chapters here carry the name of a single author, this merely reflects which of us assumed responsibility for the actual writing. We have worked jointly on the majority of the cases discussed in this volume and on formulating our ideas and hypotheses about this puzzling disorder.

# Acknowledgments

The ideas presented in this book have developed not only from the many conversations we have had regarding Munchausen by proxy syndrome, but also from the work of numerous other researchers and authors, discussions with participants at conferences, collaboration with colleagues, and, most important, our work with Munchausen by proxy perpetrators and their families. Additionally, the actual writing of the book was encouraged and supported in many ways by numerous individuals. We wish to acknowledge the contributions of the following persons.

For their collaboration at conferences, which was both enlightening and greatly appreciated, we thank Judith Libow, Ph.D.; John E. B. Myers, J.D.; Mercedes Ojeda-Castro, Ph.D.; Matthew Seibel, M.D.; Mary J. Sanders, Ph.D.; and Herbert Schreier, M.D.

For their input into various versions of the manuscript that became this book, we thank Helen Booth, M.A.; Sherrie Bourg Carter, Ph.D.; Barbara Daskam; William Daskam; Doug England, M.S.; Kay Marshall Strom; and L. Michael Honaker, Ph.D..

We also want to thank the following people, most of whom we have never met, who have published work in this area that has particularly challenged and inspired us: Kenneth Feldman, M.D.; Judith Libow, Ph.D.; Bernard Kahan, M.D.; Tona McGuire, Ph.D.; Roy Meadow, M.A., B.M., FRCP; Paul Robins, Ph.D.; Donna Rosenberg, M.D.; Martin Samuels, M.D.; Herbert Schreier, M.D.; Robin Sesan, Ph.D.; David Southall, M.D., MRCP; David Waller, M.D.; and Beatrice Yorker, J.D., R.N.

We thank the staff of Psychological Affiliates, Inc., especially Michele Simmons and Sheila Burgett, for their technical support, and the District Seven Florida Department of Health and Rehabilitative Services administrators, caseworkers, and legal department, not only for being willing to believe such abuse exists, but for working tirelessly to protect the young child-victims.

We are grateful to the Arnold Palmer Hospital for Children and Women and its Child Protection Team for recognizing this disorder, diligently working to establish a multidisciplinary team, and allowing us to be part of this groundbreaking work, and to our patients for trusting us enough to allow us to enter their secret world. We especially thank the first few mother-perpetrators whom we saw in therapy, who were aware that they were guinea pigs but allowed us to learn together.

Our thanks go also to our editor at Sage Publications, Terry Hendrix, and to senior editorial assistant Dale Grenfell, who believed in the project and gave us this opportunity.

Finally, we thank especially our families, for their patience, sacrifice, and support.

# Part I

## Identifying and Managing the Munchausen by Proxy Syndrome Case

# 1 An Overview

Teresa F. Parnell

> *Some patients consistently produce false stories and fabricate evidence, so causing themselves needless hospital investigations and operations. Here are described parents who, by falsification, caused their children innumerable harmful hospital procedures—a sort of Munchausen Syndrome by proxy.*
> *—Roy Meadow, "Munchausen Syndrome by Proxy: The Hinterland of Child Abuse," 1977*

As a pediatrician in Leeds, England, Roy Meadow (1977) encountered two young patients with puzzling symptoms that he described in a seminal paper.[1] The first case was that of a 6-year-old child, Kay, who was seen at three medical centers due to recurrent passing of foul-smelling, bloody urine throughout her young life. Since the age of 3 years, she had been on continuous antibiotics that produced secondary symptoms such as drug rashes, fever, and candidiasis. Medical professionals were especially puzzled by the intermittent nature of her symptoms. Purulent, bloody urine specimens were followed by clear ones within hours. Similarly, foul discharges on her vulva would be gone within the same day. Curiously, she otherwise appeared to be a healthy girl who was developing normally.

Kay's parents were described as most cooperative, and her mother always stayed with her in the hospital. The mother was further described as loving and concerned, but not as worried about the cause of the symptoms as were the doctors. Suspicions were thus raised by what seemed an unsolvable problem, the inconsistency of facts, and the mother's temperament.

Meadow and his colleagues decided to work under the assumption that everything about Kay's history and the subsequent medical investigations was false. They set out to test this theory by comparing urine specimens collected under strict supervision with those collected by the mother or left unattended in the mother's presence. Of the 57 specimens collected, the 45 collected by a nurse were normal, whereas the 12 collected by the mother or left in her presence were grossly abnormal. Analysis of a urine sample provided by Kay's mother further suggested that the unsupervised specimens contained some of the mother's urine.

The evidence suggested to Meadow and his colleagues that the mother had been adding her own urine or menstrual discharge to specimens of her daughter's urine. The consequences of her actions for Kay included

> 12 hospital admissions, seven major X-ray procedures . . . , six examinations under anaesthetic, five cystoscopies, unpleasant treatment with toxic drugs and eight antibiotics, catheterisations, vaginal pessaries, and bactericidal, fungicidal, and oestrogen creams; the laboratories had cultured her urine more than 150 times and had done many other tests; sixteen consultants had been involved in her care. (p. 344)

The mother denied interfering with her daughter's care. However, during the mother's outpatient psychiatric treatment, Kay's health remained good, with no urinary problems.

The second case involved Charles, who, since the age of 6 weeks, had recurrent, sudden attacks of vomiting and drowsiness associated with hypernatraemia. Upon arrival at the hospital, his plasma-sodium concentrations were elevated and his urine contained a great excess of sodium. However, extensive investigations at three medical centers showed his endocrine and renal systems were normal and that he excreted salt load efficiently. Between attacks, Charles, like Kay, appeared healthy and seemed to be developing normally.

By the time Charles was 14 months old, it became clear that his attacks happened only at home. His mother was then deliberately excluded from a prolonged hospital stay for Charles, and no illness recurred until the weekend she was allowed to visit. Thus the doctors believed that the illness must be caused by sodium administration, probably by the mother. Tragically, during the period in which arrangements were being made for the child, he "arrived at hospital one night, collapsed with extreme hypernatraemia, and died" (Meadow, 1977, p. 344).

Meadow noted that the cases of Kay and Charles were similar, and reminiscent of Munchausen syndrome.[2] However, instead of an individual presenting him- or herself to a physician with false or induced symptoms, the individual (the parent) presented her child, thus a "by proxy" form of Munchausen was described. Meadow's astute analyses and observations in this brief paper raised questions that are still being considered.

Specifically, Munchausen by proxy syndrome, or MBPS, is a form of child abuse in which a caretaker fabricates and/or induces illness in a child.[3] The caretaker then presents the child repeatedly for medical attention, all the while denying any knowledge of symptom origin. This form of child abuse can lead to physical and/or psychological damage to the victim, owing either to the direct actions of the perpetrator or to the intrusive medical procedures performed by doctors to diagnose the child's suspected illness. In 95% of cases, the child's mother is the perpetrator (Schreier & Libow, 1993a).[4]

Mother-perpetrators' actions cover a broad spectrum, from misrepresenting symptoms (Griffith & Slovik, 1989) to tampering with lab specimens (Verity, Winckworth, Burman, Stevens, & White, 1979), to actually creating symptoms of illness in their children. Symptom induction may range from seemingly innocuous under- or overmedicating (Meadow, 1982b; Schreier, 1992) to life-threatening actions such as suffocating (Boros & Brubaker, 1992), chronic poisoning (Nicol & Eccles, 1985), and injection of various substances (Halsey et al., 1983; Saulsbury, Chobanian, & Wilson, 1984). Perpetrating mothers are often quite ingenious in their techniques of misrepresenting or producing symptoms while avoiding detection. Reports in the literature include cases in which perpetrators spit into a central venous line (Rosenberg, 1987); injected oral, fecal, or vaginal excretions into an intravenous line or into the child (Halsey et al., 1983; Kohl, Pickering, & Dupree, 1978); contaminated urine or stool specimens with blood (Crouse, 1992; Outwater, Lipnick, Luban, Ravenscroft, & Ruley, 1981); and gave large doses of laxatives to the child (Berkner, Kastner, & Skolnick, 1988).

The resulting symptom profile in the child-victim often involves multiple organ systems, with a preponderance of gastrointestinal symptoms and seizures. This results in an often dizzying array of medical subspecialists becoming involved in the care of the child. The most commonly reported symptoms include bleeding, seizures, unconsciousness, apnea, diarrhea, vomiting, fever, and lethargy (Rosenberg, 1987; Schreier & Libow, 1993a). However, Schreier and Libow (1993a) have identified almost 100 additional symptoms presented in suspected cases.

The mother-perpetrator's chilling behavior often occurs against the backdrop of what is described as perfect, nurturing, self-sacrificing, and attentive parenting (Leeder, 1990). That a mother may deliberately harm her child in such a way, endangering the child's life and manipulating medical professionals, is, for many, unthinkable; the mere suggestion challenges a basic tenet of human motherhood. When expressed, these suspicions often engender passionate disbelief among physicians, nurses, and hospital administrators, who may rally to support the mother (Blix & Brack, 1988; Waller, 1983). Once this wave of resistance is partially squelched by confrontation of the perpetrator, the disbelief often extends to others who are drawn into the case, such as mental health professionals, child protection workers, attorneys, and judges (Feldman, 1994; Sheridan, 1989; Waller, 1983; Zitelli, Seltman, & Shannon, 1987). When confronted, these mothers invariably deny or seriously minimize their actions in spite of evidence to the contrary. They are quite convincing, and the literature is replete with examples of their persuasiveness.

Identification of Munchausen by proxy has been difficult at best. The mothers' attentiveness to their ill children and their cooperation with hospital staff belie their dangerous behavior. Additionally, the medical establishment has depended upon an obviously valid medical tradition of using parent-supplied medical histories and symptom reports for young child patients. As physicians are challenged with unexplained symptoms, they generally investigate more rigorously to determine the suspected illness.

In spite of detection difficulties, developing awareness and understanding of MBPS are resulting in increasing identification of cases. A library literature search completed in 1990 yielded 77 references to Munchausen by proxy syndrome between 1966 and May 1990; a similar search covering only May 1990 to July 1993 yielded 88 additional references. This included the first book on MBPS (Schreier & Libow, 1993a). More recently, even the popular media have turned their attention to these cases (Kellerman, 1993; "My Sister-in-Law," 1991; Wartik, 1994).

General guidelines for suspecting and then confirming cases of MBPS have emerged largely from the case study-based literature. They highlight aspects of the victim's illness, characteristics of the mother-perpetrator, and family dynamics. In the last of these areas there appears to be the least agreement. The dynamics of the Munchausen by proxy family system and of the perpetrator's family of origin are addressed only superficially in the early case studies. More information is currently emerging in the literature, but case studies are still being published that fail to report whether the researchers even asked pertinent questions regarding family dynamics—specifically, questions concerning perpetrators' histories of sexual and physical victimization.

Once a diagnosis of MBPS is suspected, a multidimensional approach is imperative, in order to secure confirmation of the diagnosis and plan for long-term management of the family. Confirmation of the suspected diagnosis is best obtained through a multidisciplinary panel that includes the professionals who have been working with the family and an expert consultant in this type of abuse. Only a team approach can ensure that the necessary components are present for confirmation of the diagnosis (i.e., a thorough medical evaluation of the child, verification of the child's medical history, independent review of medical records, psychosocial and psychological assessment of all family members, gathering of concrete evidence of intentional harm to the child, and ongoing collaboration of all caregivers involved with the family) while preventing continued deception by the alleged perpetrator through the splitting of professionals (Meadow, 1985; Rosenberg, 1987; Schreier & Libow, 1993a). Long-term management of the family must also include support from the judicial system.

Unfortunately, even when cases are identified, most professionals are ill equipped to deal with either the perpetrators or the child-victims of Munchausen by proxy syndrome (Kaufman, Coury, Pickrell, & McCleery, 1989). This may be especially true of psychologists and other mental health professionals. Schreier and Libow (1993a) report that only about 10% of journal papers on this topic have appeared in the psychological or psychiatric literature; the vast majority have appeared in pediatric journals. Additionally, these articles have mainly been case presentations, with little direction given regarding treatment. Nevertheless, mental health professionals are called upon increasingly, as in other types of child abuse, to help with these cases. The lack of therapy experience with MBPS is particularly problematic for clinicians, as treatment models are just beginning to be explicated.

The potentially fatal outcome of undetected Munchausen by proxy syndrome makes our understanding of this disorder gravely important. Significant accomplishments have been made in this field since Meadow's (1977) initial article. We now have some guidelines that provide direction for identification and verification of cases. However, much work is still needed if we are to understand the dynamics underlying MBPS (including the obvious gender issues raised by the predominance of mother-perpetrators) and to develop treatment models for the perpetrator, the child-victim, and the family. Additionally, efficient interdisciplinary collaboration is imperative if we hope to intervene effectively with these families. Early detection and effective intervention can be accomplished only through the continued education of all professionals who work with families of chronically medically ill children. The following chapters provide information for all practitioners who are struggling to deal with this mystifying disorder and all of its ramifications.

## Notes

1. Money and Werlwas (1976) had previously used the term *Munchausen by proxy* in describing a case of psychosocial dwarfism. In addition, cases had previously been described in the literature of parents' focus on their children's illness (Green & Solnit, 1964; Yudkin, 1961) and of nonaccidental poisoning (Kempe, 1975; Lansky & Erickson, 1974; Rogers et al., 1976). However, Meadow (1977) was the first to bring attention to the phenomenon of deliberate, persistent, and covert deception by a mother to meet her own needs with the result that unnecessary medical procedures were carried out on the child.

2. Munchausen syndrome is a psychiatric disorder in which otherwise healthy individuals seek surgical or other medical treatment for feigned or self-induced symptoms. Although there are earlier reports of fabricated illness in the medical literature, Dr. Richard Asher first applied the term *Munchausen syndrome* in 1951. Asher named the syndrome after an 18th-century German baron, Karl Freidrich Hieronymus von Münchhausen, who recounted dramatic tales based on his travels and was known as a skilled storyteller (Meadow & Lennert, 1984). These stories became the basis for R. E. Raspe's (1785) collection of fictitious tales of the travels and adventures of Baron von Munchausen (the corrupted English spelling), and the name of Munchausen became associated in general with outlandish storytelling.

3. The terms *Munchausen syndrome by proxy, Munchausen by proxy,* and *Munchausen by proxy syndrome* are used interchangeably to refer to the same disorder. However, Schreier and Libow (1993a) suggest that the name *Munchausen syndrome by proxy* erroneously implies that the syndrome is simply a variant of Munchausen syndrome. They argue that the similarity in names has engendered confusion about the relationship between these two distinct disorders. Therefore, they prefer the term *Munchausen by proxy syndrome*. Although Deborah Day and I are not sure this term provides much distinction, as the editors of this volume we have also chosen to use it throughout, in deference to the originality of Schreier and Libow's book and to the growing use of the shortened term *Munchausen by proxy*. The term *factitious disorder by proxy* is also used interchangeably with these terms, as discussed in Chapter 2.

4. Because only a small number of documented cases have involved fathers or other caretakers as perpetrators, the term *mother* is used in this volume interchangeably with terms such as *perpetrator* and *abusing parent*. Female pronouns are also used to refer to MBPS perpetrators.

# 2 Defining Munchausen by Proxy Syndrome

Teresa F. Parnell

> *For those cases that seem to fall at the edges of the definition of [Munchausen syndrome by proxy], it is worth remembering that the name applied to the child's circumstances is not as material as a careful assessment of the threatened harm to the child.*
> —*Donna Rosenberg, "Munchausen Syndrome by Proxy," 1994*

Dr. Richard Asher (1951) coined the term *Munchausen syndrome* when he saw similarities between his patients and the exaggerated storytelling of the infamous Baron von Münchhausen (see Parnell, Chapter 1, note 2, this volume). Dr. Asher worked with patients who told dramatic and plausible, but ultimately untruthful, stories about their medical symptoms, resulting in an astounding number of hospital admissions. He observed that his patients appeared to gain nothing definite from their fabrications except unnecessary, sometimes painful, medical procedures and perhaps the pleasure of deceiving many.

Asher's work directed attention to what at that time was a largely unrecognized disorder that has had many names, including *hospital addiction, polysurgical addiction,* and *factitious illness;* patients with this disorder have been called *hospital hoboes* and *peregrinating patients.* However, of all the labels, Munchausen syndrome has remained the most widely used (Sussman, 1989). Meadow references Munchausen syndrome in his classic 1977 article analyzing two cases in which parents, by falsification, caused their children innumerable harmful hospital procedures. Meadow notes the obvious similarities between the actions of Munchausen syndrome patients and the behavior of these parents, who were falsifying information regarding their children. Like Munchausen syndrome, the by-proxy form has been referred to by many names, including *Polle syndrome, Meadow's syndrome, Medea complex, child abuse, chronic nonaccidental poisoning,* and *factitious illness by proxy.* Although the terms *Munchausen syndrome* and *Munchausen syndrome by proxy* predominate in the research literature, the terms *factitious disorder* and *factitious disorder by proxy* are used in the major compendium of diagnostic categories, the *Diagnostic and Statistical Manual of Mental Disorders* (currently in its fourth edition, i.e., *DSM-IV;* American Psychiatric Association, 1994). Although the varied terminology can certainly be confusing, the connection between the terms *Munchausen syndrome by proxy* (or *Munchausen by proxy syndrome*) and *factitious disorder by proxy* is clearly established in the research literature.[1] There has also been some debate recently in the literature about shifting to the term *factitious disorder by proxy.* Starting with a discussion of Munchausen syndrome, I will explore in this chapter the formal diagnostic status of these disorders and, more important, how Munchausen by proxy syndrome is currently defined.

### Psychiatric Diagnosis of Munchausen Syndrome

Clarke and Melnick (1958) describe a classic case in their article "The Munchausen Syndrome or the Problem of Hospital Hoboes." The case involved a 36-year-old obese woman who had been admitted to the hospital as an emergency patient complaining of an earache with discharge, blurred vision, headache, and stiffness of the neck. Upon admission, she vomited, became suddenly unconscious, and had marked neck retraction. Clarke and Melnick provide the following medical details:

> An exploratory mastoidectomy was carried out but all structures reached were normal. Following this procedure she began to improve and twelve hours later was only drowsy; left-sided weakness and sensory disturbance could now be demonstrated. At this stage a functional component was suspected.
>
> Cerebrospinal fluid was normal in all respects, as was an electroencephalogram and other investigations. An x-ray of the skull, however, revealed bilateral, posterior parietal burr-holes and

she now admitted that she had been in another hospital ten years previously. The records concerning this hospitalization indicated that she had suffered a purulent meningitis but the responsible organism had not been discovered. Because of left-sided signs a ventriculogram to rule out brain abscess had been performed. She had recovered after appropriate treatment for the meningitis but left-sided signs persisted.

Gradually she improved and as she did so it became clear that many of her symptoms were either grossly exaggerated or actually feigned. The left-sided weakness and slight reflex changes however persisted and she had a constant pyrexia, occasionally a temperature of 104°F being made. In view of our suspicions, many attempts to check the thermometer readings were made, but under close observation and sampling at various sites an elevation was always recorded; however, she had none of the usual accompaniments of hyperpyrexia.

One day her belongings were searched and besides a number of broken thermometers her case record from another hospital was found. It now became clear that this woman had visited many hospitals, in each of them presenting the same problem and often staying for months. (p. 8)

After her ruse was discovered, the woman was transferred to another ward. Her temperature fell to normal, and she then left the hospital without her doctor's consent. Clarke and Melnick note that one feature of this case that was never explained was the woman's ability to produce a high temperature despite all the usual precautions of the nursing and medical staff.

In the third edition of the American Psychiatric Association's *Diagnostic and Statistical Manual of Mental Disorders* (*DSM-III;* 1980), the more generic term *factitious disorder with physical symptoms* is used to describe Munchausen syndrome, identifying it as one of three subtypes of the diagnostic category of factitious disorders. The category of factitious disorders in *DSM-III* also includes "factitious disorder with psychological symptoms," referring to the production or feigning of psychological symptoms, and "factitious disorder not otherwise specified," for patients not clearly meeting criteria for either diagnosis. Each of these three diagnoses can theoretically be made with one episode of feigning or induction. The repeated, or chronic, form of factitious disorder is still commonly referred to as Munchausen syndrome, even though this is not a *DSM* term (American Psychiatric Association, 1994; Taylor & Hyler, 1993). It is important to remember that genuine physical or psychological symptoms can coexist with factitious symptoms. In fact, complex combinations of real, exaggerated, invented, and induced symptoms can certainly occur.

The main theme for differential diagnosis of factitious disorder with physical symptoms is the intentional simulation of physical disease for the sole purpose of obtaining medical attention. The revised third edition of the *Diagnostic and Statistical Manual of Mental Disorders* (*DSM-III-R;* American Psychiatric Association, 1987) refined the criteria for factitious disorder by clarifying the central features of intentionality and motivation. The simulation of symptoms is considered intentional, but not under the conscious control of the patient. For instance, the person's ability to simulate illness while considering the timing of the simulation and planning for concealment of his or her actions suggests cognitive activity indicative of voluntary control. At the same time, the behavior has a compulsive quality in the sense that the person is unable to refrain from the behavior although aware of the potentially dangerous consequences—when facing discovery or even after confrontation. Barker (1962) remarks on the obsessional quality of these patients in his report on seven cases. He discovered that three of the patients had lengthy lists of hospitals they proposed to visit, with the symptoms to be fabricated at each hospital meticulously recorded. Voluntary control is, of course, subjective and can only be inferred by an outside observer.

In terms of motivation, *DSM-III-R* further clarifies that the person's goal is to assume the sick role in the absence of secondary gains such as those seen in episodes of malingering. Examples of secondary gain include financial compensation, avoiding work, and escaping criminal prosecution. Of course, patients may sometimes obtain such gains as a consequence of their "illness." This can make it difficult to distinguish whether this is their primary motivation for fabricating symptoms. Taylor and Hyler (1993) provide a three-dimensional model to represent three processes in factitious and related disorders: motivation, production of symptoms, and type of symptoms (see Figure 2.1). They state, "Factitious disorder is described by the space representing unconsciously motivated but voluntarily produced physical or psychological symptoms" (p. 83)

The study of Munchausen syndrome or factitious disorder has focused on physical symptoms, but has also included psychological or psychiatric symptoms, although these are far less common in patients' presentation (Feldman, Ford, & Reinhold, 1994). Further, when psychological symptoms do occur in factitious disorder, it is most often in combination with physical symptoms. The fabrication, exaggeration, and induction of physical symp-

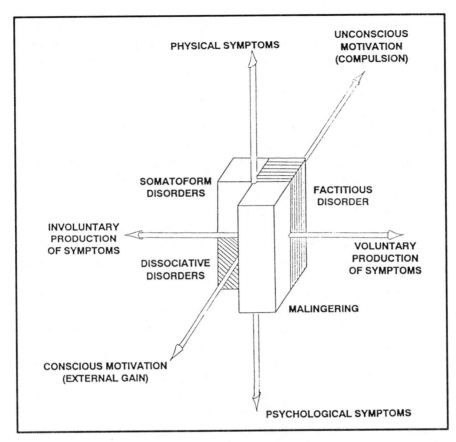

**Figure 2.1.** Factitious and Related Disorders Represented on a
Three-Dimensional Spectrum
SOURCE: Stuart Taylor and Stephen E. Hyler, "Update on Factitious Disorders,"
*International Journal of Psychiatry in Medicine,* 1993, *23*(1), 83. Copyright 1993
by the Baywood Publishing Company, Incorporated. Used by permission.

toms are difficult enough to confirm, but psychological symptoms are entirely subjective and even harder to confirm than physical symptoms. Feldman et al. (1994) report that the symptoms most commonly indicated with
this diagnosis are associated with bereavement supposedly caused by dramatic, elaborate, and generally false claims of familial death. The common
symptoms include depression, visual and auditory hallucinations, memory
loss, and suicidal thinking. However, cases of this type of factitious disorder
have involved syndromes as diverse as dementia, multiple personality disorder, and post-traumatic stress disorder. Generally, the process and goals

appear to be virtually the same as those in physical factitious disorder, but the patient exaggerates, feigns, or induces (e.g., through the use of drugs) psychological symptoms to obtain psychiatric medical care and to assume the sick role.

Pope, Jonas, and Jones (1982) have reported on nine cases of factitious psychosis. They reviewed the charts of 219 patients admitted consecutively to a research ward for the study of psychotic disorders over a 3½-year period. Of these, the researchers identified 14 patients (6.4%) with probable or definitive factitious psychosis. They excluded 5 patients who possibly exhibited real psychotic symptoms in addition to factitious psychotic symptoms. For selection of subjects, the researchers used the *DSM-III* criteria for factitious disorder with psychological symptoms, expanded to identify clear evidence of voluntary control of symptoms by the patient. These included alleged delusions or hallucinations not explained by an actual *DSM-III* psychotic disorder and clear evidence of voluntary control manifested by at least two of the following: (a) patient admission of voluntary control, (b) unconventional and fantastic symptoms lacking stereotypy, and (c) unconventional response of symptoms to the environment.

Pope et al. (1982) report many features of phenomenology, family history, and long-term outcome for the two men and seven women included in the sample. Some interesting features include the fact that no first-degree relatives (of the eight cases in which such information was available) were reported ever to have displayed psychotic symptoms, although there was evidence of other psychiatric diagnoses. The subjects all met the criteria for borderline or histrionic personality disorder (five met the criteria for both). Psychological testing performed on seven of the patients failed to diagnose factitious psychotic symptoms, even when the diagnosis was already suspected. Pope et al. remark on the serious consequences of undetected factitious psychotic symptoms. At the time of follow-up, 4 to 7 years after the index admission, the subjects scored close to a comparison group of schizophrenic patients and significantly worse than manic or schizoaffective patients on four indices of outcome (social and occupational function, level of residual symptoms, and global assessment). Eight patients spent months or years in mental hospitals during this period, four were hospitalized at the time of follow-up, and one committed suicide. All nine had been exposed to neuroleptics, and two displayed symptoms of tardive dyskinesia.

In my own experience, as an intern I treated a case of a 17-year-old female who had presented to a community mental health center over a 2-year period with symptoms of hallucinations, physical aggression, outrageous appearance, and bizarre behavior. The hallucinations consisted of her hearing voices directing her to harm others physically as well as her seeing "little green men." Due to a family history of bipolar disorder and schizophrenia, and her very convincing presentation, she was tried on numerous psychotropic medications, with no benefit, and participated in several tumultuous therapy contacts. I developed a therapeutic relationship with this patient (thanks to a very astute supervisor) by focusing on simply being in the room with her. I accepted her often outrageous presentation matter-of-factly, but also with an expectation that her everyday life problems would be addressed in the sessions. Soon the patient no longer needed to talk about "little green men" and instead dealt with familial dysfunction, a history of sexual abuse, and severe social anxiety. The psychotic symptoms rather quickly moved out of the focus of therapy, but with no direct acknowledgment of this shift. However, near termination of therapy the patient acknowledged her factitious symptoms, and we were able to address the meaning and purpose of her having promulgated these symptoms. Mainly, the patient used these symptoms simultaneously to alienate herself from painful social relationships and to seek an accepting, nurturing, and safe relationship with someone—a therapist. Of note, the patient's outrageous and histrionic physical appearance and gestures also gradually transformed during the course of therapy. Although this woman, a very talented artist, maintained a unique appearance, she became attractive rather than repulsive to her peers.

The fourth and most recent edition of the *Diagnostic and Statistical Manual of Mental Disorders* (*DSM-IV;* American Psychiatric Association, 1994) leaves the basic diagnostic criteria for factitious disorder unchanged except for the merging of the criteria for the two major categories. In order to account better for the commonly seen mixture of physical and psychological symptoms in many patients, one set of criteria is offered, from which the diagnostician then indicates the predominant type of symptoms (see Table 2.1).

## Psychiatric Diagnosis of Munchausen by Proxy Syndrome

The by-proxy form of Munchausen syndrome or factitious disorder was not specifically addressed by the American Psychiatric Association until *DSM-IV,* which acknowledges the syndrome in two specific ways. The first is inclusion of the by-proxy form of factitious disorder as an example of "factitious disorder not otherwise specified." *DSM-IV* states:

**TABLE 2.1** Diagnostic Criteria for Factitious Disorder

---

A.  Intentional production or feigning of physical or psychological signs or symptoms.
B.  The motivation for the behavior is to assume the sick role.
C.  External incentives for the behavior (such as economic gain, avoiding legal responsibility, or improving physical well-being, as in malingering) are absent.
Code based on type:
  *300.16 With Predominantly Psychological Signs and Symptoms:* if psychological signs and symptoms predominate in the clinical presentation.
  *300.19 With Predominantly Physical Signs and Symptoms:* if physical signs and symptoms predominate in the clinical presentation.
  *300.19 With Combined Psychological and Physical Signs and Symptoms:* if both psychological and physical signs and symptoms are present but neither predominates in the clinical presentation.

---

SOURCE: American Psychiatric Association (1994).

This category includes disorders with factitious symptoms that do not meet the criteria for Factitious Disorder. An example is factitious disorder by proxy: the intentional production or feigning of physical or psychological signs or symptoms in another person who is under the individual's care for the purpose of indirectly assuming the sick role. (p. 727)

The second and most important acknowledgment of Munchausen by proxy syndrome in *DSM-IV* is the category of "factitious disorder by proxy," described in Appendix B, "Criteria Sets and Axes Provided for Further Study." This appendix contains proposed categories that were suggested for inclusion in *DSM-IV* but were determined by the *DSM-IV* Task Force to require additional information prior to inclusion as official categories. This section provides a common language for researchers and clinicians who study psychiatric disorders. However, the criteria sets are considered tentative, and researchers are encouraged to study alternative criteria. The research criteria for factitious disorder by proxy are presented in Table 2.2.

Inclusion of these criteria in this *DSM-IV* appendix suggests that the psychiatric community is beginning to acknowledge Munchausen by proxy syndrome from a formal diagnostic standpoint, but that more research is needed to refine the criteria. Although *DSM-IV* is certainly the most widely accepted source of diagnostic nomenclature, the failure to include MBPS as

**TABLE 2.2**  Research Criteria for Factitious Disorder by Proxy

| | |
|---|---|
| A. | Intentional production or feigning of physical or psychological signs or symptoms in another person who is under the individual's care. |
| B. | The motivation for the perpetrator's behavior is to assume the sick role by proxy. |
| C. | External incentives for the behavior (such as economic gain) are absent. |
| D. | The behavior is not better accounted for by another mental disorder. |

SOURCE: American Psychiatric Association (1994, app. B).

a diagnosis at this time belies the fact that clinicians are "diagnosing" this syndrome out of necessity in order to protect children. Although clinicians and researchers are still grappling with the clarification of diagnostic parameters of this syndrome, significant agreement does exist within the published literature on the central features of MBPS (Meadow, 1982a, 1985; Samuels & Southall, 1992; Schreier & Libow, 1993a).

Components of the *DSM-IV* criteria raise a number of issues that must be considered and debated regarding the potential future diagnostic category of factitious disorder by proxy. First, the proposed category includes language almost identical to the factitious disorder category, suggesting that factitious disorder by proxy or Munchausen by proxy syndrome is an extension of factitious disorder. This implies more features in common between the two disorders than have been demonstrated in the research literature. Second, the traditional definition of Munchausen by proxy syndrome or factitious disorder by proxy has assumed the fabrication and/or induction of *physical* symptoms. There is virtually no support in the published literature for inclusion of *psychological* symptoms, except that these have been included for factitious disorder (Munchausen syndrome). Although psychological symptoms must be considered, a great deal of research is needed within the mental health and medical communities if we are to understand this component. (I present further discussion of psychological symptoms later in this chapter.)

Third, inclusion of the criterion that the motivation for the behavior must be "to assume the sick role" seems to reflect an attempt to explain the dynamics of the etiology of the disorder. This seems a superficial, one-dimensional explanation for the Munchausen behavior, and does not address why the perpetrator chooses the child rather than simply assuming the "sick role" herself. This criterion seems to reflect the early hypothesized explanation that perpetrators seek attention for themselves through their behavior, which is an inadequate and superficial explanation. As more cases are identified, understanding of the diverse and complex motives underlying MBPS is broadening. Clearly, more than one motive may be present, and motives may change over time. Most would agree with the inclusion of a criterion noting the absence of secondary gain for the perpetrator, such as monetary compensation. Although such external incentives for the behavior may be present, they are not the primary motivation. In its simplest form, the motivation for the behavior may be stated as follows: the maintenance of a relationship with medical practitioners to meet a plethora of psychological needs.[2]

Finally, the issue of intentionality arises again. As described previously in the case of Munchausen syndrome, the behaviors appear to be carefully planned and consciously concealed. Cases in which mother-perpetrators have been videotaped appear to support this description (Epstein, Markowitz, Gallo, Holmes, & Gryboski, 1987; Frost, Glaze, & Rosen, 1988; Rosen et al., 1983). My own clinical experience also suggests that these mothers know exactly what they are doing when they perpetrate these behaviors. In treatment, mother-perpetrators have acknowledged, described, and discussed their intents. They have revealed their thought processes before, during, and after perpetration. However, as indicated earlier, there is a compulsive quality to the behavior, such that even in the face of discovery and possibly dire consequences, these mothers are unable to stop themselves. Again, these mothers in therapy have indicated their awareness of the need to stop their behaviors but also their lack of self-control. Additionally, some evidence of dissociation exists (see Day, Chapter 9, this volume). Further, it seems that some mothers truly believe their children to be ill, or come to believe their own fantastic stories (Fisher, Mitchell, & Murdoch, 1993; Orenstein & Wasserman, 1986; Waller, 1983; Warner & Hathaway, 1984), even using the physicians' treatment as proof their children must be ill (Sanders, 1995b). It is difficult to detect when this becomes delusional; some authors have referred to the "delusional intensity of parental concern" (Woollcott, Aceto, Rutt, Bloom, & Glick, 1982) and to "quasi-delusional" thought processes (Ravenscroft & Hochheiser, 1980).

## The Relationship Between Munchausen Syndrome and MBPS

Although it is true that there are similarities between Munchausen syndrome and Munchausen by proxy syndrome, the latter should not be considered simply a variant or subset of the former. As noted above, both disorders obviously involve patients whose psychopathology is centered on simulating illness to bring them into contact with the medical profession in order to meet psychological needs. This central similarity does suggest a possible connection between the underlying dynamic motivations of the disorders. In fact, 10-25% of Munchausen by proxy perpetrators also produce or feign illness in themselves (Rosenberg, 1987). However, there seems to be a fundamental difference between the psychopathology of an individual who is willing to make herself suffer and that of one who is willing not only to watch but to create suffering in another human being, particularly her own helpless child. The sacrifice of another's physical well-being, and possibly his or her life, is far different from the sacrifice of one's own well-being. Munchausen by proxy syndrome is more a pathology of the parent-child relationship than a pathology of the self. We simply do not know enough about MBPS to assume that it involves the same dynamic formulation or motivation as that seen in Munchausen syndrome cases.

Whereas Munchausen syndrome patients (usually) stop short of suicide, the mortality rate for Munchausen by proxy victims, although impossible to gauge accurately at this time, has been reported to range from 9% (Rosenberg, 1987) to 31% (Alexander, Smith, & Stevenson, 1990) in samples where follow-up was available. An estimated 98% of Munchausen by proxy perpetrators are female (Rosenberg, 1987); in contrast, Munchausen patients are at least equally divided among men and women (Hyler & Sussman, 1981), although some sources suggest a higher incidence in men (American Psychiatric Association, 1987; Taylor & Hyler, 1993). The victims of Munchausen by proxy syndrome are also equally divided among male and female children (Rosenberg, 1987).

Of interest is a phenomenon noted in which some mother-perpetrators exhibit signs of Munchausen syndrome not only preceding the Munchausen by proxy abuse but following confrontation and removal of their children (Lee, 1979; Schreier & Libow, 1993). In one case in which my colleagues and I were involved, a mother of four children was alleged to have victimized two of her children with her Munchausen by proxy behavior. Her 20-month-old son had had 28 emergency room visits and hospitalizations in his young life, beginning shortly after birth. His purported medical problems included asthma, bronchitis, reflux, diarrhea, seizures, reactive airway disease, apnea, meningitis, and giardiasis. He had had an adenoidectomy and bilateral myringotomies with tube placement. He also had physical injuries secondary to possible physical abuse and neglect. The majority of his symptoms were not observed once the child was hospitalized. An older sibling, a 3-year-old girl, was allegedly sexually abused by two perpetrators on multiple occasions. As a result, the child underwent numerous investigations, including four pelvic examinations.

At the time of the initial child protective services investigation for Munchausen by proxy, the mother in this case reported little significant medical history for herself. She described a tonsillectomy as a child, hospitalizations for the births of her children, and allergies to three medications. She reported having an "extra mild" case of mitral valve prolapse with chest pains and kidney stones that caused her no problems. She claimed difficulties with her third pregnancy due to "secondary smoke" and "magnesium poisoning." However, the mother described herself during the psychological evaluation interview as being in good medical condition, with no medical problems and taking no medication. After removal of the children, their medical health improved rapidly, whereas the mother's medical well-being rapidly deteriorated. Within months of the evaluation, she had surgery to remove a kidney, which turned out to be a healthy, vital organ. This is a classic instance of a Munchausen by proxy mother who has lost access to her children and turned her medical obsession on herself.

Certainly, some Munchausen by proxy mother-perpetrators appear to have such a focus on illness that the object of their focus may be strongly related to opportunity or other factors (Smith & Ardern, 1989). Sigal, Gelkopf, and Meadow (1989) describe a situation in which a 2½-year-old child with factitious seizures was the subject of a case conference and supervision order. Several months later, there was an investigation regarding the child's sibling for blood-stained vomit and rashes. This lasted until the mother was treated for undiagnosed back problems. Then the original child was reported to be having seizures again, which were investigated for a lengthy period before it was determined that they were not occurring. At that time, the mother developed problems with her knee.

Waller (1983) also describes a case in which, after the mother was confronted, she did not keep a follow-up appointment. She had apparently been admitted to another hospital, "writhing in pain" and claiming she had appendicitis. She was so convincing in her portrayal of symptoms that she was taken to surgery in spite of being afebrile and having a normal blood count. Her appendix was normal.

At this time, the perpetrator of the Munchausen syndrome by proxy abuse would be given the diagnosis of "factitious disorder not otherwise specified." The child-victim would be given the diagnosis of "physical abuse of child." Of course, other Axis I or Axis II diagnoses may also be given for the perpetrator or victim when appropriate.

## The Continuum of Munchausen
## by Proxy Syndrome Cases

What behavior constitutes Munchausen by proxy syndrome? The research literature is a more useful source at this time for answering that question than any one diagnostic compendium. The central features of the definition of MBPS have remained fundamentally the same since Meadow's 1977 article and are captured in Rosenberg's landmark 1987 article (see Table 2.3.). Although the essential features have remained consistent over the past two decades, attempts to refine this diagnosis have raised interesting differential diagnostic issues, such as the continuum of severity of cases, induction of psychological symptoms, and the falsification of sexual abuse allegations.

A number of authors have suggested that the boundaries of what is considered Munchausen by proxy syndrome should be broadened (Rand, 1989, 1993); others argue that some parental behaviors are being considered variants of MBPS when they should not (Baldwin, 1994; Eminson & Postlethwaite, 1992). There is a continuum of parental response to a child's physical condition, be it ill or well, that ranges from adaptive to maladaptive. Maladaptive responses encompass both ends of a continuum, such that neglecting to seek medical attention for a child may be just as damaging as seeking medical attention for fabricated illness. These concepts have been presented diagrammatically by several authors in their attempts to delineate various parental patterns of health care seeking for their children. Eminson and Postlethwaite (1992) consider the parents' desire to consult for their children's symptoms, the agreement between parents and professionals on the need to consult, and the ability of the parents to distinguish their children's needs from their own. The result is a spectrum of health care seeking by parents for children (see Figures 2.2 and 2.3). Waring (1992) presents a "persistence algorithm" for consideration of the spectrum of parent persistence in seeking medical consultation for the child (see Figure 2.4). When a parent is persistent in seeking medical attention, the physician must ask whether that persistence is consistent with the reported symptoms and medical diagnosis. Thus, referring to Yudkin's (1961) suggestion that the physician must make two diagnoses (i.e., What is wrong with the child, if anything? and Why is the child being brought at this time?), Waring suggests that there should be congruence between the child's morbidity and the level of parent persistence. The first and second diagnoses are identical if persistence and morbidity are congruent. However, after the first diagnosis is made, if there is incongruence, then the physician must consider other second

**TABLE 2.3** Rosenberg's Definition of Munchausen by Proxy Syndrome

---

1. Illness in a child that is simulated (faked) and/or produced by a parent or someone who is in loco parentis;
2. presentation of the child for medical assessment and care, usually persistently, often resulting in multiple medical procedures;
3. denial of knowledge by the perpetrator of the etiology of the child's illness; and
4. acute symptoms and signs in the child abate when the child is separated from the perpetrator.

---

SOURCE: Rosenberg (1987, 1994).
NOTE: This definition excludes physical abuse only, sexual abuse only, and nonorganic failure to thrive only.

diagnoses, which may include parental falsification of symptoms, to explain the parent's persistence.

Cases of Munchausen by proxy syndrome fall somewhere along the continuum of parental response to a child's general physical condition, and within Munchausen by proxy cases there is certainly a continuum of severity. There is some disagreement as to where on this hypothetical continuum we should label the behavior Munchausen by proxy syndrome, with some extremists arguing that "true" MBPS involves only those cases in which symptoms are actually induced (Eminson & Postlethwaite, 1992). Generally, published discussions have attempted to divide Munchausen by proxy behavior into roughly three levels, suggesting mild, moderate, and severe MBPS (Baldwin, 1994; Kinscherff & Famularo, 1991; Libow & Schreier, 1986; Meadow, 1985). However, the parameters of these levels are not consistent among authors, and a variety of terms have been used to describe the activities and actors involved (e.g., doctor shopping, perceived illness, fabricated illness, enforced invalidism, help seeker, doctor addict, active inducer, extreme illness exaggeration, symptom overemphasis, misperception). The categories are determined on the basis of such factors as symptom frequency, potential lethality, and motivation of the perpetrator. Also considered is the method of symptom simulation, such as exaggerating real illness, fabricating illness, fabricating plus nonintrusive actions (e.g., altering lab specimens), or induction of symptoms. These categorizations generally exclude cases in which the mother-perpetrator is using the child to communicate emotional distress, the fabrication is not considered chronic or severe, and the perpetrator readily acknowledges her behavior and accepts help when confronted.

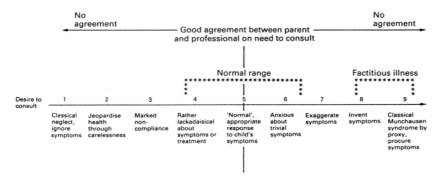

**Figure 2.2.** Parent's Desire to Consult for Their Child's Symptoms
SOURCE: D. M. Eminson and R. J. Postlethwaite, "Factitious Illness: Recognition and Management," *Archives of Disease in Childhood,* 1992, *67,* 1511. Copyright 1992 by the BMJ Publishing Group. Used by permission.

In general, these categorizations have not proven useful, and they may in fact be counterproductive to the goal of protecting children. First, many cases of Munchausen by proxy syndrome are mixtures of exaggeration, false reporting, and induction (Geelhoed & Pemberton, 1985; Hvizdala & Gellady, 1978). Second, the motivation of the perpetrator is often unclear until much later in the therapeutic process. Generally, perpetrators are quite manipulative and deceptive; they can easily present explanations for their behavior that seem benign and plausible (e.g., "I just wanted help for my child"; "The hospital is the only place I felt wanted"; "I just couldn't handle the kids on my own anymore"; "I didn't understand the doctor's instructions"). In fact, my colleagues and I are discovering in therapy with this population that one common component in these cases is alleviation of intrapsychic or familial distress (see Chapters 8, 9, and 10). However, this does not lessen the potential for harm to the child from the parent's actions, regardless of the motivation.

Third, the willingness of the perpetrator to acknowledge her behavior and accept psychological assistance is, of course, vital to rehabilitation and prognosis. However, this should not be used to determine type or severity. I am familiar with cases in which the perpetrators, once confronted, confessed, but vehemently insisted that the incidents in which they were caught were the only incidents of fabrication or induction in which they had participated. However, these mother-perpetrators have much later, in the safety of the therapeutic relationship, acknowledged additional incidents.[3] Of most con-

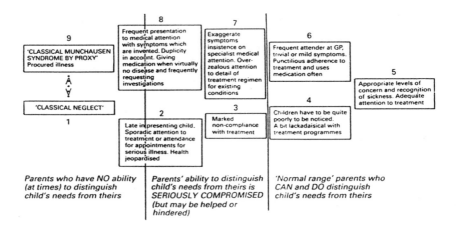

**Figure 2.3.** The Spectrum of Health Care Seeking by Parents for Their Children
SOURCE: D. M. Eminson and R. J. Postlethwaite, "Factitious Illness: Recognition and Management," *Archives of Disease in Childhood,* 1992, *67,* 1511. Copyright 1992 by the BMJ Publishing Group. Used by permission.

cern, however, is the tendency to minimize a mother-perpetrator's actions by indicating that the case involves "one episode" or "only exaggeration." Consider the case described below.

For almost 3 years, concerns regarding a diagnosis of Munchausen by proxy syndrome appeared in the medical records of a boy who was removed from his mother's care at almost 4 years of age. The child reportedly exhibited colic, croup, gagging and choking, chronic diarrhea, blood in his stool, blood in his mouth, fevers, apnea, cyanosis, staring spells, blue spells, drop attacks, possible seizures, sinusitis, chronic rhinitis, asthma, dust allergies, food allergies, salmonella enteritis, mild eczema, and hematemesis. He had multiple medical workups, including gastroenterology, neurology, allergy, and audiology, on an inpatient and outpatient basis. Multiple tests and laboratory studies resulted in normal or unremarkable findings, a number of his medical difficulties had no known etiology, and seizure activity was never witnessed or confirmed by physicians. In spite of all his problems, the child continued to grow and thrive. Following confrontation of the boy's parents and referral to therapy (but before the abuse report was made), this child was being referred by his parents for social security disability. The boy's 6-year-old brother also had problems, including vomiting, diarrhea, coughing,

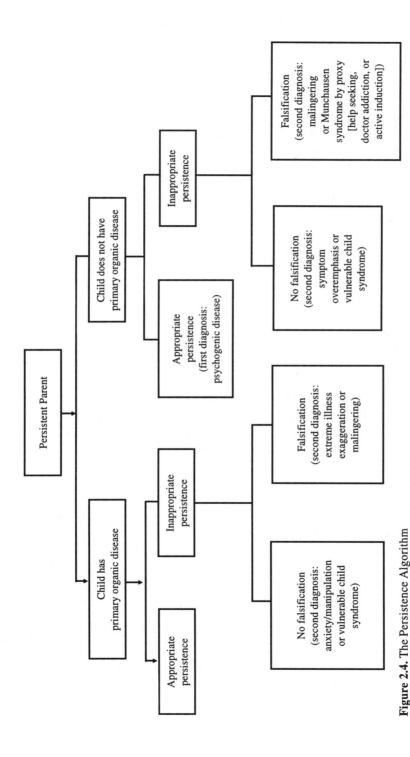

**Figure 2.4.** The Persistence Algorithm

NOTE: The most common pathway is depicted with arrowheads.

SOURCE: William W. Waring, "The Persistent Parent," *American Journal of Diseases of Children*, 1992, *146*, 754. Copyright 1992 by the American Medical Association. Used by permission.

crying, and sleep difficulties as an infant. Multiple episodes of otitis media were followed by surgery for insertion of tubes. Fluctuating hearing loss was recorded, with bilateral amplification suggested at one point. However, the child had normal hearing for a year prior to the investigation. In spite of this, the mother reportedly sought techniques and special education programs not recommended by the audiologist. The child continued to wear amplification devices in spite of normal hearing until his school ultimately refused to allow this. An abuse report was eventually made, accusing the mother of falsely reporting or exaggerating medical symptoms and of excessively medicating the two boys.

In this case the mother agreed that she was excessively anxious regarding the children's physical well-being, may have overreacted to symptoms, and had difficulty communicating effectively with physicians. The court appointed a consultant with experience in Munchausen by proxy cases to assist the therapist and the psychiatrist treating the perpetrator. The psychiatrist assured the consultant that he was an "expert" on Munchausen by proxy syndrome due to his experiences with several cases as a resident. He insisted that a diagnosis of Munchausen by proxy should be applied only to cases of induction of symptoms, and therefore this mother-perpetrator was only an anxious, caring mother who had difficulty communicating with physicians. The doctor went so far as to suggest that the mother was being victimized by the child protective system and that her psychiatric depression would remit if only she could be reunited with her children. The court ultimately agreed, and the children were returned home prior to any acknowledgment by the mother of her behavior. No further information about the case has been available.

Cases involving "only one episode" or "just exaggeration" can still be dangerous. The potential for iatrogenic harm exists any time a false medical history is provided to a physician. Additionally, a mother's need to have a sick child, combined with simulation of illness, can lead to actual physical illness in the child. Also, even "single episodes" or cases of "only exaggeration" hide other intrapsychic or intrafamilial issues that are not being addressed and place children at risk for psychological morbidity, including Munchausen syndrome in the child-victim (Croft & Jervis, 1989; McGuire & Feldman, 1989). Of most concern is the potential for the Munchausen by proxy behavior to escalate. Such a case may progress from the exaggeration of episodes of real illness to the fabrication of symptoms, to the induction of symptoms, all with a single child-victim. This escalation may occur as the mother-perpetrator finds that her needs are met through this behavior and thus wishes to ensure continuation of her contact with the medical profession. Conversely, if the physician response to the child's "illness" is not satisfying to the mother, she may become desperate enough to escalate her behavior. There are also cases in which the "single episode" is one in which the mother begins with a serious or life-threatening form of induction, with apparently little or no history of fabrication. It is interesting to note that these cases rarely involve other forms of physical abuse that are not within the context of MBPS.

Subsequent to their article "Three Forms of Factitious Illness in Children: When Is It Munchausen Syndrome by Proxy?" (Libow & Schreier, 1986), Schreier and Libow (1993a) state clearly that a mother does not need to induce illness to be classified as displaying Munchausen by proxy syndrome; rather, an individual can manifest the syndrome through such actions as misrepresenting history, fabricating symptoms, and altering lab specimens (p. 66). They suggest that, as with Munchausen syndrome, there may be forms of Munchausen by proxy syndrome that are less dramatic, less compulsive, and less serious than others. Additionally, they state that persons displaying MBPS may range from mothers who resort infrequently to the behavior during periods of stress to those who pursue the behavior compulsively as a course of life. Ultimately, all of these variations constitute serious and potentially lethal child abuse.

So how do we classify these patients? Certainly, as with all categorical systems, such distinctions have some utility for identification, communication, and research as we grapple with understanding this disorder. While recognizing that each mother-perpetrator is unique, we can hope to further our understanding by looking at the similarities among these women. However, we must also view each case in light of its own unique set of circumstances, considering the actions taken by the mother, the risk to the child, the actual physical and psychological harm to the child, the mother's ability to acknowledge some or all of her behavior, and the mother's involvement in treatment. Additionally, for this information to be useful in treatment planning and case management, we must also take note of such factors as the parent-child bond, other parenting skills, and overall functioning of the family system. Consideration of each of these issues can be especially useful in those cases that seem to fall around the edges of Munchausen by proxy syndrome. It can serve to keep us focused on the experience of the child, regardless of what we try to label the mother. None of these issues alone can be used to categorize a mother-perpetrator in any meaningful way.

## Psychological Munchausen by Proxy Syndrome

One emerging issue in the Munchausen by proxy syndrome classification arena is the inclusion of fabricated or induced psychological symptoms as mentioned in the *DSM-IV* research criteria. The research literature to date has defined and discussed Munchausen by proxy in terms of physical symptoms in child-victims. Virtually nothing is known about the fabrication or inducement of psychological symptoms. The psychological impact or consequences for child-victims of Munchausen by proxy abuse is beginning to be discussed in the literature (Bools, Neale, & Meadow, 1993; McGuire & Feldman, 1989; Schreier & Libow, 1993a; see also Day and Ojeda-Castro, Chapter 12, this volume), but that is a separate issue from the mother-perpetrator's intentionally inducing such symptoms. Only one case, discussed below (Fisher et al., 1993), really meets the criteria if the guideline is "factitious disorder with psychological symptoms" in the *DSM-IV* compendium. However, if we broaden that perspective because of the unique nature of Munchausen by proxy syndrome, several potentially troubling forms emerge.

First, as with Munchausen syndrome, psychological Munchausen by proxy can refer to fabricating, exaggerating, or inducing the child-victim's emotional symptoms or behavioral problems to obtain psychological or psychiatric care for the child. Second, it can refer to the perpetrator's actually inducing the psychiatric illness of factitious disorder with physical symptoms by teaching the child to simulate or induce physical symptoms on his or her own. This may also include covert manipulation that leads the child to develop psychogenic symptoms—in other words, genuine symptoms whose origins are emotional (e.g., psychogenic vomiting).

Fisher et al. (1993) describe the first case reported in the literature of psychiatric illness as the focus of the Munchausen by proxy mother-perpetrator. However, the case actually represents a complex situation involving fabricated allergies, "confirmed" sexual abuse, and coached psychotic symptoms.

The child, 10 years old by the time he met Fisher and colleagues, was apparently a healthy infant who was fed a strict vegetarian diet until 4 years of age, due to supposed allergies. The child was seen by multiple doctors, who found no objective evidence of allergies. A developmental assessment was requested because of behavioral problems, and the assessment revealed normal development at 4 years old. However, by the time the child was 7 years old, his behavioral problems apparently escalated to the point where he was placed in foster care for 6 months. After being returned to his mother, he alleged sexual abuse by his mother's stepfather, which Fisher et al. indicate was "confirmed." The boy responded well to therapy, and the mother obtained services and support from many agencies. Throughout this time, the mother insisted that no one else appreciated the severity of the child's difficulties; she also maintained that allergies were the cause of his problems.

Shortly after the boy's therapy was terminated, his mother began reporting that he was exhibiting bizarre behavior, including hallucinations of jungles and animals, and an apparition of his mother coming to attack him with a knife. Fisher et al. (1993) note, "The 'apparition' (his 'bad mother') would leave his room and he would call for his 'good mother' to come to him—which she would immediately do" (p. 701). Because of the child's fear of these hallucinations, he and his mother reportedly developed a system of "passwords." His mother further described the boy as oppositional, destructive, and a compulsive stealer of food. Following a psychiatric consultation, he was diagnosed as paranoid schizophrenic. His treatment included large doses of multivitamins, psychotropic medication, and visits to medical doctors, faith healers, spiritualists, and priests.

When the child was seen on an outpatient basis, his mental status examination was normal; further, he could produce only vague reports of his experiences. Due to the discrepancy between these observations and his diagnosis, he was hospitalized, and during his hospitalization he was observed to be physically healthy and able to tolerate foods to which his mother said he was allergic. He exhibited no psychotic symptoms, even with termination of his medication, and exhibited few behavioral problems, except during visits from his mother. Fisher et al. report that it was later learned that the mother provided detailed descriptions of symptoms to her son because she insisted he had "total amnesia." The mother was confronted with the doctors' suspicions of fabrication and coaching, which she denied. However, she participated in psychotherapy and achieved what would be considered a somewhat favorable outcome.

Fisher et al. (1993) make some interesting observations regarding the spectrum of parental behavior with fabricated symptoms and possible Munchausen by proxy. They describe the child as being maintained in a "position of illness" (medical or psychiatric) in order to deflect attention from other issues. An example seen commonly by mental health professionals is the dysfunctional family system that demands a psychiatric diagnosis for a child to avoid acknowledging familial causal factors. Alternatively, parents may insist that a child's behavioral disturbance has a medical cause, to avoid the fear of accepting a diagnosis of a chronic psychiatric condition. When the parents' position is not validated or their demands for treatment are not met, they may exhibit a pattern of changing physicians until they find one who will agree with their perspective, give the child the preferred diagnosis, or perform some validating treatment such as medication or out-of-home placement. The parents further blame the physicians they leave for forcing them to find other professionals because the physicians refuse to perceive the child's problem accurately or to treat the child's problem correctly. Fisher et al. suggest that these somewhat more common parental behaviors "may be the beginning of movement along an increasing spectrum of factitious disorder from belief in illness to actual falsification" (p. 703).

Another case report that may be considered under this category is presented by Katz, Mazer, and Litt (1985), who report a case of "anorexia nervosa by proxy." They describe a 17-year-old female with self-induced weight loss of 12.3 kg, reducing her weight to 39.6 kg over a 2-month period. The girl accomplished this by restricting her caloric intake to 300-400 calories a day, undertaking 2 hours of aerobic exercise per day, and participating in team sports. Of note, Katz et al. indicate that the adolescent displayed no evidence of severe body distortion or preoccupation with body size. In fact, she acknowledged she was too thin and reported having difficulty increasing her food intake because of her mother's close observation. Rather, the mother was perceived as preoccupied with food and dieting and was herself quite thin. As the patient's treatment progressed, including weight gain, she was satisfied and comfortable with her appearance, whereas her mother fretted that her daughter would look too heavy and complained about her own weight gain. Katz et al. propose that the patient's development of anorexia nervosa was the result of "parental preference for extreme thinness." In other words, the parent's expectations regarding weight, transmitted through overt and covert pressure, were sufficient to cause symptoms of a psychiatric illness with serious physical consequences.

The second manifestation of psychological Munchausen by proxy syndrome is the psychological induction of physical symptoms. The psychiatric problem the parent is able to induce in the child is factitious disorder with physical symptoms; the parent accomplishes this by coaching the child to simulate or induce physical symptoms. This may range from encouraging illness behavior through overt or covert parental manipulation to directly teaching the child to simulate or induce physical symptoms. The child may or may not be fully aware of this process and the expectations for production of symptoms. Some child-victims may be able to articulate that their mothers told them to display symptoms, whereas other children may display emotionally driven symptoms (e.g., vomiting when stressed) that have their origins in covert maternal manipulation. There is certainly a fine line between factitious disorder with physical symptoms, which develops in a child independent of the parent, and parent-induced factitious disorder with physical symptoms.

Croft and Jervis (1989) present a case of a 4-year-old boy who repeatedly feigned epileptic fits after a history of his mother's first fabricating and then coaching such fits. He reportedly presented at 2 years of age to a hospital's outpatient pediatric department for episodes of cyanosis, but no abnormality was found. Again at 3 years of age he presented with episodes of shaking and unconsciousness, with no abnormality found. At 4 years of age a diagnosis of epilepsy was made after the mother continued to report that he had fits, and he was treated with sodium valporate. He was admitted to the hospital 3 months later because of these fits and was independently observed to have episodes of apparent unconsciousness and trembling. However, curiously, he could be easily aroused with the mention of a favorite food. Feigning was suspected, and the diagnosis of epilepsy, as well as the treatment, was withdrawn. No mention was made at this point of psychotherapy or of intervention by child protective services.

The mother apparently continued to claim the child was having fits, however, which resulted in a referral for psychiatric intervention. In spite of this intervention, the mother continued to bring the boy to the hospital reporting fits, and he continued to feign further fits upon hospital admission. A very enlightening case conference was conducted that included the family doctor and the head teacher of the boy's school.[4] The family doctor reported that the child had been "brought to the surgery 130 times," which was in addition to "35 visits to the hospital accident and emergency department" (Croft & Jervis, 1989, p. 740). Additionally, the teacher reported that the boy told her his mother "trained him to simulate epileptic fits by falling off his chair, shivering, and flickering his eyes" (p. 741). Of additional concern, the child apparently feigned fits at school even with his mother not present, "because mummy said I should" (p. 741). He further suggested that his mother rewarded him with food or drink when he feigned these fits.[4]

Croft and Jervis (1989), noting that Munchausen syndrome had not been previously described in a child of this age, point out that their 4-year-old patient displayed features typical of Munchausen syndrome in adults, albeit trained by his mother, perhaps sufficient to warrant such a diagnosis. Munchausen syndrome has been reported to develop independent of a parent's encouraging symptoms or coaching symptoms (Reich, Lazarus, Kelly, & Rogers, 1977; Sale & Kalucy, 1980; Sanders, 1995b). Tec, in 1975, stated that he was reporting the first case to his knowledge of Munchausen syndrome in a child in his brief report on a 10½-year-old. The case presents a timid, unathletic boy who feared bodily injury and whose father wanted him to be a powerful football player. The boy's symptoms began before football practice, although they were sufficiently mild that his father insisted he play. His symptoms escalated over the following months to include stiff neck, muscle spasms, headaches, abdominal pains, unusual gait, and anorexia nervosa. Following a psychiatric consultation with the family, Tec recommended a vacation away from home; during this vacation, the boy was almost symptom free. The mother and child later resisted Tec's recommendation that the boy go to a boarding school, and the child minimized the improvement he had experienced on his successful vacation. Apparently, the family did ultimately accept Tec's recommendations, and the boy returned to school and did well. Interestingly, this article, written before Meadow's classic article on MBPS in 1977, also mentions that the parents requested exploratory laparotomy on the child and restricted the activity level recommended by the physician because the child did not feel well.

Sneed and Bell (1976) have reported a case of a 10-year-old boy who fabricated symptoms and presented pebbles as factitiously passed renal stones. Although the child was credited with producing the symptoms and physical evidence of a medical condition, the authors also raise questions about the possible collusion of the child's mother. Gilbert, Pierse, and Mitchell (1987) report a case of a 13-year-old boy who presented with a complaint of persistent otalgia resulting in numerous unnecessary investigations and two unnecessary operative procedures. The boy ultimately admitted placing beetroot juice in his ear to simulate a cerebrospinal fluid leak. Although suspicions of the mother's involvement were not proven, the authors report a number of concerns, such as the medical sophistication necessary to create this fabrication, the mother's domineering handling of her son, her presence at his bedside, her support of the hospital staff, her previous employment in health care, and her reaction upon detection of the boy's ruse. The question arises: Are early reports of Munchausen syndrome in children actually extensions of undiscovered previous perpetration of Munchausen by proxy syndrome? At the very least, we must consider the possible role of the parent in inducing such disorders.

Once a parent has successfully induced factitious disorder psychogenic symptoms in the child, who now maintains the factitious disorder with physical symptoms, the parent's responsibility becomes invisible—the parent's original behavior becomes both difficult to detect and impossible to confirm. If this is a calculated plan by the parent, the possibilities are chilling.

Schreier and Libow (1993a) describe the case of Danny, who presented to the hospital in moderate respiratory distress after coming in contact with three asthma-inducing conditions when his mother dropped him off at a park. A nurse overheard Danny's mother, who was sitting on his bed, say to him several times, "You can't breathe." Soon after, Danny suffered a respiratory arrest resulting in moderate to severe brain damage and profound memory loss. Schreier and Libow (1993a) note that the mother was completely calm during the respiratory arrest. There were other troubling observations as well, such as the child's adopting "a sickly, helpless position" when the mother was emotionally withholding and throwing himself from his hospital bed, causing a self-induced fracture.

Danny's case is an example of the difficulty of "proving" Munchausen by proxy in cases in which physical induction is not confirmed, but the symptoms are dangerous nonetheless. Parents in some cases may be able to manipulate their children subtly, in ways that may never be detected. It was only by chance that Danny's mother's behavior was observed, and the observation came too late to help Danny.[5] Schreier and Libow suggest that when Munchausen by proxy behavior starts early and continues through childhood, the continuance of the behavior is ego-syntonic for mother and child. Although Danny displayed behaviors consistent with Munchausen syndrome (e.g., self-injury, taking extra medication, claiming an allergic reaction to food), Schreier and Libow caution against applying the diagnosis of Munchausen syndrome to the child, because the behavior serves to perpetuate a different relationship—one with the mother, not the doctor.

The dynamics described by Schreier and Libow (1993a) were present in a case of psychogenic vomiting in which my colleagues and I were involved. By the age of 6 years, Tammy had in excess of 40 hospitalizations for a range of symptoms, including fever of unknown origin, chronic vomiting, chronic diarrhea, and repeated sepsis. She had 14 central lines placed, and both the central line and her nasogastric tube were repeatedly discovered to have been pulled out. Her mother stated to various individuals that Tammy had respiratory arrest every year, had suffered nerve damage due to a virus and so would never eat like a normal person, had never been able to eat solid foods, and needed a multiple organ transplant. Further, because she allegedly had a damaged immune system, Tammy was unable to attend school or social activities. By 17 months of age, Tammy was observed to induce vomiting when stressed or in the presence of the mother. She had been seen in five major medical centers along the West Coast, and had received a broad range of diagnoses, including severe neuropathic motility disorder, pseudo-obstruction syndrome, gastroenteritis with persistent vomiting, sinusitis, tacigastria, food aversion, psychogenic vomiting, central line infection, cardiac arrest, thrombocytopenia, seizures, and anemia. In spite of all this, she had multiple normal medical workups, and was initially well nourished and appeared healthy. She would improve upon admission, but shortly before discharge or right after discharge she would become gravely ill again. She failed to respond positively to any changes of diet. However, her condition improved on three occasions when she was separated from her mother. Further, she would eat solid foods with the encouragement of other family members, but never in the presence of her mother.

Tammy's mother, who had been trained as a nurse, initially reported an unremarkable and happy childhood. Upon closer inquiry, however, she did acknowledge to the home health care nurses a history of anger and neglect in the household. Additionally, she and each of her four female siblings had become pregnant and left home before completing high school. She reported that she had had 12 operations as a child for nonspecific conditions, although no records were obtained. She openly admitted that she met all of her emotional needs through her three children, indicating that they were her only happiness and that only they cared about her. Yet, curiously, when asked to provide her marital history, she referred to her children by number and not by name. Further, she could not remain focused on her marriage, but instead drifted to Tammy's medical history. She repeatedly used plural first-person pronouns (we, us, our) in speaking about Tammy's medical conditions and treatment. Her persistent flat affect changed only when she was relating her daughter's medical history, during which she became increasingly animated and was quite detailed in her descriptions. However, she lied about and/or embellished several aspects of this history. She described her husband as uninvolved with the family. Her only friendships were with several mothers she had met in the hospital, one of whom was later accused of Munchausen by proxy.

A possible diagnosis of Munchausen by proxy was considered several times, but could not be confirmed. On one occasion, the possibility was raised by a resident physician, who was promptly corrected in the medical records by the senior physician. Finally, at 6 years of age, at the end of a 4-month hospitalization, Tammy's condition was as follows: She was totally dependent upon hyperalimentation for nutrition, wore a surgical mask at all times, was receiving sandoglobulin shots for a damaged immune system, wore diapers, and sucked a pacifier constantly. She stated upon admission that she would die during her stay. When a central line was to be removed, she stated that her mother would be angry. She disclosed that she vomited when her mother wanted her to and that she knew when this was based on various cues her mother gave her. Another abuse report was made, and Tammy was again separated from her mother.

Before she left the hospital, Tammy was thriving on a combination of tube feedings and voluntary intake by mouth. She received no sandoglobulin and discontinued wearing a surgical mask. She played with other children and was quite energetic, with no illness. She did not wear diapers or use a pacifier except during the weekends when her mother was allowed to visit her in the hospital. On several occasions when other people were talking about her mother in her presence, she spontaneously gagged until she vomited. Also, she continued to be preoccupied with her body and to feign pain as a method of avoidance. In spite of these continued behaviors, she began to thrive; within 2 months of discharge, she was receiving all of her nutrition from solid foods. Upon follow-up, her primary care physician stated that the only treatment she was receiving was "no treatment" and the removal of her mother. Tammy today remains a physically healthy young girl with no eating problems.

Although Tammy's extensive medical history is certainly suggestive of more than induced psychogenic vomiting, fabrication, or exaggeration, no evidence of induced physical symptoms was ever obtained. Tests conducted on her blood, stool, and urine were negative on three occasions. No one ever observed any direct inducement of symptoms by Tammy's mother. Speculation remains that at some point the mother induced physical illness, but at the point of removal of the mother Tammy's symptoms had come under her own control, although clearly with overt and covert encouragement from her mother. Both Tammy and her mother had become invested in Tammy's remaining ill, with Tammy seeking to maintain the only mother-daughter relationship she had ever known. Unfortunately, the cost to Tammy was brain damage, which she sustained during a medical procedure.

A number of articles addressing Munchausen by proxy syndrome mention the children's appearing to adopt their parents' perceptions of illness and the children's complicity with the bogus symptoms. This may range from a child's simply believing the parent's perspective, to not telling about the parent's secret activities, to fabricating symptoms him- or herself. Children believe what they are told by adults, and they model adults' behavior, especially learning from their interaction with parents. It is not feasible to expect young children to make differentiations about the illness perspectives of their mothers that even doctors sometimes cannot detect. Waller (1983) questions whether a young child is capable of colluding in a parent's scheme to produce the appearance of illness. However, in a case he reports, the child was aware his mother was placing blood in his urine specimens but never volunteered the information. When finally asked about it, the child stated clearly, "Mommy put it in there."

Crouse (1992) notes that there is a strong tendency for the child-victim to "adopt the mythic symptoms as genuine and to begin to express them as his or her own" (p. 250). Sigal et al. (1989) discuss children's loss of the ability to distinguish the reality of symptoms within their own bodies due to continued fabrications and exaggerations. It becomes impossible for children to tell when and if they are sick if their perceptions have constantly been invalidated. Sigal et al. also suggest that child-victims may participate in the production of symptoms because they fear abandonment by their mothers if they stop being sick. Warner and Hathaway (1984) propose that the mother molds the child into an invalid and the child becomes extremely dependent on the mother.

Woollcott et al. (1982) present four cases of "doctor shopping" with older victims in which the child-victims' complicity is quite evident. Two of these cases in particular involved teenage patients with complex medical histories, excessive school absences, and no peer relationships who "co-operated" in the illness presentation. The presentation was clearly driven by the mother in one case and by both parents in the other. One teenager, a 17-year-old male, had not attended school for 5 years, thought he might die, fainted several times, was preoccupied with physical discomforts, and was symbiotically bonded to his mother. The other, a 13½-year-old female, was described as believing she was ill and overly dependent on her mother to the exclusion of her peers. These case reports suggest clear damage to the psychosocial development of these children as a result of the illness focus in their lives.

Single and Henry (1991) describe another interesting parent-child dyad. In this case, the father presented his 11-year-old son to school and child protection professionals as having cystic fibrosis and as having been abused by his stepmother. The father appeared more interested in financial gain and the opportunity to discredit his wife than in deceiving medical professionals, leading Single and Henry to question a Munchausen by proxy diagnosis. Of concern for this discussion, however, is that the boy genuinely believed he had a serious illness. He talked about having had life-threatening cystic fibrosis, which was now cured (after the father's ruse had been detected), while also indicating that he had a new illness. His father apparently had informed him that as a result, he would be unable to walk and would die.

Further, the boy believed the illness was caused by his stepmother's hitting him in the head, which was supported by his recent history of "fever and headaches."

Meadow (1984) describes cases of fictitious epilepsy among 32 children and 4 adults. For 21 of the children, the presentation consisted only of a story of seizures, with no symptom induction. The consequences for the children were the typical array of unnecessary investigative procedures, referral to specialists, prescription drugs, and so on. The children were also excessively absent from school, and many were kept from typical childhood activities. Of lasting concern, however, is what Meadow terms "chronic invalidism" as a result of being brought up to believe one is ill. Meadow discusses several children who, although now over 18 years old, continued to live with their mothers and believed they had epilepsy because their mothers continued to report false seizures. Further, he describes children who had independently adopted the illness presentation and others who now spent their adulthoods presenting themselves to doctors with false illness stories. The most unconscionable example Meadow provides concerns a young man who, although physically normal, does not walk because he was brought up to believe he could not. Although it may seem incredible that some adults cannot determine the presence or absence of physical illness symptoms within their own bodies, Meadow reminds us: "A child who has been told for more than 10 years that he or she has disabling epilepsy will most likely carry permanent illness behaviour into adulthood. Only the more resilient will manage to escape from the family pressures and become independent and healthy in adult life" (p. 26). Meadow describes these patients as having been programmed into permanent illness behavior.

The most thought-provoking and integrated discussion of these issues in the literature to date is found in the work of psychologist Mary Sanders. In a recent paper, Sanders (1995b) discusses older child-victims who are invited to collude or participate in their illness stories.[6] She defines symptom coaching as "the invitation the parent may give to the child to participate in symptom production" (p. 423). She asks of the case, Is the child colluding with the parent or actually unaware that the parent is creating or inducing illness? Sanders suggests a continuum with regard to the level of collusion:

1. *Naïveté:* Children who do not know their symptoms are being produced. This probably accounts for most child-victims.
2. *Passive acceptance:* Children who are somewhat aware of the deception or abuse but go along without offering information about how they

may appear ill. However, if directly asked, these children may reveal their knowledge. (It is important to note that asking children directly is a frequently overlooked tool.)

3. *Active participation:* Children who actively participate in creation of their illness stories by fabricating or exaggerating symptoms. Sanders points out, however, that these children are unlikely to appreciate the serious consequences of their behavior. Therefore, they may be active with regard to illness behaviors but naive as to the consequences. These children may also genuinely believe the illness stories when they participate.

4. *Active harm:* Children who actually participate in creating their own symptoms and engage in self-harm. The motivation of such children may be to maintain their relationships with their mothers, not with doctors.

Sanders further questions the extent of intentionality on the child's part in colluding with symptom production by reminding us that it is difficult to diagnose intentionality in the adult or the child. She therefore suggests that clinicians should remain aware of both conscious and unconscious factors when making treatment decisions. The child-victim's motivation for collusion appears to revolve primarily around maintaining the relationship with the mother in some way or avoiding the threatened alternative. A child may collude in order to maintain the only life he or she knows. Further, Sanders summarizes some of the suggestions regarding symptom collusion mentioned in the case literature. As described above, this includes such issues as the child seeking to retain his or her mother's love, fear of object loss, and wanting to protect the parent by hiding the abuse. A *folie a deux,* or shared delusion, may also develop, in which the child-victim takes on the parent's false illness belief in the context of their enmeshed relationship and the child's isolation from others due to his or her "illness."

Consideration of the subtle interactions surrounding illness presentation reaffirms the need for full family assessment (as discussed elsewhere in this book) in order for the clinician to understand the Munchausen by proxy allegations. Additionally, when a child presents with Munchausen syndrome, a careful analysis should still be done that considers all possible explanations in the context of the parent-child relationships. This second type of induction of psychological symptoms, such as the induction of factitious disorder, is particularly troubling due to the obvious long-term psychological consequences for the child. When the child begins to participate in the illness presentation, the ability of outside agencies (e.g., child protective services) to intervene becomes increasingly difficult. The arena of "psychological Munchausen by proxy" needs considerable analysis before we will know how to differentiate these cases and understand all of their implications.

## MBPS and False Allegations of Abuse

Another area coming to the forefront in the study of Munchausen by proxy syndrome is that of false physical and sexual abuse allegations. Libow and Schreier (1986) describe the following case:

Jessica was [a] five-year-old Hispanic girl who lived with her mother, Ms. T., and an older brother. An actively involved grand-mother lived nearby. According to Ms. T., this child had been sexually abused by a female relative when she was left with her for a month at age two. Since that time, Ms. T. had repeatedly brought Jessica to the emergency room with complaints of painful urination and vaginal irritation. Following several examinations in the emergency room and outpatient visits over the course of several months with no physical findings, the family was referred for psychiatric services. Ms. T. reiterated her concerns that the child had been permanently damaged by the molestation and indicated that she would never work again, allow no babysitters except the grand-mother, and protect Jessica by preventing any further contact with other children.

In a play session, the child separated easily from her mother, did not appear to be uncomfortable or distressed, and was able to play in a relaxed manner with a family of anatomically correct dolls. Ms. T., however, appeared highly anxious and paranoid, and voiced fears that the therapist would have her child removed from her by Protective Services. After two follow-up visits, Ms. T. started to miss therapy appointments and began taking Jessica to a new private physician. With some misleading clinical data she convinced this pediatrician to do a vaginal examination of the child under anesthesia and two 24-hour observations at the hospital. There were no significant findings and when finally identified and contacted by the therapist, this physician expressed frustration and outrage at having been tricked by the mother. Numerous efforts to resume therapeutic visits with Ms. T. and Jessica met with refusals and appointment failures. At last contact Ms. T. indicated she was seeking yet another physician to diagnose her child's problem. (p. 607)

Concerns regarding false allegations of sexual abuse are not new (Benedek & Schetky, 1985; Goodwin, Sahd, & Rada, 1978; Jones & McGraw, 1987; Peters, 1976), but a fervor has been created with recent debates regarding false abuse memories (see Loftus, 1993; Myers, 1994). Although children are certainly capable of telling untruths (Bussey, Lee, & Grimbeek, 1993), they are not generally inclined to create false statements of abuse outside of parental influence (Green & Schetky, 1988). False allegations of child abuse promulgated by parents may arise for a variety of reasons, including revenge against the accused, the desire for leverage in child custody disputes, and mental illness in the parent. False allegations encompass intentional fabrication, false belief that the child has been abused, and unintentional misinterpretation or distortion. Parents may induce physical signs of sexual trauma to bolster their sexual abuse allegations.

Situations do arise, especially with young children, when parents believe their children have been sexually abused due to some reasonable external signs, but confirmation cannot be obtained. If a child's contact with a suspected perpetrator continues, such as in a shared custody arrangement following divorce, the parent may feel frantic to know the truth and to protect the child. Although such a parent may become anxious and hypervigilant, he or she is usually relieved by negative findings, maintains consistent medical and mental health contacts, and seeks to follow the directives of clinicians. This is certainly more difficult in those cases where the allegations remain unclear, even from a professional standpoint. The parent's reaction to this uncertainty, or to abuse suspicions that are not confirmed, is of concern when the parent begins to engage in behaviors that are potentially damaging to the child in order to prove that abuse has occurred. This may involve repeatedly questioning the child, including audiotaping or videotaping the child's play and/or statements. Sometimes parents are encouraged by attorneys, therapists, or agencies involved in investigating abuse allegations to record their children's statements. A parent who suspects abuse may also present the child for repeated medical and/or psychological evaluation. Although obtaining a second opinion may certainly be appropriate in some cases, sometimes parents obtain multiple opinions. Rather than being relieved by negative findings, some parents may become increasingly agitated when their suspicions are not confirmed. This scenario may be most likely to occur in a custody or visitation dispute, but that is not always the case.

As in Waring's (1992) conceptualization of the persistent parent, if the child in such a case truly has been abused, then the parent's persistence is warranted. However, if the child has not been abused, then the persistence becomes pathological. Unfortunately, it is not always possible to establish definitively whether or not a child has been abused. Therefore, the clinician must look at how the parent interacts with the child and with medical/mental health professionals to determine whether the parent is seeking intervention for the benefit of the child as opposed to furthering her own agenda. Differentiation between the overly anxious parent and the pathological parent is, again, based upon what the parent does to confirm or deny the allegations. How far does she go? Does she lose the child's best interest in the process? As in medical Munchausen by proxy, does the child merely become an object, with each new intervention designed to meet the parent's needs rather than to confirm or disprove the abuse? Further, can the parent accept reasonable reassurances from competent evaluators? Thus sexual or physical abuse allegations may become the focus of the fabrication and the manner in which the mother-perpetrator maintains her relationship with the medical (or mental health) community.

Herman-Giddens and Berson (1989) describe 17 cases in which parents' focus on their children's genitals resulted in bizarre, invasive, and abusive genital care practices. The sample came from a retrospective review of 790 cases (over a 4-year period) presenting to a child protection team with suspicion of sexual abuse. The parents' behaviors included painful washing of the children's genitalia, frequent and ritualistic inspections of the genitalia, and applications of creams and medicinal preparations. Herman-Giddens and Berson describe the parents' behaviors as falling into three categories. Type I cases, of which there were 8, were those that included a ritualistic focus on and handling of the child's genitals. All of these cases involved a mother and/or grandmother, with a father also participating in one case. Type II cases, of which there were 6, involved a genital focus with a Munchausen by proxy syndrome component. In these cases, the parents gave long histories of their children's genital problems, resulting in numerous medical examinations and procedures, but without documentation of the alleged problems. Six mothers and/or grandmothers and one father participated in these cases. In Type III cases, of which there were 3, the behavior masked overt sexual abuse. Only one mother or grandmother participated in these cases; three fathers were involved. Parents in the Type I group most frequently reported that their genitals had been washed or inspected this way when they were children, or that these "hygiene" practices were necessary to stop odor. These parents were the most amenable to changing their behaviors with guidance on appropriate genital care. Type II and Type III parents described events such as diaper rashes or urinary tract infections as "legitimating" their behavior. However, this included situations in which years had passed since the initial events.

Although the child-victims were being evaluated for sexual abuse, Herman-Giddens and Berson do not clearly indicate whether the perpetrating parents, specifically the Type II parents, were presenting the children with false abuse allegations. Rather, they suggest more that the parents were focused on the children's having medical conditions involving the genito-urinary system. The authors do clearly state that the behavior in all cases constituted abuse. As is typical with Munchausen by proxy syndrome, there was poor compliance among the parents with referrals for mental health services. Additionally, there was a lack of understanding on the part of mental health professionals regarding the harmful consequences of the behaviors and confusion on the part of child protection agencies as to whether the practices constituted abuse or "acceptable, medically indicated care."

Although the parallel between false allegations of abuse and Munchausen by proxy syndrome had been drawn previously by several writers (Goodwin, 1982; Guyer & Ash, 1986; Libow & Schreier, 1986), Rand (1990) was the first to discuss false sexual abuse allegations as a variant of Munchausen by proxy syndrome termed "contemporary-type" MBPS. The mother-perpetrator fabricates or induces the idea that the child has been molested, then presents the child to professionals in the victim rather than the patient role. Rand (1990, 1993) has largely discussed contemporary-type Munchausen by proxy in the context of divorce and child custody disputes. Schreier and Libow (1993a) assert that the behavior Rand addresses does not constitute Munchausen by proxy behavior, because of the context and motives of the allegations. However, they consider that false sexual abuse allegations may be part of Munchausen by proxy presentation when the motivation for the fabrication is the maintenance of a relationship with the medical system. Their perspective is similar to Meadow's (1993a) sample of cases in which false sexual abuse allegations occurred in the absence of a child custody dispute and in the context of other Munchausen by proxy abuse.

I concur with Meadow's (1993a) definition (and Schreier and Libow's opinion) of false allegations of abuse related to Munchausen by proxy syndrome as referring to allegations of abuse, predominantly sexual, fabricated by the mother but not in the context of parental separation, divorce, or child custody disputes. In some way the mother generally encourages or teaches the child to substantiate the allegations of sexual abuse. The false allegations of abuse occur in the context of the Munchausen by proxy syndrome, and therefore often accompany factitious medical illness. These presentations usually involve older children who can be indoctrinated to believe that abuse occurred and can therefore provide stories of abuse "independent" of the mothers' stories during investigation. Meadow (1993a) describes 14 children in seven families with false sexual or physical abuse allegations. The subjects for this study were culled from Meadow's vast experience with 300 child-victims of factitious medical illness over a 14-year period. Although Meadow identified other potential cases of false abuse allegations within the 300 child-victims, he included in this study only those cases in which the sexual abuse allegations were proven to be false or were considered, with a "very high degree of probability," to be false. Meadow describes the false abuse allegations as one of several factitious problems invented by the mothers for their children, adding that in each case the false allegations of abuse probably caused more stress and abuse of the child than the associated factitious illness.

Of the 14 subjects in Meadow's study, 13 also experienced factitious medical illness abuse. The other victim's sibling had incurred factitious medical illness abuse. In five of the seven families represented, all the children suffered both factitious medical illness and factitious abuse allegations. In 12 of the index children the allegations were of sexual abuse; in 1 the allegations were of physical abuse, and in 1 the allegations included both sexual and physical abuse. In 3 of the children, the physicians were aware of possible factitious medical illness, and then the abuse allegations were forthcoming. In the remaining 11 children, factitious medical illness was undetected prior to the investigation of the sexual/physical abuse allegations.

All of the allegations were made by the natural mothers, with whom the children resided. For 7 children, perpetration by more than one individual was alleged. For 13 children, allegations involved unrelated men not living in the home; of these, 4 children were alleged to have been abused by the mother's former boyfriend or husband not living in the home. For the remaining individual, the alleged perpetrator was the mother's current husband living in the home. For 6 children there was circumstantial evidence of abuse in addition to the mother's allegations, because the children were trained by the mother to disclose realistic stories. Tapes were found in two homes that indicated the child was being helped or taught by the mother to disclose sexual abuse. Two of the children even had minor injuries of the perineum not characteristic of sexual abuse, which were believed to be caused by the mother. For 8 of the children the allegations were ongoing for less than 6 months; for 4 children, they were ongoing for 1 ½ to 4 years. Each of these cases went through the usual investigation process, including physical examinations and interviews for the victims as well as police interrogation of the alleged sexual perpetrators. Many of the children underwent massive and repetitive investigations.

Meadow reports that it was only during the course of prolonged investigation that the stories of abuse became suspect. Factors arousing suspicion included the lack of detail and authenticity in the stories, the fact that the children's stories contained language inappropriate to children, and the fact that the children did not have or express appropriate associated emotions. Additionally, the mothers were more active in telling the abuse stories than were the children, the mothers sought further assessment even if it would be unpleasant for the children, and the mothers did not show usual empathy or concern regarding their children's being abused. Details of the fabrications emerged over 2 years' time. For 7 of the children, certainty was reached that the abuse allegations were false, either due to confession of the mother or because the circumstances and details of the abuse were proved to be impossible. In the remaining 7 cases, Meadow reports, repeated evaluation by professionals with expertise in the diagnosis of sexual abuse made it virtually certain that the allegations were false.

The preceding discussion is not intended to be an overview of issues surrounding false allegations of sexual abuse or the methods of interviewing alleged victims of such abuse. Any clinician attempting to determine the veracity of sexual abuse allegations, and secondarily a possible diagnosis of Munchausen by proxy syndrome, should have considerable professional education and experience. The circumstances surrounding such cases are extremely complex and difficult, and opportunities for deception do exist. The clinician may never determine the "truth" without a confession in either of these scenarios, thus he or she must take into consideration all relevant factors. The clinician involved in such cases must have an understanding of the dynamics of Munchausen by proxy and of sexual abuse, must possess appropriate interviewing skills, must be knowledgeable regarding child development, and must understand the literature on children's memory and false allegations of abuse. Further, the clinician must be able to combine and apply all the methods that he or she would use separately to investigate sexual abuse and Munchausen by proxy. Of course, it is also important for the clinician to remember that sexual abuse can occur in the context of divorce as well as in the context of Munchausen by proxy syndrome medical illness. The primary issue in any case of sexual abuse is to determine the veracity of the allegations, even if the "motivation" behind the false allegations is never completely understood.

## Notes

   1. In spite of the clear connection in the research literature, problems with this disparate nomenclature can arise. I am aware of one case in which an alleged perpetrator's attorney actually attempted to discredit a psychologist witness by arguing that Munchausen by proxy syndrome does not even exist, supported by the fact that the specific term is not included in *DSM-IV.*

   2. According to Lori McQueen (personal communication, August 31, 1995) of the American Psychiatric Association, the work group for this section of the *DSM-IV* revision did not publish a paper. However, Joe Fagan, M.D. (personal communication, January 1996), has provided some enlightening and important information about the group's decision making. First, the findings of the work group led to the recommendation that factitious disorder by proxy be included in *DSM-IV* as a new diagnostic category. However, the final committee did not approve this recommendation. Second, the similarity between the diagnostic criteria of factitious disorder and factitious disorder by proxy reflects the perspective that the by-proxy form is on a continuum with factitious disorder. Although he pointed out the lack of adequate historical information in many of the published articles, Dr. Fagan indicated there is sufficient information to suggest that perpetrators may have been victims of factitious disorder by proxy in childhood, often have factitious disorder prior to the by-proxy abuse perpetration, and frequently manifest factitious disorder again after confrontation and removal of their child-victims. The inclusion of psychological symptoms as the focus of feigning or induction was a reasoned conclusion given the presence of such symptoms in factitious disorder, the lack of a sharp demarcation between psychological and physical factitious disorder, and knowledge of unpublished cases. Finally, the inclusion of the criterion that the individual's motivation is to assume the sick role helps to delineate factitious disorder by proxy from malingering and conveys the essence of the diagnosis.

   3. In their study of the comorbidity associated with factitious illness, Bools, Neale, and Meadow (1992) found that in addition to the detected factitious illness incident, 64% of child-victims had other illnesses fabricated by their mothers.

   4. This is an excellent example of an often overlooked resource for confirming suspicions of Munchausen by proxy syndrome: the child's school. The school is in a unique position with older victims of expecting daily contact with them. The vital role played by the school is discussed by Karen Palladino in Chapter 15 of this volume.

   5. This is only a small portion of a complex case that highlights many of the difficulties with Munchausen by proxy syndrome, including treatment by multiple uncoordinated health care professionals, the changing of professionals due to dissatisfaction, disappearance from medical care, possible serial Munchausen by proxy

syndrome, sibling death, coexistence of real medical problems, and inability to persuade child protective services to pursue out-of-home placement for the child. The reader is referred to Schreier and Libow's (1993a) book for a complete review of the case.

6. Sanders (1995b) approaches Munchausen by proxy syndrome from the perspective that we all have stories about ourselves that result from the events in our lives to which we have assigned meaning. In turn, these stories direct us to pay attention to certain life events and to choose certain life events in the future. According to Sanders, we coauthor these stories with others, and we obtain meaning for events through our interaction with others. Munchausen by proxy syndrome, therefore, is seen as a story in which the lead characters are the "illness," the physician, the parent, and the child. The parent "invites" the physician and the child to coauthor a story of illness. The physician does his or her part by attempting to diagnose and treat the "illness." In so doing, the physician creates the text of the story in the form of a written medical chart. The child-victim may not even be aware of the illness story. However, as the child grows older, he or she is increasingly likely to become aware, and may actually be invited to participate.

# 3  Guidelines for Identifying Cases

Teresa F. Parnell

> *The universal identification of factitious disorders is that almost everyone can admit either to having played sick to get sympathy (instead of asking directly for attention, nurturing, and/or lenience) or to having fantasized about how people would react to their serious illness and possible imminent death. . . .*
>
> *Factitious disorders are an exaggerated outgrowth of a relatively harmless, normal behavior—"playing sick." And that's what makes it at once frightening and familiar. The primary distinction, however, between most people and those with full-blown factitious disorders is that factitial patients take playing sick to* **pathological extremes,** *profoundly affecting their lives, as well as the lives of others who support them.*
>
> —M. D. Feldman, C. V. Ford, and T. Reinhold, **Patient or Pretender: Inside the Strange World of Factitious Disorders,** *1994*

Munchausen by proxy syndrome cases usually present with an astounding array of information. It is important for practitioners to determine what information is most relevant to a suspicion or confirmation of the diagnosis. It would certainly be helpful for health care professionals to have some kind of "map" to aid them in selecting the most salient details of such cases, but such a clear-cut path has not yet been developed. However, some guidelines for identification of Munchausen by proxy syndrome were first explicated by Meadow (1982a) and have continued to evolve. Deborah Day and I have

47

developed the following guidelines based on our own experience and the contributions of other writers (e.g., Meadow, 1982a, 1985; Rosenberg, 1987; Samuels & Southall, 1992). We divide these 18 guidelines, which have provided us with a useful framework, into three categories: child-victim features, mother-perpetrator features, and family features. The practitioner can apply these guidelines at the time he or she first forms a suspicion, to determine whether an intervention is warranted, and then again after all the data have been gathered, to confirm or dispute the diagnosis. Some indicators, especially those involving familial issues, may be clarified only after confrontation and during the psychological evaluation or therapy process. The indicators most salient for proper identification of Munchausen by proxy syndrome are those in the child-victim category. Certainly, not all cases that exhibit these features will ultimately be labeled as MBPS cases, nor will every MBPS case demonstrate all of these features. Ultimate diagnosis of Munchausen by proxy syndrome is not as simple as "counting" a set of indicators.

## Guidelines

### Child-Victim Features

1. *Persistent or recurrent illness that cannot readily be explained by the consulting physician despite thorough medical workup.* The illness presents as an atypical pattern, even to experienced clinicians. Physicians may remark that they have never seen a case like it before.
2. *A "diagnosis" that is merely descriptive of the symptoms, or diagnosis of an extremely rare disorder.*
3. *Symptoms that do not respond to the usual treatment regime.* This may mean the treatment simply does not work as expected. However, other responses may occur that interfere with treatment effectiveness, such as intravenous lines coming out, repeated line infections, or persistent vomiting of medications.
4. *Physical or laboratory findings that are not consistent with the reported history.* This may include laboratory findings that are unusual or physiologically impossible. Examples include unexplained pharmacological substances or bacteria in the child's blood, urine, stool, or stomach. There may be unusual or even multiple organisms obtained upon culture.

5. *Physical findings and reported symptoms that are at odds with the child's generally healthy appearance.*

6. *A temporal relationship between the child's symptoms and the mother's presence.* The reported symptoms fail to occur in the mother's absence and may not have been observed by anyone other than the mother.

7. *Pertinent medical history that cannot be substantiated.* The parent may be unable to provide sufficient information about previous physicians to obtain records, or the records obtained do not reflect medical care consistent with the parent's report.

8. *Presenting complaints that include bleeding, seizures, unconsciousness, apnea, diarrhea, vomiting, fever, and lethargy.* These symptoms are considered to be the most commonly reported and can serve as warning signs that a physician might consider this diagnosis. Allergies to foods or drugs also appear to be extremely common associated symptoms, but are not generally the primary concern.

## Mother-Perpetrator Features

9. *Reluctance to leave the child while the child is in the hospital.* The mother may refuse to leave the child's bedside for even a few minutes or to take care of her own personal needs. She will frequently attend to the child-victim to the exclusion of her other children, to the point that it is detrimental to them.

10. *Development of close personal relationships with hospital staff.* The mother may spend the little time she does leave her child's side becoming very involved with the medical staff or socializing with parents of other ill children. Physicians may find themselves very emotionally involved with her, and may experience blurring of physician/patient boundaries. This may take the form of the mother's giving gifts to physicians and providing them emotional support.

11. *Educational or employment background in the medical field or the desire to be employed within the medical field.* As a result of her background, the mother is medically knowledgeable and well versed in medical terminology and procedures.

12. *Unusual calm in the face of problems with the child's care.* In spite of expressed concern for the child, in the face of an emergency the mother remains calm, unaffected, and does not appear worried. She may actually be highly supportive and encouraging of the physician, even when the physician is baffled about the child's problems and

how to treat them. A minority of mothers go to the other extreme of being angry, degrading medical staff, and demanding additional procedures that are not medically indicated.

13. *Medical problems similar to those of the child, or other unusual symptoms.* A substantial minority of these mothers exhibit some or all of the features of Munchausen syndrome.

14. *Fabrication of information about many aspects of her life.* The fabrication may not be confined to the child's symptoms or history but may include aspects of the mother's family, education, previous employment, illnesses, and other historical data.

## Family Features

15. *Unexplained illness or death in a sibling of the victim or in another child in the mother's care.* Siblings may also exhibit similar, but less serious, forms of illness as the child-victim is currently experiencing, or may have also had unusual health problems.

16. *A marital relationship that is emotionally distant.* The perpetrator's spouse is often described as physically unavailable, uninvolved, and seemingly unaware of the falsifications. Although not frequently reported in the literature, perpetrators' marital relationships may also be abusive, controlling, and overinvolved.

17. *Perpetrator's family of origin marked by emotional, physical, or sexual abuse.* Neglectful, emotionally abusive family environments that devalue women are most frequently described in the literature, although some authors have described histories of physical and sexual abuse.

18. *Perpetrator's family of origin exhibits a pattern of illness behavior.* This may include a family history of unusual or frequent medical ailments or of family interactions that respond to illness with nurturance, attention, or other rewards. This may be most commonly present in cases where the perpetrator also exhibits Munchausen syndrome.

## Epidemiology

Determining the incidence and prevalence of Munchausen by proxy syndrome is difficult for many reasons. Although cases have been reported predominantly in the United States and England, there have been many references in international journals as well (Abe, Shinozima, Okuno, Abe, &

Ochi, 1984; Bourchier, 1983; Geelhoed & Pemberton, 1985; Ifere, Yakubu, Aikhionbare, Quaitey, & Taqi, 1993; Lim, Yap, & Lim, 1991; Lyall, Stirling, Crofton, & Kelnar, 1992; Main, Douglas, & Tamanika, 1986; Oppenoorth, 1992; Pickford, Buchanan, & McLaughlan, 1988; Proesmans, Sina, Debucquoy, Renoirte, & Eeckels, 1981; Roth, 1990; Sigal, Altmark, & Gelkopf, 1991; Single & Henry, 1991). The case reports suggest that Munchausen by proxy is a worldwide phenomenon, occurring even in countries without organized health care. Some attempts have been made to estimate incidence, but no widespread population-based accounting has been conducted. However, estimates within specific pediatric diagnostic groups have been obtained. For example, Godding and Kruth (1991) found that 1% (17 of 1,648) of asthmatic patients in their sample were identified as Munchausen by proxy syndrome victims. Light and Sheridan (1990) estimate that 2.7 per 1,000 infants (0.27%) on apnea monitors might be victims. In 1984, Warner and Hathaway reported on their work in the allergy clinic of a hospital that had served approximately 1,600 children. Of those, 301 had received detailed dietetic assessment for presumed food allergy or intolerance. They identified 16 children from these 301 (5%) as victims of Munchausen by proxy syndrome (an additional child from the 1,600, with suspected aero-allergens, was also identified).

Researchers have also established estimates by polling professionals likely to have had contact with MBPS cases. In a survey of various professionals attending a conference who routinely worked in medical facilities or community service agencies, Kaufman, Coury, Pickrell, and McCleery (1989) found that 40% of the respondents had seen a case they suspected to be Munchausen by proxy syndrome within the previous year. A total of 77 possible cases were seen by 86 professionals. Schreier and Libow (1993b) surveyed 870 pediatric neurologists and 388 pediatric gastroenterologists, surmising that these physicians would be likely to see the most common presentations of Munchausen by proxy syndrome. The response rate was 21.8% for the neurologists, or 190 respondents, with 107 of these reporting contact with a Munchausen by proxy syndrome case. The response rate for the gastroenterologists was 32.4%, or 126 respondents, of which 103 reported contact with a Munchausen by proxy syndrome case. Together, these physicians reported 273 confirmed cases and 192 seriously suspected cases. Schreier and Libow do not include in their report an estimated number of total pediatric cases in which these physicians had been involved in their careers, however. Although studies such as those mentioned here are of interest, none provides a valid estimate of incidence or prevalence of Munchausen by proxy syndrome.

The true incidence of Munchausen by proxy syndrome is difficult to determine because many cases go undetected. Physicians are reluctant to acknowledge that they could be deceived in such a manner, although they concede that the syndrome exists—apparently suggesting that it happens, but only to other physicians (Sheridan, 1994). Often there are case suspicions, but insufficient evidence exists or is gathered, so that these cases are never officially reported or investigated (Porter, Heitsch, & Miller, 1994; Sullivan, Francis, Bain, & Hartz, 1991). Further, the diagnosis of MBPS takes some time; the estimated average time for diagnosis ranges from 6 months (Schreier & Libow, 1993b) to 14.9 months (Rosenberg, 1987). Additionally, the number of unexplained child deaths that accumulate on a yearly basis, including those of known Munchausen by proxy syndrome child-victims' siblings, is likely to include some Munchausen by proxy-related deaths. Finally, the research literature is likely to represent only the most severe cases and those cases that are confirmed on some level. Of course, many professionals who see cases of Munchausen by proxy syndrome never contribute to the published literature. As with other forms of child abuse, incidence must be largely inferred until more complete data are available, but the syndrome is unlikely to be rare.

Jani, White, Rosenberg, and Maisami (1992) examined the discharge records of pediatric inpatients for indicators of possible Munchausen by proxy syndrome. They compared the 14 AMA (against medical advice) discharges and 24 transfers that occurred in the specified 2-year period with 41 randomly selected regular discharges. Using six criteria culled from the literature, the researchers found indications of a suspicion for Munchausen by proxy syndrome in 64% of AMA cases, 8% of transfer cases, and none of the regular discharges.

## Deaths

In a curious twist, Meadow reported in 1994 that a 53-year-old woman, during consultation with a psychiatrist the previous year, had admitted killing her son with salt poisoning nearly 20 years before. That mother was the perpetrator in one of the first two examples of Munchausen by proxy syndrome abuse Meadow had described in his 1977 article. The knowledge that MBPS child-victims die from this abuse is not new; many authors have reported child-victim's deaths. As with incidence figures, however, the frequency of death resulting from Munchausen by proxy abuse is not completely known. Rosenberg (1987) found that 9% of the child-victims in her meta-analysis sample of 117 cases died. This figure has been criticized for a number of reasons (see Meadow, 1990a), such as the belief that the most severe cases are likely to appear in the literature and concern over possible duplication of cases in Rosenberg's sample.[1] However, a number of reports support concern over the possibility of death as a result of Munchausen by proxy abuse.

Meadow (1982a) compiled cases from pediatricians and his own work to study the characteristics of 19 child-victims and their families. Of these, 2 children were known to be dead. Meadow (1990b) later compiled 27 cases of child suffocation by the mother. In this sample, 9 child-victims were dead and one had severe brain damage. Additionally, the 27 child-victims had 15 live elder siblings, but 18 dead siblings. These siblings died suddenly and early in life, 13 with histories of apnea, cyanosis, or seizures. Most of the deaths were certified as sudden infant death syndrome. Meadow (1993b) has also reported 2 deaths in 12 cases of nonaccidental salt poisoning.

Waller (1983) reviewed 23 case reports of Munchausen by proxy and nonaccidental poisoning. Of these, 5 children were known to be dead. Light and Sheridan (1990) report that of 24 infants with apnea who probably represented cases of Munchausen by proxy, 3 were dead (another was severely brain damaged). Further, 5 of their siblings were known to be dead, supposedly of sudden infant death syndrome. Alexander, Smith, and Stevenson (1990) have noted especially high rates of death among children in families of serial Munchausen by proxy syndrome. They describe five families in which more than one sibling was the victim of Munchausen by proxy syndrome; 13 children were affected within these families, and 4 of the children died. Mitchell, Brummitt, DeForest, and Fisher (1993) reviewed the cases of 11 children in five families. Among these children with factitious apnea, there were 2 deaths. Lastly, in Schreier and Libow's (1993b) survey of pediatric gastroenterologists and neurologists, 9.7% of suspected victims had died.

Child-victims of MBPS may be killed by perpetrators directly or indirectly. That is, a child may die due to some manipulation by the mother or as the result of complications of medical tests or treatment. The question arises, Did the mother mean to kill the child? Early in our work, Deborah Day and I believed there was no death wish, and we separated such cases from Munchausen by proxy. It seemed that death of the child was not the goal, but rather a consequence of the mother-perpetrator's compulsive behavior. The death of the child did not seem to be a real possible outcome in the mother-perpetrator's mind, in spite of the realistic likelihood of such an outcome given her behavior. However, over time in the therapy process we have found that some MBPS mothers do wish for, or at least fantasize about, the death of their children. In fact, this preoccupation with the child-victim's death includes the mother's fantasizing about what she will wear to the funeral, how to dress the deceased child, and how her affect should appear to others in the context of the child's death. In 12 cases of nonaccidental salt poisoning, Meadow (1993b) found that three mother-perpetrators out of seven who had confessed to poisoning their children admitted a wish to kill.

## The Major Participants

Perpetrators of Munchausen by proxy syndrome abuse may be in any care-taking role, such as biological mother, foster mother, adoptive mother, stepmother, father, foster father, stepfather, nonmarried parent figure, baby-sitter, nurse, or other relative. However, most perpetrators are in some sort of "mother" role, and roughly 90% of these are biological mothers of the child-victims. The risk of these perpetrators to children outside of the perpetrators' families appears to be minimal, although some cases have been reported. Additionally, many cases have been reported in which more than one child in the family has been victimized (see below). Fathers in these families are very rarely involved as perpetrators.

The same difficulties as are found in epidemiology apply to attempts to obtain descriptive data regarding MBPS family members. Only one large meta-analysis, which is now several years old, has been published (Rosenberg, 1987). Although there are other published series that provide descriptive data (Bools, Neale, & Meadow, 1992, 1993, 1994; Light & Sheridan, 1990; Meadow, 1982a, 1990b, 1993b; Samuels, McClaughlin, Jacobson, Poets, & Southall, 1992; Waller, 1983), these represent smaller samples, and the possible overlap among them is unclear. I review the information available below, but the reader is cautioned that, as Rosenberg (1994) aptly points out, "as with all statistical methods, meta-analysis has limitations, and no statistic based on sample population studies is entirely applicable to an individual patient" (p. 267).

### The Mother-Perpetrator

The MBPS mother-perpetrator is usually described in overtly positive terms as a nice, loving, tender, and caring individual. She seems totally devoted to her child and his or her medical care. When the child is hospital-ized, the mother may be reluctant to leave the child's bedside for any reason. She stays for extended periods of time, to the point that hospital staff often notice the difference between her presence and that of other parents. She is also very pleasant and interactive with staff, displaying appreciation and support for their efforts. Further, she is likely to be quite helpful to busy medical staff by involving herself actively in the child's care. In fact, she may claim that she is the only one for whom the child will eat, drink, or allow medical procedures. Her level of medical knowledge and sophistication is generally quite high, but such acumen is not seen in other areas of her life. She seems actually to enjoy the hospital environment and often forms close personal relationships with physicians, nurses, and other hospital staff. Additionally, she may bond with the parents of other child patients.

Often, the most striking element of the mother-perpetrator's interaction is how "normal" she appears. On closer examination, however, it may become clear that she has presented elaborate and unlikely medical histories, lied about easily verifiable personal history, encouraged or even demanded painful diagnostic procedures for the child, and solicited media attention for the child's condition. Curiously, when a staffing is finally conducted on the case, many staff may realize that they have had interactions with the mother or obtained information from her that is quite troubling as well as informative. These pieces of information, when brought together, often cast an entirely new light on the case.

It is important to remember that not all mother-perpetrators fit this prototypical presentation. For instance, some will appear uneducated and unsophisticated. In others, their psychopathology may be quite noticeable from the beginning of contact. Deborah Day and I have seen mothers in a substantial minority of our cases who presented as dramatic, erratic, and emotionally labile. They embellished, elaborated, and told obvious lies. Their presentation as well as their lives would be best described as chaotic. They were capable of tremendous irritability and rage when thwarted, and their anger took the form of harassment, threats, and multiple ongoing lawsuits. It seems that Munchausen by proxy perpetrators have a higher incidence of threatening and actually filing lawsuits and licensing board complaints than do most clinical populations. The lawsuits may be unrelated to the Munchausen by proxy case (e.g., they may sue attorneys, insurance companies, or schools) or related to the case (e.g., malpractice). In fact, Deborah Day and I are aware of several pending lawsuits against physicians in cases in which we were involved.

In her 1987 meta-analysis, Rosenberg reported on 97 mother-perpetrators of 117 child-victims. She found no primary father-perpetrators in her review of the literature, although paternal collusion was indicated in 1.5% of cases once the deception by the mother was discovered. Of the perpetra-

tors, 98% were biological mothers; 2% were adoptive mothers. The occupa-
tions of 40% of the mother-perpetrators were unknown, and those of the other
60% broke down as follows: 27% worked in nursing or a health-related field,
20% worked at home, 4% were unemployed, 3% were medical office workers, 2% were social workers, and 1% worked in each of the categories of
schoolteachers, home helpers, baby food demonstrators, and orderlies. Information regarding psychiatric or psychological treatment history was
incomplete, with very few formal assessments ($n = 3$). However, the perpetrators were generally described as affable, friendly, and socially adept.
Psychosis was not a prominent feature. Emotional distance in the marriage
as well as themes of isolation and loneliness were indicated. A total of 10%
were diagnosed with Munchausen syndrome, and another 14% were reported
to have some features of Munchausen syndrome. Of the psychiatric disorders
described, depression was most common, followed by hysterical personality
disorder. Borderline personality, narcissistic personality, and unspecified
personality disorder were all noted very occasionally. Regarding suicidal
thoughts, 12 of the perpetrators reported being suicidal before disclosure of
the deception and 5 were suicidal after disclosure. Another 47 reported being
suicidal as well, but it is unknown whether the thoughts of suicide occurred
before or after disclosure.

The mother-perpetrator admitted the ruse completely in 15% of the 117
cases. A partial admission was obtained in 7%, and complete denial was
offered in 18%. The reaction of the mother-perpetrator was unknown in 60%
of cases. Legal follow-up was also largely unknown (87%); 8% of the cases
were known to result in criminal conviction, and 5% were known to have no
criminal conviction. A total of 20% of the mother-perpetrators had been
previously suspected and confronted, but the children were sent home.

As will be discussed below, a small portion of perpetrators are fathers.
In these families, we know virtually nothing about the mothers as nonperpe-
trators. They are generally described as passive and less involved than the
father-perpetrator in the child-victim's care. In these cases, the mothers do
not appear to build relationships with medical staff as previously described
for mother-perpetrators.

### The Child-Victim

In Rosenberg's (1987) analysis, there were roughly equivalent numbers
of male and female child-victims. The victims were generally quite young,
usually infants and toddlers. The age at diagnosis ranged from 1 month to

252 months ($n = 117$), with a mean age of 39.8 months at diagnosis ($n = 67$). The time from onset of symptoms to diagnosis ranged from days to 240 months ($n = 117$), with a mean of 14.9 months ($n = 67$). Information regarding simulation (faked without the mother directly causing harm) or production (actually inflicted on the child by the mother) of illness was available for 72 cases. Signs of illness were exclusively simulated in 25% of cases, exclusively produced in 50% of cases, and both simulated and produced in 25% of cases. Most of the simulation and production actually took place in the hospital, with 72% for simulation only, 95% for production only, 84% in simulation/production cases.

Symptoms covered a broad spectrum, with many children having more than one presenting problem. The most common presentations were bleeding (44%), seizures (42%), central nervous symptom depression (19%), apnea (15%), diarrhea (11%), vomiting (10%), fever (10%), and rash (9%) (see Table 4.1 in Seibel & Parnell, Chapter 4, this volume). Short-term morbidity, defined as pain and/or illness that resolved, was described as 100%; 75% of resolution was accomplished by the perpetrator and medical staff, and 25% by the medical staff alone as the result of investigations and procedures. Ten (9%) of the child-victims died. All of these victims for whom age was reported ($n = 8$) died at a young age, under 3 years. Of the remaining 107, long-term morbidity, defined as pain and/or illness that caused permanent disfigurement or permanent impairment of function, was at least 8%. Very little information was available on the psychological functioning of these children, including the psychological effects of the Munchausen by proxy abuse (see Day & Ojeda-Castro, Chapter 12, this volume). In Rosenberg's sample, sexual abuse and physical abuse were each reported in only 1% of cases. Failure to thrive was indicated in 14%, generally due to the illness produced by the perpetrator.

It is possible that many cases of Munchausen by proxy syndrome actually begin when the child-victim is still in utero. Obstetric complications and feigned obstetric symptoms are reported in the literature, as well as numerous pregnancy-related problems for the child-victims and their siblings (Alexander et al., 1990; Berkner, Kastner, & Skolnick, 1988; Goss & McDougall, 1992; Meadow, 1977; Outwater, Lipnick, Luban, Ravenscroft, & Ruley, 1981; Porter et al., 1994; Ravenscroft & Hochheiser, 1980; Sullivan et al., 1991). Jureidini (1993) explores these issues in a recent review of obstetric complications in Munchausen syndrome and Munchausen by proxy syndrome. Jureidini found no mention in major obstetric textbooks of factitious disorder or feigned contractions. However, he found 19 patients in the literature with obstetric factitious disorder whose primary presentations he describes as antepartum bleeding, feigned premature labor, feigned rupture of membranes, induced postpartum bleeding causing anemia, self-induced vomiting presenting as hyperemesis gravidarum, false claims of reduced fetal movements, feigned pyrexia, feigned trophoblastic disease, and feigned seizures. Two of these papers reported major problems or damage to the child as a consequence of the factitious behavior, including the death of at least one baby. With regard to the Munchausen by proxy syndrome literature, Jureidini found no review of obstetric complications, and less than half of the case reports have even documented obstetric histories. However, Jureidini makes several observations based on his review. First, he concludes that significant obstetric complications are common, stating, "In roughly 70% of those cases where history was available, there had been delivery at 37 weeks or earlier, antepartum hemorrhage, or emergency cesarean section" (p. 135). Second, he reports a significant incidence of obstetric factitious disorder (i.e., factitious symptoms during pregnancy), with or without significant obstetric complications. Third, he notes the presence of previous perinatal bereavement, such as stillbirth or sudden infant death syndrome, in a number of cases.

Jureidini also reports on his own experience with six Munchausen by proxy mother-perpetrators. These mothers had 19 children, 14 of whom were Munchausen by proxy victims. Eight pregnancies in three of the mothers were complicated by significant obstetric events, and five of the mothers showed evidence of factitious behavior during pregnancy that affected 13 pregnancies. Jureidini concludes that (a) there is a link between obstetric complications, be they real or genuine, and Munchausen by proxy syndrome; (b) obstetric complications are common in the histories of Munchausen by proxy syndrome perpetrators and can contribute to the development of Munchausen by proxy syndrome; and (c) pregnancy can facilitate the transition from Munchausen syndrome to Munchausen by proxy syndrome.

Jureidini offers some interesting hypotheses regarding the contribution of pregnancy and obstetric complications to the development of Munchausen by proxy syndrome. He suggests that the obvious disruption in the mother-child relationship that is evident in Munchausen by proxy cases may occur with unresolved grief from previous perinatal bereavement or the production of a damaged child. This produces not only a disruption in the relationship but a simultaneous focus on external illness for the mother, given the nature of the disruption. In cases where the mother already exhibits Munchausen syndrome, Jureidini asserts that a transition may be facilitated from self-focused hostile behavior to externally focused behavior as the fetus inside the mother becomes a separate person.

Deborah Day and I have also noted obstetric complications, factitious obstetric symptoms, and perinatal bereavement in many cases in which we have consulted. Complete obstetric histories of suspected MBPS mother-perpetrators, including verification of reported problems, have generally not been obtained, but we are now pursuing these issues more diligently. Mother-child attachment problems often begin with ambivalence about the particular pregnancy or even a desire to terminate the pregnancy. A mother's fabrication that her pregnancy is high risk suggests that she is already formulating that something is wrong with the child. In such a case, the focus is more on what the mother is experiencing than on concern for the fetus. In one particular case with which I am familiar, the disturbance in mother-child attachment was present from conception. The mother did not want the child and attempted to abort the child herself in the third trimester. Labor was induced as a result of her actions, and the baby subsequently became the victim of MBPS abuse. In another case, the mother reported numerous abortions and miscarriages prior to the birth of her only child. She described obstetric complications and then fetal distress during labor. The child was born with serious medical problems and a chromosomal abnormality, and the mother subsequently induced serious symptoms in the child-victim.

It is important for researchers and practitioners to consider the possible relationship of mothers' reported obstetric complications to later MBPS behavior. In the overall context of MBPS abuse, considerable study needs to be conducted in this area before we will be able to draw firm conclusions.

## The Father

The nonperpetrating father in the Munchausen by proxy family is generally viewed as minimally involved in the life of the family. He may be emotionally and physically distant, perhaps being very involved in his work or holding a job that requires long periods of absence from the home. The mother-perpetrator may reveal feelings of emotional abandonment and lack of support from her partner if the interviewer can get past her initial presentation of a perfect family environment. In our experience, my colleagues and I have often found severe and long-standing but well-hidden marital discord in MBPS families.

Once the mother-perpetrator is confronted, the father generally claims that he did not know of the abuse. The father usually has tremendous difficulty believing the allegations, although initially he may express concern and may cooperate with interventions. However, once the shock has worn off, he will usually align with the wife against the perceived attack by physicians and other professionals. It is interesting to note that in the therapy cases in which Deborah Day and I have been involved, although the nonperpetrating fathers initially aligned with the mother-perpetrators, these couples are all now divorced.

Not only is the nonperpetrating father generally distant from the family, he appears distant from the child-victim's supposed chronic illness as well. While the child is in the hospital, he maintains a low profile and may rarely visit. His wife generally makes all the medical decisions and confers with physicians. Some fathers are not even aware of their children's outpatient visits to physicians. Of note, this lack of involvement appears to be rarely noticed, let alone challenged, by medical professionals, until they begin to suspect Munchausen by proxy syndrome.

An incredible and dangerous passivity has been noted in some cases in which nonperpetrating fathers appear to have known or should have known about their wives' abuse of their children (Orenstein & Wasserman, 1986). There have also been reports of some cases in which fathers seem to have been actively involved in their children's illness (Woollcott, Aceto, Rutt, Bloom, & Glick, 1982), to the point of colluding with the mother-perpetrators (Light & Sheridan, 1990). Schreier and Libow (1993a) report two such cases. In one case of a 5-year-old with supposed failure to thrive, the boyfriend of the child-victim's mother put his finger down the boy's throat to induce vomiting. This apparently occurred in the mother's presence. In the other case, involving an 8-year-old also with failure to thrive, secondary to ipecac poisoning, the father and mother were both suspected of being actively involved. Interestingly, it was also suspected that the paternal grandmother might have been playing a role.

Biological fathers are considered to be perpetrators of Munchausen by proxy syndrome abuse in an estimated 5% of cases. There have been 13 cases of father-perpetrators discussed in the literature (Bath, Murty, & Gibbin, 1993; Boros & Brubaker, 1992; Dine & McGovern, 1982; Godding & Kruth, 1991; Jones, Badgett, Minella, & Schuschke, 1993; Kovacs & Toth, 1993; Makar & Squier, 1990; Meadow, 1990b; Morris, 1985; Mortimer, 1980; Samuels et al., 1992; Single & Henry, 1991; Zohar, Avidan, Schvili, & Laurian, 1987). Light and Sheridan (1990) also found one father-perpetrator (and one mother and father combination) out of 24 cases in their survey of apnea monitoring programs; however, they provide no separate information about this case. Mitchell et al. (1993) also report a probable case of father-perpetration, but without conclusive evidence.

Table 3.1 summarizes information about the father-perpetrators discussed in the literature, and their child-victims. As for mother-perpetrators, all pertinent information is not available in the articles describing father-perpetrators. The information available does suggest some issues of note, however. Several of these fathers had inadequate or questionable employment histories, and some are specifically described as unemployed at the time of the detection (Boros & Brubaker, 1992; Jones et al., 1993; Makar & Squier, 1990; Samuels et al., 1992). Others were seeking and/or receiving financial assistance related to the child's illness (Kovacs & Toth, 1993; Single & Henry, 1991). Interestingly, the father-perpetrator in many cases is viewed as the more dominant parent, or at least as very actively involved in the child-victim's day-to-day caretaking (Boros & Brubaker, 1992; Jones et al., 1993; Makar & Squier, 1990; Single & Henry, 1991). Several father-perpetrators had unrelated criminal histories (Bath et al., 1993; Single & Henry, 1991) and possible factitious illness in themselves (Kovacs & Toth, 1993; Samuels et al., 1992). Only one study specifically notes that a particular father-perpetrator had training in a health care-related field (Jones et al., 1993).

Jones et al. (1993) consider some factors that may contribute to the recognition of males as perpetrators of Munchausen by proxy abuse. First, they mention the increased awareness and attention being paid to male caretakers in these families. They also consider the changing role of fathers in U.S. society in general, including the fact that increasing numbers of nonworking fathers are taking responsibility for primary caretaking of their children. Jones et al. suggest that this role shift may leave fathers open to the same stresses of caregiving that lead to Munchausen by proxy behavior in mother-perpetrators. They further suggest, however, that it is the father's need to feel like the protector of the family that is manifested in his first perpetrating illness on and then rescuing the child.

Schreier and Libow (1993a) have suggested that father-perpetrators are a more overtly pathological group, exhibiting bizarre behavior or symptom reports, with possible psychosis. They do not consider the case reports they reviewed as fitting the profile of a seemingly devoted, concerned parent. Of the 13 cases of father-perpetrators I have reviewed, 2 had psychiatric treatment histories and 2 exhibited self-injurious behavior. Again, the amount of information available concerning these documented father-perpetrator cases varied widely.

**TABLE 3.1** Father-Perpetrators

| Age of Victim | Gender of Victim | Presenting Complaint | Method | How Discovered | Response by Perpetrator | Outcome |
|---|---|---|---|---|---|---|
| 4 months | male[a] | apnea | unknown | detailed history; separation | unknown | convicted; 5 years in jail |
| 10 months | female | apnea | smothering | video surveillance | denied; arrested; admitted after learning of tape | convicted of felonious third-degree assault; 10 months in workhouse, 5 years probation; no contact with daughter; no unsupervised contact with children |
| 10 months | male | asthma | withheld treatment | forced child to leave emergency room | unknown | police called; lost to follow-up |
| 6 months | female | apnea | held tightly | video surveillance attempted; confrontation | confessed, then recanted | unknown |
| 14 months | male | diabetes mellitus, spontaneous hypoglycemia | fabricated medical history | testing; physical exam | denied, went to another physician | abuse investigation in progress; lost to follow-up |
| 2 months | female | apnea | unknown | observation; parent visits, reduced and supervised | unknown | protective services notified; placement out of home |
| 2 months | male[a] | apnea | smothering | unknown | unknown | unknown |
| 1.5 months | male | apnea | smothering | observed | denied, then admitted | unknown |
| 1.5 months | male[a] | cyanotic episodes | suffocation | video surveillance | denied, then admitted when told of tape | convicted of attempted murder; convicted of murder for sibling death |
| 11 years | male | cystic fibrosis | fabrication | medical testing; review of records | relinquished diagnosis easily but adopted another | case being prepared for court; fled |
| 5 years | male | external otitis | insertion of chalk | father's history of Munchausen syndrome | angrily discharged son | unknown |
| 7 months | male | pneumonia lethargy | Doriden poisoning | tested blood for poisons | unknown; mother confessed that father poisoned child | infant released to mother; father committed suicide |
| 4 years | male | seizures | water intoxication | elimination of other diagnostic possibilities | unknown; admitted other physical abuse | convicted of assault |

NOTE: a. This victim had a sibling who died with a history of unexplained apnea.

62

## The Siblings

In Schreier and Libow's (1993b) survey of physicians, a sibling was believed to be involved in the Munchausen by proxy abuse in 120 of 465 possible cases (25.8%). In Rosenberg's (1987) seminal review, of 117 child-victims, 10, or 8.5%, had siblings who were also victims. Just as the incidence of Munchausen by proxy syndrome in general is unknown, the incidence of multiple-child MBPS has yet to be calculated. As previously indicated, the diagnosis of Munchausen by proxy syndrome is often difficult and/or delayed, thus perpetrators have many opportunities to continue victimization. Also, as their children age, perpetrators may realize that it is easier to continue their deception with infants, who cannot tell. In some cases, Munchausen by proxy syndrome appears to occur as the result of the dynamics of a particular parent-child relationship, or a particular time in the parent's life. In other cases, however, this is not so clear.

I have noted how difficult it is to detect ongoing Munchausen by proxy abuse; identifying possible past abuse is even more difficult. The most a practitioner may be able to determine is that a suspicion of Munchausen by proxy syndrome is warranted. However, a review of the medical records (or even the death certificate) of a suspected child-victim's siblings may reveal the same condition or symptoms similar to those exhibited by the suspected child-victim. Additionally, many authors suggest associated sibling involvement in the abuse via factitious illness, unexplained death, failure to thrive, suspicious poisoning, and nonaccidental injury abuse (Meadow, 1984, 1990b, 1993b; Rosen et al., 1983; Stevenson & Alexander, 1990)

Alexander et al. (1990) describe five families in which more than one child in the family was victimized by Munchausen by proxy abuse. Of the 18 children in these families, 13 (71%) were victimized. Of the abused children, 4 (31%) died. Interestingly, all of the victimized children within each family exhibited the same or very similar symptoms. The mother-perpetrators displayed a higher incidence of health profession backgrounds, Munchausen syndrome in themselves, histories of psychiatric treatment, and histories of suicide attempts than previously reported (Rosenberg, 1987). Although their sample was relatively small, Alexander et al. (1990) suggest that mother-perpetrators of serial Munchausen by proxy may have more psychopathology than single-victim perpetrators. Alternatively, they suggest that these pathology indicators may reflect the deterioration in the perpetrator and family when Munchausen by proxy abuse is allowed to continue without detection and intervention.

Bools et al. (1992) studied the comorbidity associated with Munchausen by proxy syndrome in 56 families. The 56 index children had 103 siblings, although there was sufficient information on only 82 of them available for study. Of these, 39% were also victims of fabricated illness by the mother. Thirteen (11%) died in early childhood, with the cause of 11 of these deaths not medically conclusive. Among the studied siblings, 17% were also affected by failure to thrive, nonaccidental injury, inappropriate medications, or neglect. Bools et al. conclude that the high morbidity rates for siblings are likely an underestimate, for at least two reasons. First, they were unable to obtain full data for one-fifth of the siblings. Second, some siblings had been protected by legal orders or were not living with their mothers at the time of the study, thus their risk of abuse was reduced.

## Other Perpetrators

As I have noted, the typical relationship between perpetrator and victim is that of mother and child. However, other cases have been reported that involved adult perpetrators in child caretaking roles. These include individuals in parent roles, such as foster mothers (Baldwin, 1994; Frederick, Luedtke, Barrett, Hixson, & Burch, 1990), adoptive mothers (Jones et al., 1986), and stepmothers (Atoynatan, O'Reilly, & Loin, 1988; Sutphen & Saulsbury, 1988). The involvement of grandmothers has also been reported (Baldwin, 1994; Godding & Kruth, 1991; Samuels et al., 1992). Individuals in other caretaking roles, such as baby-sitters (Emery, Gilbert, & Zugibe, 1988; Richardson, 1987) and nurses (Carrell, 1984), have also been reported to be perpetrators, although these are often cases of serial abuse, often resulting in death for the victims (Darbyshire, 1986; Davies, 1993; Elkind, 1989). One case of serial deaths involving a caretaker in a mother role has also been reported (Egginton, 1990).

## Adult Victims

A number of more unusual manifestations of Munchausen by proxy-type behavior have been identified in which the unsuspecting victims have been adults (Sigal, Altmark, & Carmel, 1986; Smith & Ardern, 1989; Meadow, 1984). These cases have dynamics similar to those already described—that is, perpetrators seek to meet their own psychological needs by keeping adult-victims in the patient role.

## Intergenerational Munchausen by Proxy Syndrome

Intergenerational Munchausen by proxy syndrome has appeared in several of the cases with which my colleagues and I have been involved. Each of these cases has been discovered after the second-generation Munchausen by proxy mother-perpetrator (our patient) was revealed to be perpetrating abuse against her own child. Through careful investigation, we found that these mother-perpetrators had long medical histories as children, often seeing their family physicians one to two times a month from birth until age 18. Families explained away the doctor visits, calling the first-generation mothers "over-anxious" or "overprotective." We found many unusual symptoms and diagnoses in the records. In one case, hysterical blindness was reported in a 10-year-old child's medical records. In the child-victims' teenage years, the medical records reflect significant documented psychological issues, such as depression, anxiety, anorexia, and bulimia. In our practice, we have found that the first-generation MBPS mothers exaggerated symptoms, and their daughters fell into the categories of active inducers and symptom exaggerators. In one case, the mother-victim did not perpetrate against her children, but presented with a somatization disorder.

## Some Closing Thoughts

The Munchausen by proxy syndrome case usually involves multiple physicians, due to the consultations various practitioners seek to "figure out" the mysterious case. Sometimes one or more of these consulting physicians will strenuously disagree with the ultimate Munchausen by proxy syndrome diagnosis. The result is a very tense situation, due to the intensity of the mother's denial, the intensity of support for her among the medical caregivers with whom she has developed relationships, the intensity of emotions related to such abhorrent allegations, and the physician's role in the abuse of the child-victim. Even more physicians, and other professionals, are thrown into the mix once a legal case begins to unfold. Waller (1983) describes one case in which five physicians were found to testify on the mother-perpetrator's behalf as to her integrity as a parent. In another case, nine physicians and five nurses testified for the mother (Schreier & Libow, 1994). Light and Sheridan (1990) tell of one instance in which a physician's life was threatened following confrontation of the mother-perpetrator.

An allegation of Munchausen by proxy syndrome abuse is extremely serious and potentially life altering for the suspected perpetrator, regardless of the outcome of the case. Therefore, practitioners must conduct competent, thorough, professional, and well-documented investigative work before they levy any such allegation. A hastily formed and incorrect diagnosis can and will be challenged, and should be challenged. Practitioners should also be aware that the MBPS mother-perpetrator is capable of creating a circuslike atmosphere around her case, involving physicians, other medical staff, attorneys, the media, and politicians. This can shift the focus from the horrendous abuse suffered by the child to suspicions of and attacks on the physicians making the diagnosis, which can often lead to dangerous mismanagement of the case. For example, in one case, the psychiatrist evaluating the mother after detection was not allowed to communicate with the physicians who had brought the case to the attention of child protection workers (Waller, 1983). Shortly thereafter, the diagnosing physicians learned that the clinic evaluating the mother-perpetrator had engaged in its own investigation to determine what was "really wrong" with the child medically.

Mother-perpetrators have often been known to pull government officials into their plight, through letters to the governor, the state head of protective services, and groups opposing the practices of the state's child protective services. As I have noted, mother-perpetrators are often quite articulate, and they have been known to misrepresent their case data persuasively enough to get responses from these unsuspecting officials. When this occurs, the professionals who have investigated the case and the practitioners who have made the diagnosis are placed under pressure to respond to the mother's allegations and defend themselves. This creates chaos, deflects attention from the real issue of the mother's abuse, and drains the energy of the medical and investigating professionals. Not only do they feel attacked, but delays are created in the case. Professionals who have found themselves in this position often no longer want to be involved in such cases. This means that the hospital, child protective services, the prosecutor's office, and the mental health community may lose the help of the very people who are best trained to deal with these bizarre and challenging cases.

## Note

1. Rosenberg (1987) includes only those cases that clearly conform to her definition of Munchausen by proxy syndrome (see Table 2.3 in Parnell, Chapter 2, this volume). Excluded are some cases in which there was simply insufficient information to make the diagnosis or it was unclear that the case fit the definition, and Rosenberg specifies which articles have been excluded. In a personal communi-

cation, Dr. Rosenberg indicated that there was no duplication of cases from the literature in her meta-analysis. She also indicated that she agrees with Dr. Meadow's objection to generalizing the 9% death rate found in her study to the entire population of Munchausen by proxy victims.

# 4 The Physician's Role in Confirming the Diagnosis

Matthew A. Seibel
Teresa F. Parnell

> *Characteristics of physician training and personality usually make it quite difficult for him to assume the role of policeman or district attorney, and start questioning patients as if he were investigating a crime.*
> —*C. H. Kempe, F. N. Silverman, B. F. Steele, W. Droegemueller, and H. K. Silver, "The Battered-Child Syndrome," 1962*

Munchausen by proxy syndrome is a relative newcomer to the collection of medical problems of child abuse and neglect. The classic article by Dr. Roy Meadow in 1977 spawned the subsequent publishing of more than 250 articles and a book, most describing the medical details of single case studies. Excellent review articles have also been written (Leonard & Farrell, 1992; Meadow, 1982a, 1985; Rosenberg, 1987; Samuels & Southall, 1992), but the literature has contained few resources describing how physicians and other medical providers can systematically consider and confirm the diagnosis of MBPS through medical records. Our purpose in this chapter is to guide the physician through the steps of confirming the diagnosis of Munchausen by proxy syndrome using review of the medical records and in-hospital observation. Although the medical diagnosis is paramount, we should note that the physician should not take the steps described below outside of the context of the multidisciplinary team (see, in this volume, Parnell, Chapter 5; Wilkinson & Parnell, Chapter 13; Whelan-Williams & Baker, Chapter 14).

## Approach to Diagnosis

A major deterrent to accurate identification of Munchausen by proxy syndrome cases is the failure of medical personnel even to consider the diagnosis. Primary care providers are often ill equipped to deal with deception by patients or their patients' parents, because they are trained to depend on the histories that patients or patients' parents provide. Only care providers with specialty training in child abuse are likely to have experienced the level of manipulation and lying evident in MBPS cases. The presence of Munchausen by proxy syndrome is incomprehensible to most medical personnel (Blix & Brack, 1988; Epstein, Markowitz, Gallo, Holmes, & Gryboski, 1987), and there remains a lack of awareness of this disorder among many professionals (Hochhauser & Richardson, 1994; Kaufman, Coury, Pickrell, & McCleery, 1989). Over the past few years, however, Munchausen by proxy syndrome has become much more widely discussed, and medical providers who work with children are increasingly realizing that they need to consider carefully the veracity of information given to them by their patients' parents. Surely physicians cannot stop listening to the parents of their child patients, but perhaps they must learn to listen in different ways.

Physicians do not tend to believe that their patients will fabricate symptoms (Sheridan, 1994) and often have difficulty accepting their own inability to resolve patients' clinical presentations (Meadow, 1994; Schreier & Libow, 1994). For many doctors, suspecting a patient's mother in the absence of being able to resolve the medical dilemma may feel far too frightening. In fact, the more uncertain the medical situation, the more investigation a physician usually orders in an attempt to solve the problem. Munchausen by proxy mother-perpetrators who present either as demanding of further investigation and treatment or as incredibly supportive of the now frustrated primary care provider only heighten the physician's tendency to pursue zealously more and more tests, procedures, and consultations. Primary care providers who do consider the diagnosis of MBPS may feel a tremendous amount of self-doubt about their suspicions.

Primary care physicians need to be open to the input of their colleagues, including other physicians, nurses, and physician's assistants, in considering this diagnosis. Sometimes the primary physician is extraordinarily reluctant to consider Munchausen by proxy syndrome even when faced with many signs (see Schreier & Libow, 1993b, for a discussion of the dynamics influencing this resistance). There have been cases in which primary physicians have so staunchly refused to consider the diagnosis that other professionals have been forced to intervene. Generally, even if the primary physician suspects such abuse, it is not recommended that he or she attempt to confirm the diagnosis. Rather, the primary physician should consult a neutral physician—the consulting physician reviewer, to whom the bulk of this chapter is directed. The primary care physician is likely to be too close to the situation and too emotionally involved with the family to proceed toward confirmation or denial of the diagnosis with any objectivity. The physician's involvement in the suffering of the child through repeated, intrusive medical investigations arouses strong emotional reactions, making this especially difficult. Additionally, from a legal perspective, a primary physician who makes a diagnosis of MBPS may be accused of resorting to that diagnosis only because he or she cannot find the "real" cause of the illness.

Once a physician considers a diagnosis of MBPS, the foremost issue from a medical standpoint becomes the protection of the child. Medical personnel are mainly involved with ensuring the health of the child, and this responsibility must not be compromised. If Munchausen by proxy syndrome is suspected and the nature of the child's illness is such that the physician believes that further parental contact could be harmful to the child, then the physician must take immediate action to protect the child. At the same time, the physician is often faced with the reality that intervening at the point of suspicion may mean that child protective services or law enforcement will not have enough evidence to ensure the continued safety of the child.

When a physician is trying to gather information to convince others who are vital to the future handling of the case, there can be quite a discrepancy between the amount of information needed to make a medical diagnosis and the amount required to protect the child legally (Hanon, 1991). Often this leads to the physician's being asked to cooperate in actions that place him or her in direct opposition to the physician's role of protecting the child, at least in the short term. An example would be a situation in which there is suspicion that the parent is introducing a foreign substance to the child, perhaps through tampering with the hospitalized child's intravenous fluids. Video surveillance could record such actions, allow law enforcement to proceed, and probably provide the evidence necessary to compel a long-term child protective plan (Williams & Bevan, 1988). However, this means that the physician must delay confrontation of the parent and allow the child to be placed in a dangerous situation; a bacterial infection in the bloodstream is potentially fatal, even if treated quickly. There are no easy answers to such dilemmas. Physicians must certainly be guided by their mission to preserve their patients' health at all costs—but which approach best meets this goal?

Medical personnel are usually the professionals who initiate investigation in Munchausen by proxy cases, and they must be willing to step forward and take a leadership role in the diagnostic process. However, as with other forms of child abuse, a multidisciplinary approach to diagnosis ensures that all aspects of how to proceed in these puzzling cases will be considered (Hanon, 1991; Mercer & Perdue, 1993). It is impossible for physicians to intervene successfully from a purely medical standpoint without the support of other individuals and agencies; therefore, a doctor who suspects Munchausen by proxy syndrome must contact a multidisciplinary team of professionals. Together, these professionals can identify the information needed to confirm or deny the diagnosis and any steps that must be taken to intervene on the patient's behalf. Depending on availability, a consulting physician reviewer may or may not be involved immediately in the case. Therefore, the primary care physician may have an active role until safety of the child can be assured based on the suspicions. From that point, the primary care physician's role in confirmation of the diagnosis may diminish as the consulting physician reviewer becomes more actively involved. (A multidisciplinary response protocol is discussed in depth in Whelan-Williams & Baker, Chapter 14, this volume.)

Nursing personnel represent very valuable resources for confirming a diagnosis of Munchausen by proxy syndrome. Nurses can provide accurate information about medical/clinical issues, and can participate actively in the diagnostic process. Of all the professionals in the hospital setting, nursing personnel spend the greatest amount of time with child patients and their parents, and have many opportunities to observe their interaction. Nurses may observe subtle signs suggestive of Munchausen by proxy syndrome, such as a mother's enmeshed interaction with the families of other ill children, a mother's misperceptions of her child, and certain kinds of statements made by a mother during conversations. Nurses may be the only persons to whom a mother makes statements that, when considered along with other pertinent information, are incriminating and sometimes bizarre.

Smith and Killam (1994) describe the case of Robert, who had severe weight loss and developmental delay. After 20 months of exhaustive evaluation by pediatricians, neurologists, geneticists, endocrinologists, and gastroenterologists, it was determined that Robert's condition was essentially the result of starvation; Robert's mother was suspect of withholding food and fluids. Nursing personnel were crucial to the ultimate diagnosis and management of Robert's case. Their observations included the following:

- His mother complained that Robert was running a high temperature, although his temperature was in the low to normal range.
- His mother described Robert as being very "edematous," when there was no edema.
- Despite Robert's weight gain, his mother complained that no tests were being done.
- When Robert was bagged for a urine specimen, his mother complained that he should be catheterized.
- When Robert's social interactivity and playfulness increased, his mother complained that the hospitalization was causing Robert to become depressed.
- When Robert would point to his juice cup, his mother would respond, "Oh, he doesn't want that."
- When Robert was observed to eat "ravenously," his mother would attempt to remove the food tray from his room.
- When Robert was leaning or lunging toward food, his mother would remark that he was "just playing" and move the food.

Involvement of nursing staff in steps to confirm a diagnosis of MBPS may be vital. Often, because of the close relationships Munchausen mother-perpetrators tend to build with nurses, the nurses may initially find such allegations unfathomable. If a nurse is asked to provide information or to be involved in interventions such as those described later in this chapter, he or she must support the efforts to confirm the diagnosis. If the nurse does not believe he or she can provide this support, often without the family's knowledge, then he or she may need to ask to be removed from the care of the child. (For a discussion of nurses' reactions to their participation in MBPS abuse, see Whelan-Williams & Baker, Chapter 14, this volume.)

Child protection workers and hospital social services also need to be involved when Munchausen by proxy syndrome is suspected, to ensure the child's ongoing safety. Various issues, such as placement of the child after the diagnosis as well as research into other family dynamics, need to be addressed before the physician should proceed with techniques to confirm the diagnosis. Law enforcement personnel, including state attorneys, also need to be part of the multidisciplinary team, to ensure the proper gathering of evidence. Although law enforcement involvement at such an early point has generally been rare, we believe that it is vital. Prosecution, through the dependency and/or criminal courts, may be required to protect the child adequately from further harm. A legal decision may need to be made to hold the child where those aware of the situation can monitor his or her well-being. Otherwise, nothing prevents the confronted parent from moving to another jurisdiction and beginning the process of abuse again.

Psychological or psychiatric assistance is a mandatory part of the diagnostic process as well. The multidisciplinary team should include individuals with an understanding of family dynamics as well as an understanding of the issues surrounding intervention with the alleged perpetrator. There are times when the medical diagnosis is not certain, and the presence on the team of an authority with psychological information about the background of the mother or the dynamics of the relationship between the mother and the child allows the team to proceed more confidently.

Although multidisciplinary collaboration is vital, ultimately the diagnosis is a medical one, and the physician must be prepared to assert the diagnosis with confidence. A physician who suspects or confirms a diagnosis of Munchausen by proxy syndrome is likely to be confronted by tremendous resistance, and may find him- or herself attacked by others involved in the case, including medical colleagues. It is also not uncommon for a physician to doubt his or her own medical evidence when confronted with the persuasive denial of the perpetrator (Waller, 1983). The physician who reaches a diagnosis of MBPS must clearly articulate for others who are called on to protect the child his or her process of reaching *this* medical diagnosis in *this* case.

## Diagnosis

Diagnosis of Munchausen by proxy syndrome is made when a cluster of situations can be shown to exist. These have been presented in earlier articles (see, e.g., Rosenberg, 1987) and elsewhere in this book (see Parnell, Chapters 2 and 3). Confirming the diagnosis of Munchausen by proxy syndrome can be a very difficult task. It is important to remember that genuine illness and Munchausen by proxy syndrome may coexist. Most medical caregivers would agree that the true incidence of Munchausen by proxy syndrome is much higher than once thought, and that the disorder is currently underdiagnosed (Kaufman et al., 1989; Schreier & Libow, 1993a). The secrecy and deception surrounding the disease process require that the physician use all methods available to arrive at an accurate diagnosis. Most MBPS child-victims show remarkable medical improvement after diagnosis and placement in a safe environment. However, accuracy in diagnosis is vital, because of the potential morbidity and mortality of this disease process (Rosenberg, 1987). Physical morbidity is difficult to measure in the short term, but technically all victims experience some immediate short-term morbidity when they suffer needless, painful medical procedures. The limited literature available on the lasting physical effects of Munchausen by proxy syndrome suggests that at least 8% of surviving victims show some degree of long-term medical morbidity (Rosenberg, 1987). This does not address the psychological morbidity present in these children, which is even more difficult to assess (Bools, Neale, & Meadow, 1993; Croft & Jervis, 1989; McGuire & Feldman, 1989; Porter, Heitsch, & Miller, 1994; see also Day & Ojeda-Castro, Chapter 12, this volume). These cases also involve the issue of mortality, which has been reported to be as high as 31% (Alexander, Smith, & Stevenson, 1990).

Accuracy of diagnosis is also important because of the potential harm caused by false allegations. As with any case of child abuse, false allegations can be devastating to the family. The suspected child-victim and possibly his or her siblings may be separated from the parents for a lengthy period of time. Alternatively, the parents may be separated, with the alleged perpetrator forced to leave the home. The legal costs involved in fighting such allegations far exceed most families' financial resources. These concerns are compounded by the typical scenario of frequent and lengthy delays in the legal process before closure is reached. In the meantime, the family system is inordinately stressed. Although cases with similar dynamics may be inaccurately identified, usually after careful scrutiny or when swift action is believed necessary for child safety, sometimes misidentification may be due to carelessness on the part of the medical professional. This is usually seen when physicians make firm diagnoses without obtaining all the available information or without personally reviewing the records.

We recommend two basic methods through which a physician should confirm a medical diagnosis of MBPS. The first involves retrospective diagnosis based on review of the child's medical records. The second involves prospective analysis based on manipulation of the child's environment so as to gather evidence of the suspected abusive behavior.

## Review of the Medical Records

A Munchausen by proxy syndrome case usually involves a significant past medical history. Although it is important for the physician to speak directly with the persons involved with the child's care, the child's medical records stand as a tremendous source of information. These records include documentation of medical symptoms reported by the family, the history given by the family, the tests and procedures conducted as a result of the history given, physicians' thoughts and notes, and nurses' observations.

Medical records can contain information that can help to confirm a diagnosis of Munchausen by proxy syndrome, but not all physicians may be qualified to discover that information within the records. When MBPS is suspected, the child's medical records should be reviewed by someone who has experience with this disorder, because an inexperienced reviewer may overlook certain subtleties. Additionally, even though failure to diagnose Munchausen by proxy syndrome is more prevalent, inexperienced physicians may be quick to diagnose MBPS when other medical possibilities remain.

When a review of medical records is to be conducted for purposes of diagnosis, the physician must consider three issues: What is the best way to organize such a voluminous task? What in the records might be considered as evidence of factitious symptoms? What is the best way to communicate the findings of the records review to others?

### Organizing Medical Records for Review

The physician must obtain *all* medical records for the patient from *all* sources. In addition to asking the suspected mother-perpetrator, the physician should speak with the child's father as well as other family members (grandparents, aunts, uncles, adult siblings, and so on) regarding possible locations for records. However, the physician reviewer should never assume that the family has provided full and accurate information regarding the location of records. Cases of MBPS often involve records from multiple medical personnel and facilities. If the family has lived in other locations, the physician needs to look for records there.

If the family has medical insurance, the physician can contact the insurance company to discover where claims have been paid in order to find out where records should be available. Managed care insurance plans can be especially helpful with the location of medical records. Most of these plans encourage the primary care physician to be the central figure in all medical care, thus the reviewer may find a central location for information. Traditional insurance plans, on the other hand, allow patients to seek medical attention without the knowledge of a medical coordinator or primary care physician. This can lead to a situation where one hand doesn't know what the other hand is doing. Physicians seeking records for review must keep in mind the Munchausen by proxy mother's propensity for deception and creativity. For instance, even with coordinated medical care, in some cases the mother-perpetrator's need for contact with medical professionals is so insatiable, she secretly goes outside of her geographic area, without utilizing the insurance plan. This is obviously difficult to detect; in fact, this information may not emerge until later, when the perpetrator has acknowledged her behavior. Interestingly, the 24-hour availability of walk-in clinics and emergency rooms makes it easy for mother-perpetrators to access medical personnel when the compulsion arises. We are aware of one case in which a child's guardian ad litem, on a hunch, canvassed walk-in clinics in the family's neighborhood and found additional medical records.

Obtaining a child's complete medical records may be difficult for a number of other reasons as well. The parents may refuse to sign releases for all of the records. In such a case, it is crucial that the physician involve child protective services and/or law enforcement in order to obtain the consent or a court order allowing access to the records. Other difficulties include the tendency of most doctors' office and medical center personnel to handle requests for records quite slowly. Further, it is not uncommon for doctors and medical centers to send out only portions of medical records or treatment summaries, despite their being presented with release forms that clearly request *all* records. (The second author of this chapter has had the experience of having to request records repeatedly from hospitals that send information only on the patient's most recent admission.) Thus pursuit of a child's complete medical records often requires tremendous time on the part of someone's office staff. Further, some institutions charge fees of hundreds or thousands of dollars for the release of records. Alternatively, they may insist that the reviewer come to their location due to the amount of records.

In a Munchausen by proxy syndrome case, the entirety of the child's medical records is often voluminous, and the logical and orderly review of these records can seem overwhelming. (In one case in which the first author of this chapter was involved, the patient's records occupied 10 feet of shelf space in the hospital's records room—and this was only one of several facilities in which the child had received care.) Complicating the issue is the sometimes frustrating task of deciphering various medical professionals' handwriting and the fact that photocopies of original records are often difficult to read at all. When records are impossible to decipher, the physician reviewer must not skip over the information. He or she should consider obtaining permission to review the original records whenever feasible, or should try to talk directly with the medical provider who made the records.

The records review process must proceed in an organized manner from the beginning, so that the reviewer can avoid amassing useless bits of data from which no diagnostic conclusions can be drawn. It may be helpful for the reviewer to enlist the assistance of another physician, nurse, or medical resident in organizing the review. However, given the legal conflicts in many MBPS cases, the physician reviewer should be aware that he or she may be expected to have reviewed virtually every piece of the medical records personally.

It is not sufficient for the reviewer to read only the medical summaries in the records. It may be helpful, however, for the reviewer to start by reviewing admission, discharge, and consultant summaries for each hospitalization and the intake summaries and physician correspondence for outpatient care. From these, the physician reviewer should develop a chronology of medical care, with dates of service, presenting symptoms (both those observed by medical professionals and those reported by parents), the diagnoses considered, diagnostic and therapeutic procedures, and complications. The reviewer can also develop a brief summary of each hospitalization from nurses' and other medical personnel's observations in the medical records. The broad scope provided by the chronology will give the reviewing physician a base from which to begin to look at details of the hospital records from specific admissions. He or she will have developed questions or hypotheses regarding possible organic or nonorganic explanations for the child's condition from the initial cursory review of the records. A more thorough, and now well-organized, review of the details of the records will serve to answer questions and to confirm or dispute the various hypotheses.

Along with the child's records, the reviewer should look closely at the medical records of the child's siblings, as certain similarities may be evident. An offending parent may direct abuse toward one child for a period and then move to another, and the induced or invented symptoms may suggest conditions that statistically would be very unusual within the same family. An example of this is a recent case in which a child presented with symptoms that turned out to be the result of ipecac poisoning. A sibling of this child had previously presented with similar symptoms and subsequently died. Only then was it learned that the first child died as a result of complications of ipecac poisoning. The physician reviewer should also investigate sibling deaths by talking with other family members, reviewing autopsy reports, and obtaining death certificates. If at all possible, the reviewer should also obtain the medical records of the suspected mother-perpetrator, including her childhood records. A review of sibling and perpetrator records similar to the review of the child-victim's records can help to illuminate a pattern of deception over time and generations.

### Evidence of Factitious Symptoms

The illnesses of children suffering MBPS abuse often involve respiratory, neurological, gastrointestinal, infectious, and hematological problems. More than 100 physical symptoms have been associated with Munchausen by proxy cases (see Table 4.1), but the most common symptoms reported are bleeding, seizures, central nervous system (CNS) depression, apnea, diarrhea, vomiting, fever, rash (Rosenberg, 1987), and lethargy (Schreier & Libow, 1993). Table 4.2 shows various methods of fabrication/induction as well as methods of diagnosis for each of these common symptoms. The diagnostic strategy a physician utilizes will of course depend upon the type of perpetration suspected. The physician may use a number of laboratory tests; toxicology screens and checks of blood, urine, stools, and vomit should always be conducted. The physician consultant must recognize, however, that not all agents can be identified through laboratory testing. Additionally, Munchausen by proxy perpetrators are extremely crafty; the physician may not even be able to ponder the type of falsification occurring in a particular case.

The written medical records may contain evidence of false medical history of the child or family, exaggeration of the child's medical condition, exaggeration of physician statements regarding the child's medical condition, reports of symptoms that never occurred, faked or simulated symptoms, and actual induction of symptoms. The distinction between exaggeration and fabrication is often difficult to make, as is a determination of simulation versus induction, through consideration of the symptom presentation or report alone. Induced symptoms are generally much more difficult to detect, especially because induction tends to create actual physiological conditions. At the same time, once detected, the induction of symptoms may be easier to confirm or prove than fabrication of symptoms. It is important for the physician to remember that the same symptom presentation may result from fabrication, faking, or inducing. For example, a child with a history of vomiting blood may have a mother-perpetrator who (a) has simply lied about seeing the episode, (b) has presented her own blood as evidence, or (c) has scratched the back of the infant's throat. Of course, the physician must also be aware that these alternatives are not mutually exclusive, and that they may also overlay genuine illness.

*Accuracy of medical history.* Careful review of medical records often suggests a tendency on the part of medical personnel simply to repeat medical history from document to document, without verification. This results in the appearance of factuality for a piece of family or victim medical history owing to the credibility lent it by its repetition in the medical records. The reviewer

**TABLE 4.1** Symptoms, Signs, and Prominent Laboratory Findings in MBPS Victims

Abdominal pain
Abuse dwarfism
Anorexia
Apnea
Arthralgia (painful joints)
Arthritis (swollen joints)
Asthma
Ataxia (dyscoordination)
Bacteriuria (bacteria in urine)
Biochemical chaos
Bleeding from ears
Bleeding from ears due to abuse
Bleeding from mouth
Bleeding from other sites (NG tube, ileostomy)
Bleeding tendency
Bleeding from upper respiratory tract
Bleeding from vagina, rectum
Bradycardia (slow heart-beat)
Catheter contamination, sepsis
Central catheter sepsis
Chest pain
Cerebral palsy
Cutaneous abscesses
Cyanosis (turning blue)
Cystic fibrosis
Contaminated/altered urine
Coma
Dehydration
Delirium
Dermatitis artefacta (lesions, scratches, bruises)
Diabetes
Diaphoresis (sweating)
Diarrhea
Difficulty breathing
Ear infections
Easy bruising
Eczema

Edema (peripheral)
Epistaxis (nosebleeds)
Esophageal burns
External otitis
Failure to thrive
Feculent vomiting
Feeding difficulties
Fetal distress
Fevers
Food allergy
Glycosuria (sugar in urine)
Hallucinations
Headache
Hearing loss
Hematemesis (vomiting blood)
Hematochezia or melena (blood in stool)
Hematuria (blood in urine)
Hemoptysis (coughing blood)
Human immuno-deficiency virus
Hyperactivity
Hypernatremia (high blood Na+)
Hypertension
Hypoglycemia (low blood sugar)
Hypokalemia (low blood K+)
Hyponatremia (low blood Na+)
Hypothermia
Hypotonia
Hypochromic microcytic anemia
Immunodeficiency
Insomnia
Irritability
Leaking urine
Lethargy
Leukopenia (low white blood cell count)
Morning stiffness
Mouth lesions

Muscle aches
Nocturia
Nystagmus (jerking eye movements)
Obstetric or pregnancy complications
Painful urination
Personality change
Poisoning (includes MBPS and intentional poisoning)
Polydipsia
Polymicrobial bacteremia
Polyphagia (eating a lot)
Polyuria
Prolonged sleep
Pseudo-obstruction/ dismotility syndrome
Psychogenic vomiting
Pyelonephritis
Pyuria (pus in urine)
Rash
Reflux
Renal failure (acute)
Renal stones
Respiratory distress
Respiratory symptoms
Seizures
Sepsis
Septic arthritis (infected joint)
Shock
Starvation diarrhea
Stupor
Unconsciousness
Unimicrobial bacteremia
Urination difficulty
Urination from umbilical micropenis
Urine gravel
Vaginal discharge
Vaginal irritation
Ventricular tachycardia
Vomiting
Weakness
Weight loss
Yeast infections

SOURCE: Adapted from Schreier and Libow (1993a); originally adapted from *Child Abuse and Neglect, 11,* D. Rosenberg, "Web of Deceit: A Literature Review of Munchausen Syndrome by Proxy," p. 553, copyright 1987, with kind permission from Elsevier Science Ltd, The Boulevard, Langford Lane, Kidlington OX5 1GB, UK.

**TABLE 4.2** MBPS: Methods of Fabrication and Corresponding Diagnostic
Strategies

| Presentation | Method of Simulation and/or Production | Method of Diagnosis |
|---|---|---|
| Bleeding | 1. warfarin poisoning | 1. toxicology screen |
| | 2. phenolphthalein poisoning | 2. diapers positive |
| | 3. exogenous blood applied | 3. blood group typing (major and minor) |
| | | 3. $^{51}$Cr labeling of erythrocytes |
| | 4. exsanguination of child | 4. single blind study |
| | | 4. mother caught in the act |
| | 5. addition of other substances (paint, cocoa, dyes) | 5. testing; washing |
| Seizures | 1. lying | 1. other MBPS features/retrospective |
| | 2. poisoning (phenothiazines, hydrocarbons, salt, imipramine) | 2. analysis of blood, urine, IV fluid, milk |
| | 3. suffocation or carotid sinus pressure | 3. witnessed |
| | | 3. forensic photos of pressure points |
| CNS depression | 1. drugs (Lomotil, insulin, chloral hydrate, barbiturates, aspirin, diphenhydramine, tricyclic antidepressants, acetaminophen) | 1. assays of blood, gastric contents, urine, IV fluids; analysis of insulin type |
| | 2. suffocation | 2. See "Apnea" and "Seizures" |
| Apnea | 1. manual suffocation | 1. patient with pinch marks on nose |
| | | 1. mother caught |
| | | 1. video camera (hidden) |
| | | 1. diagnosis of exclusion |
| | 2. poisoning (imipramine, hydrocarbon) | 2. toxicology (gastric/blood) |
| | | 2. chromatography of IV fluid |
| | 3. lying | 3. diagnostic process of elimination |
| Diarrhea | 1. phenolphthalein or other laxative poisoning | 1. stool/diaper positive |
| | 2. salt poisoning | 2. assay of formula/gastric contents |
| Vomiting | 1. emetic poisoning | 1. assay for drug |
| | 2. lying | 2. admit to hospital |
| Fever | 1. falsifying temperature | 1. careful charting, rechecking |
| | 2. falsifying chart | 2. careful charting, rechecking |
| | | 2. duplicating temperature chart in nurses' station |
| Rash | 1. drug poisoning | 1. assay |
| | 2. scratching | 2. diagnosis of exclusion |
| | 3. caustics applied/painting skin | 3. assay/wash off |

SOURCE: Reprinted from *Child Abuse and Neglect, 11,* D. Rosenberg, "Web of Deceit: A Literature Review of Munchausen Syndrome by Proxy," p. 554, copyright 1987, with kind permission from Elsevier Science Ltd, The Boulevard, Langford Lane, Kidlington OX5 1GB, UK.

should not assume that just because a piece of medical information is contained in more than one document it is true; he or she should take care to review the place in the records where the observation or diagnosis was originally made. The records may also show that either the child's or the family's medical history has seemed to expand with each new admission or consultation. When the history is directly related to the child, the reviewer may find that there is a notable absence of intervening records to support the "new" information or diagnosis. When the history is related to a family member, it may resemble the child's current symptom presentation. The physician reviewer must question everything, no matter how seemingly small or insignificant.

Another interesting feature that has been found in many cases is that the diagnosis of Munchausen by proxy syndrome has been considered previously. Often a consultant or resident has suggested that the diagnosis be ruled out as part of differential diagnosis. In some cases the reviewer will find that there has simply been no apparent follow-up to the recommendation. In other cases, a senior physician has intervened, usually suggesting some rare diagnosis, which sets off another round of tests.

The physician reviewer can usually confirm reports of false medical history or exaggeration of primary care providers' statements about medical conditions by conducting a thorough attempt to secure the actual records. In this way, the reviewer can determine whether or not a reported diagnosis was actually ever made. Unfortunately, uncovering this information is often more challenging than one might expect. A mother-perpetrator may insist that a diagnosis was given verbally, claim she cannot recall the name of the medical provider who made the diagnosis, or, in the case of family history, insist that the records have long since been lost or destroyed. The situation is actually more troublesome when the mother-perpetrator is exaggerating the medical condition in general rather than attempting to misrepresent a physician's findings. In some cases, the mother holds a false belief about the child's medical condition (rather than participates in deliberate prevarication) that is difficult to discourage, even with clear medical evidence. Certainly if the mother refuses to authorize the release of medical records or portions of the medical records for herself, the child-victim, or her other children, this is a serious problem. Additionally, the records obtained sometimes will refer to treatment by other providers whom the mother-perpetrator has omitted from the medical history given.

*Fabrication of symptoms.* Confirmation that symptoms reported by the mother-perpetrator never occurred usually evolves over time. As a mother-perpetrator reports repeated symptoms of seizures or apnea, for instance, the likelihood that these would occur in front of someone other than the mother increases. An illness or condition that happens "all the time" or only when unobserved at home but never happens in the hospital or when nurses are present is suspect. However, the mother might claim that the act or condition has in fact been witnessed by a neutral person, which would appear to make the illness or symptom more valid. The medical records may indicate that an episode occurred in the presence of someone else, but only because the mother provided this history. It is important, therefore, that the reviewer establish who has actually witnessed the child's medical problems. He or she should always attempt to confirm a symptom observation with the actual person who was allegedly present. It is essential that the reviewer check the story by speaking directly with the witnessing individual and comparing the accuracy of that person's statements with the parent's report. In particular, it is important that the reviewer question whether the beginning of the symptoms, such as a seizure, was directly observed. General information about the child's physical condition can also be obtained, with proper permission for the release of information, from collateral sources such as extended family members, friends, neighbors, day-care workers, teachers, and baby-sitters.

   *Temporal relationship of symptoms and mother's presence.* The relationship between the alleged mother-perpetrator's presence and the child's symptoms may be documented through nurses' detailed, accurate notes made during the course of the child's hospitalization. These notes should reflect not only the mother's report of symptoms but the mother's presence, along with the presence or absence of symptoms as observed by the nurse. Documentation of the mother's involvement in the feeding, medicating, diapering, collecting of specimens, and treatment regime of the child can also be helpful if carefully detailed. Hospital records may also include descriptions of the mother's handling of intravenous lines or other hospital equipment in an effort to "help" the staff. If interviews are conducted with hospital staff, these types of questions should be asked. Of course, in order to draw conclusions from this information, investigators would also need to document the presence of any other individuals who had access to the child or involvement in the child's care.

   *Inconsistencies and contradictions.* Inconsistencies and contradictions among findings may also point to reported symptoms that never occurred. One kind of inconsistency might be that the presentation of the child does not match the symptom report. Frequently, the records will refer to a "robust" or "well-appearing" child on examination although the child has a supposed history of refusal to eat as well as frequent and chronic vomiting and diarrhea. A child with such a history is unlikely to appear so healthy over time. Another kind of contradiction is evident in the case of a child who repeatedly appears to the physician only in a diaper and T-shirt because, according to the mother, the child has just vomited, yet there is no evidence of emesis on the child's clothing or breath.

Another type of inconsistency involves medical testing that does not confirm or that contradicts the clinical situation. An example of this would be a child who is reportedly vomiting blood when a stool guaiac continues to be negative. If a child is vomiting blood from a source in the child's nose, throat, or stomach, there will always be some trace that presents in the child's stool. If stool tests are negative, one must question the source of the blood, even when the parent provides a sample, as well as whether the child is even vomiting. In one recent case that we know of, a mother placed her own blood on the child's burp cloth and claimed that it had been vomited by the child.

A final example of contradiction or inconsistency would be a child who did not respond in the anticipated fashion when medication or other treatment was provided. Failure to respond as expected to a treatment regime known to be effective with a given symptom or diagnosis may suggest that no real condition exists. Alternatively, a genuine condition may exist for which medication has been prescribed, but the mother may not be giving the medication to the child or may be overdosing the child.

*Differential diagnosis.* As the physician reviewer examines the medical records, he or she should be alert to proposed illnesses where there is a great deal of difficulty in making the diagnosis. Often, the records of MBPS abuse victims show symptoms that appear to be consistent with one diagnosis, but that turns out not to be the correct diagnosis. The child's physician might think he or she has found a new disease process, because none of the usual or common disease processes seem to fit. In fact, it seems that many physicians are more likely to consider the possibility of a new disease than a diagnosis of Munchausen by proxy syndrome. Although it may be possible that new disease processes will be discovered in the mid-1990s, this would represent an extraordinarily unusual situation. A more likely cause of such difficulty in diagnosis is the presence of Munchausen by proxy syndrome.

One example of an interesting disease process in which there is difficulty making the diagnosis is that of pseudo-obstruction syndrome. Hyman, DiLorenzo, Beck, Hamilton, and Zelter (1994) describe chronic intestinal pseudo-obstruction as a rare clinical condition based on signs and symptoms of bowel obstruction in the absence of a liminal lesion detectable by laparotomy or radiology. They report on 19 children referred for chronic intestinal pseudo-obstruction of sufficient severity to require special means of nutritional support (11 TPN, 8 tube feeding). Hyman et al. diagnosed Munchausen by proxy syndrome in 8 of the 19 children, based upon (a) a medical history that did not fit any pattern of disease, (b) repeated documentation of maternal exaggeration or lying, and (c) relief of symptoms due solely to maternal separation. When the researchers compared these 8 cases to the remaining 11, the following emerged:

> Children with MBP were clustered in the 18-36 month age group. Mothers had healthcare-related jobs or were in nursing school in 5 of 8, compared to none of the children with organic disease. In no case were gastrointestinal symptoms congenital, but in all the severity of symptoms increased during infancy. . . . All children with MBP had normal antroduodenal and colonic manometries; all but 1 child with organic causes for CIP had abnormal antroduodenal and/or colonic manometry. All 8 victims of MBP, but only 2 children with organic CIP, had chronic visceral pain. (p. 332)

The potentially disastrous effects of Munchausen by proxy syndrome are highlighted by Hyman et al.'s following statement: "These 8 children had 65 surgeries, including 7 fundoplications, 8 gastrostomies, and 39 central venous catheters." Schreier and Libow (1994) remark in their review of a case, "Because chronic intestinal pseudo-obstruction is a relatively new diagnosis and there is a lack of consensus among gastroenterologists as to what constitutes normal gastrointestinal motility, it is a 'set up' for the elaboration of a MBPS process" (p. S114)

*Family dynamics.* A final important aspect to which the physician reviewer should be alert in examining the medical records is evidence of the family dynamics. Relevant information can often be found in nurses' notes and sometimes in social workers' evaluations. Is the mother inappropriately invested in the child's illness? Does she seem to welcome additional invasive procedures? Does the mother live in the hospital with the child? Does she develop overly close bonds with the medical staff and the parents of other ill children? Does she comfort the physician who is bewildered by her child's illness? Is the father notably absent from the hospital or generally uninformed about the child's condition? The reviewer can find answers to these questions and more in the notes, if he or she looks carefully. None of these features alone confirms the diagnosis of Munchausen by proxy syndrome, but each adds to the emerging clinical picture.

## Communicating the Medical Findings

The findings of the medical records review must be carefully communicated to several parties. First, if the child is hospitalized during the review, the physician should clearly and thoroughly document all steps taken in the consideration of a diagnosis of Munchausen by proxy syndrome. These steps would include all medical procedures, alternative diagnoses considered, consultations requested, multidisciplinary staffings, meetings with nursing staff, conversations with parents, and abuse reports made. Second, medical personnel are often asked to interpret medical information for nonmedical individuals and to provide expert testimony. The physician reviewer may first be asked to present his or her findings in an understandable form to the multidisciplinary team, later to child protection workers, and ultimately to a judge.

Legal intervention in Munchausen by proxy syndrome cases is vital for long-term management and rehabilitation of the mother-perpetrator (see Parnell, Chapter 5, this volume). The medical chronology compiled by the reviewer will aid the physician's preparation of a written report. This report should articulate the physician's medical conclusion regarding the current episode while documenting as many previous episodes of suspected and confirmed exaggeration, fabrication, and induction as possible. Each step taken in the process of reaching the diagnosis should be clear to any reader of the report. The medical chronology helps the physician reviewer to assess the degree of past harm to the child and potential future harm if the child remains in the care of the mother, which must also be indicated in the report. The medical chronology and the written report may also provide useful groundwork for preparation of a dependency petition, for criminal prosecution, and for testimony by the physician reviewer. However, this format is likely to be overwhelming in most settings. Therefore, the physician reviewer must also be able to reduce the information to a concise summary of the evidence supporting a theory of symptom fabrication or induction, the harm to the child, and the future risk to the child in the custody of the parent.

## When More Evidence Is Needed: Prospective Analysis

Although many Munchausen by proxy syndrome cases can be confirmed within a reasonable degree of medical certainty through review of medical records, others remain elusive. Records may raise suspicions in a knowledge-able individual, but more information may be needed to prove the case to others. In some cases, it may be that the medical expert is not convinced, or it may be that the medical expert is convinced, but does not feel that he or she can be convincing in a legal proceeding if the parent denies the deception. Generally, perpetrators do initially deny their behavior when confronted, react with anger, and may immediately remove the child from the physician's care. Therefore, additional evidence is often needed to support the allegations and protect the child. This is where the second type of diagnostic method, prospective analysis, is useful. Prospective analysis of a case involves directed monitoring of the child's environment to gather evidence of the suspected mother-perpetrator's Munchausen by proxy behavior.

When deciding how to proceed with prospective analysis of a case, the physician is faced with interesting operational problems that may also be dangerous. When Munchausen by proxy syndrome is strongly suspected, it is inappropriate for professionals simply to continue observing the child to gather evidence to confirm or dispute the hypothesis. Without video surveillance or 24-hour nursing care, it is impossible to observe the child closely enough, and this places the child at the same risk of continued harm as if no actions were taken. If the physician elects to proceed by ignoring the child's symptoms, in the hope that the mother will abandon them when she does not receive gratification, this may lead the mother to increase the severity of her actions. Implying to the mother that suspicions have been aroused may only heighten her interest in continuing the ruse. Proesmans, Sina, Debucquoy, Renoirte, and Eeckels (1981) have reported on one case in which a child suffering recurrent attacks of renal failure was allowed to go home from the hospital for a weekend visit after his mother had been interviewed and her handbag searched. When the child returned to the hospital, the mother produced a pair of the child's underpants with evidence of a fluorescent yellow discoloration of his urine and challenged the physicians by stating, "There it is again, you have done nothing!" (p. 208). The mother later admitted to systematically poisoning her child with glafenin.

Clearly, the possibility of escalating symptoms and even death of the child exists with any of the above options. If the multidisciplinary team does not consider immediate confrontation of the mother viable, then the team must take direct steps to gather more evidence. This may involve either setting up a situation in which the mother is likely to simulate or induce symptoms while being videotaped or separating the mother from the child.

## Directed Monitoring

Meadow (1977) describes a plan that was used to test the theory that abnormal urine specimens obtained from a 6-year-old patient were actually the result of her mother's adding her own urine or menstrual discharge to the specimen. Meadow and his colleagues believed that each of the abnormal specimens had been left unsupervised in the mother's presence at one stage or another. They tightened the supervision under which the specimens were collected for the next several days, and then slightly relaxed the supervision so that the mother had access to some specimens. Meadow reports that on the first occasion when the mother was left to collect the specimen, she brought back "a heavily bloodstained specimen containing much debris and bacteria" (p. 343). Over a 7-day period, the 45 specimens collected by the nurse were all normal, whereas the 12 collected by the mother or left in her presence were grossly abnormal. Although the mother did not admit tampering with the specimens, Meadow reports that enough evidence was deemed to exist to support the theory that the mother's story about her daughter's condition was false.

Meadow's example involved a case in which evidence could be obtained in a short period of time due to the mother's ongoing behavior. Some symptoms will occur only when the mother-perpetrator feels stressed by the likelihood that the child will be discharged from the hospital or when she believes the child is not getting enough medical attention. Thus where there are strong suspicions of Munchausen by proxy, it may be necessary for the multidisciplinary team to create an environment in which the parent will be likely to repeat her behavior. For instance, the mother-perpetrator might be told that the child will be discharged if the symptoms do not occur soon or that further testing will be done if the symptoms recur. Of course, controlling the environment to induce the mother to abuse the child again in order to obtain confirmatory evidence places the child at risk, and thus requires stringent monitoring.

Covert video surveillance is one method of monitoring the child and gathering further evidence at the same time. Visual evidence of the actual induction of behavior or simulation of symptoms can be extremely powerful in convincing skeptics of the existence of this bizarre abuse. Seeing these acts can allow people to believe what may be very difficult for them to conceive. This visual evidence also provides confirmation of the diagnosis sufficient for legal purposes, if it is collected appropriately (see Wilkinson & Parnell, Chapter 13, this volume). Video surveillance is currently being viewed with increasing favor, both domestically and abroad, and issues surrounding this technique have been debated in the literature (Byard & Burnell, 1994; Epstein et al., 1987; Foreman & Farsides, 1993; Myers, 1994; Southall & Samuels, 1992; Southall et al., 1987; Williams & Bevan, 1988; Zitelli, Seltman, & Shannon, 1988). Opposition centers mainly on concerns for the privacy rights of families, breach of trust in the medical relationship, and allowing the child to suffer further assault in the interest of obtaining forensic evidence. Proponents of video surveillance argue that the child's right to protection from abuse and the duty owed to the child as a patient supersede the parent's rights to privacy. Additionally, the often life-or-death nature of these cases suggests that extraordinary measures may be required to protect the child in the long term. Other authors have argued that the public has a diminished expectation of privacy in settings such as hospitals anyway, and that surveillance can be focused only on the child. Parameters to guide the decision to utilize covert video surveillance have also been discussed. Suggested parameters include the following requirements: that a strong suspicion of Munchausen by proxy syndrome abuse exists, that definitive proof cannot be obtained in any other way, that a multidisciplinary staffing decision for video surveillance has been made, and that a court order has been obtained.

We concur that when a physician begins to consider video surveillance, his or her first course of action should be to work with the multidisciplinary team (Mercer & Perdue, 1993; see also Whelan-Williams & Baker, Chapter 14, this volume). Cooperation of the team with the hospital administration, head of nursing staff, and the legal department is necessary to preserve both patient and parent rights and confidentiality. The team should obtain a court order before undertaking video surveillance whenever possible. This can be done with reasonable suspicion of Munchausen by proxy syndrome and may prevent any future legal action against the hospital involving privacy and confidentiality. A court order will also relieve medical and nonmedical personnel of anxiety concerning future possible civil litigation. The multidisciplinary team members should remember that the team's ability actually to obtain a court order may depend largely on the information provided by the primary care physician or physician reviewer supporting suspicions of child abuse.

Covert video surveillance requires that someone monitor the camera feed from the child's room at all times during recording, to prevent harm to the child. For instance, strict monitoring can allow swift intervention when the perpetrator is observed injecting materials into or smothering the child, even as the evidence is being gathered.

Video surveillance must be arranged and conducted with as much secrecy as possible. Only those persons who absolutely must know should be told, and the personnel with knowledge of the surveillance will vary from case to case. The primary care physician and other actively involved physicians usually should be informed, but nursing personnel who care for the child daily should not be, because the emotions experienced by medical staff who suspect Munchausen by proxy syndrome are quite powerful, and this may interfere with nurses' ability to interact in a natural way with the child's parents. Of course, some primary care physicians may also be too close to the family to participate in planning covert surveillance. The more people who know, the more likely the parents are to detect that they are being watched. Interestingly, we know of one hospital where the families became aware that a particular room was equipped with video equipment; this room became known as the "Munchausen room."

### Establishing the Temporal Relationship

Another way the multidisciplinary team may obtain the necessary documentation to confirm the diagnosis is by establishing a temporal relationship between the presence of the parent and the child's symptoms. As discussed above, carefully kept, comprehensive medical records, especially nurses' notes, may reflect this temporal relationship. A next step would be to limit the mother-perpetrator's involvement in the child's care and then document any changes in the child's condition. Again, a differentiation must be made between symptoms reported by the mother and those independently observed by the medical staff. Steps must be taken to prevent the mother's access to any records or nursing observation notes, which are often kept at bedside. The mother must be prevented from bringing the child any food or drinks, and from participating in feeding the child from the hospital tray. Around-the-clock surveillance, with the mother-perpetrator's knowledge, may be necessary to assure that the mother's access to the child is being monitored adequately. However, the most effective way to establish a temporal relationship between the mother-perpetrator's presence and the child-victim's symptoms is to remove the child from parental care.

The removal of the child from parental care is usually best done in a hospital setting, where the child can be observed closely and any real medical issues dealt with properly. The primary care physician should explain to the parents the need to observe the child in a closely monitored situation away from family members. The physician should already have the preliminary child protective service and legal work done to enforce the request if the parents refuse to cooperate. The mother-perpetrator will often not agree, saying that the child needs her for care or is too ill to go through such an emotional ordeal. Separation in such a case usually does require a court order, and having the child in a medically protected placement such as the hospital will make it easier for a judge to issue the needed order. If the child's symptoms resolve or improve substantially after the child is separated from the mother, this gives adequate confirmation to the diagnosis.

Rubin, Angelides, Davidson, and Lanzkowsky (1986) provide an excellent example of the usefulness of parent-child separation in diagnosing Munchausen by proxy syndrome. They describe the case of an 11-year-old girl who developed progressive upper gastrointestinal ulceration of unknown origin and recurrent episodes of intravenous catheter-associated polymicrobial septicemia. These problems ostensibly began with a fever, cough, and protracted vomiting. Over the next 15 months, the patient had 24 hospital admissions, totaling 375 hospital days. Rubin et al. describe a pattern in which the child would develop an exacerbation of gastrointestinal disease while at home, and then develop fever with bacteremia in the hospital while an intravenous catheter was in place. Exhaustive evaluation failed to establish a cause for these problems.

Rubin et al. report that the mother was at the child's bedside constantly, that she applauded the medical staff's efforts despite her daughter's deterioration, and that she resisted suggestions to seek additional evaluation at another tertiary care center. The mother was eventually confronted with the suspicion that she was instrumental in the production of the bacteremias, which she denied, although she reportedly responded, "I can see how you might think that" (p. 904). Several months after this confrontation, Rubin et al. report, the child became critically ill and the parents were subsequently prohibited from visiting. The child was kept under constant surveillance in the hospital for the next 2 months, during which she was afebrile, began to eat and drink, and gained 9.5 kg, before being discharged to foster care. In the 15 months she was followed after discharge, the child returned to school and had no further hospital admissions. The parents were found guilty of child abuse.

Rubin et al. (1986) conclude that the child's mother was probably responsible for inducing the child's illness, and that the severity of the symptoms prompted multiple invasive medical procedures. They point to the child's remarkable recovery after separation from her parents and her good health while in foster care as the strongest evidence of exogenously induced illness. They also comment that without separation from her mother, the child may have died. It is important to note that it took more than a year for the practitioners dealing with this case to form a strong enough clinical impression that the child's illness was induced that they took steps to exclude the parents.

As with other techniques used to confirm a diagnosis of MBPS, separation of the suspected perpetrator and the child can have inconclusive results if the child does not improve completely. The process can be complicated when real illness is present, either due to preexisting medical conditions or resulting from the abuse the child has already suffered. Additionally, some symptoms occur infrequently, and thus separation must continue for an adequate amount of time to confirm the diagnosis. Older children who are colluding in the fabrication of their symptoms and children who have had psychological symptoms induced, such as coached vomiting, may continue to exhibit symptoms even after being separated from their mothers.

When the diagnosis is certain, intervention is the next logical step. Whelan-Williams and Baker discuss intervention strategies in depth in Chapter 14 of this volume, and we will not duplicate that effort here. In terms of the physician's role in particular, however, a few comments are warranted. When Munchausen by proxy syndrome has been diagnosed, someone needs to confront the mother-perpetrator with this finding. Sometimes the primary care physician, who often has an ongoing, usually long-term relationship with the family, will want to participate in the confrontation. Sometimes this family physician will want only to introduce the mother to law enforcement and social service personnel, who will generally conduct the confrontation. If the physician is involved in confronting the mother, he or she will usually begin by providing her with an explanation of the medical evidence leading to the suspicions of MBPS. The physician may or may not remain for the entire confrontation after law enforcement takes over. The physician may also want to spend some time with other members of the child-victim's family, to explain the situation.

The monitoring techniques we have described above for confirmation of the MBPS diagnosis occur in the hospital for several reasons. Most Munchausen by proxy syndrome abuse occurs in the hospital, and it is easier to maintain the control necessary for confirmation, and to use directed monitoring, in such a setting. Often the first suspicions of MBPS in a case arise during a hospitalization. In other cases, the child is hospitalized for the purpose of confirming or denying the diagnosis. However, current trends toward managed care may render such situations less likely to occur. As it becomes more difficult to hospitalize children, outpatient medical providers will increasingly be relied upon to detect and confirm cases of Munchausen by proxy syndrome. The medical records review may be the only technique available to those investigating suspected cases of MBPS, and, as we have noted, confirmation of the diagnosis with this technique alone can be difficult. However, although a records review may not produce enough evidence for criminal prosecution, it may produce sufficient evidence for the physician to protect the child through an abuse report.


## Education

More than 35 years ago, Yudkin (1961) suggested that when a child is brought to a doctor, the doctor can make two different diagnoses, answering two questions: (a) What is the matter with the patient? (b) Why is this child being brought for care at this moment? The parent's persistence in bringing the child to the doctor may be incongruent with the first diagnosis, thus providing the need for the doctor to search for the second diagnosis (Waring, 1992). Yudkin notes that the doctor is trained to answer the first question in medical school and residency, but the ability to answer *both* questions is "the beginning of real medicine" (p. 563).

Children enter the medical system through many sources—emergency rooms, primary care physicians, hospital-based subspecialists, and surgeons. Medical personnel who care for children must be aware of the existence of Munchausen by proxy syndrome and its many facets. However, many of the medical professionals currently seeing children were trained before this syndrome was recognized. The possibility of a diagnosis of Munchausen by proxy syndrome is often difficult for physicians and other professionals to comprehend. The syndrome places their beliefs and emotions in conflict with the cognitive reality of the situation, and this can create strong disbelief that may be difficult to overcome. The key to the identification of and proper intervention in MBPS cases is the education of those professionals who will be asked to make decisions that affect these families. Education will also make it possible for professionals to refer potential MBPS cases more rapidly for review and/or consultation.

Education of the medical community can be done in many ways. The first step is the introduction in formal medical school training of Munchausen by proxy syndrome as a possible diagnosis. Physicians and other medical personnel are taught to listen to the history provided by the patient or the patient's parent and then incorporate this history into a search for the appropriate medical diagnosis. Nowhere in medical training is the issue raised of the practitioner's questioning the validity of a history as it is presented, and certainly no interrogation techniques are taught. Medical training that includes information on the warning signs of Munchausen by proxy syndrome need not include interrogation techniques; however, these cases suggest the importance of caution on the part of the practitioner. Rather than jumping for the next test or procedure in a zealous search for a diagnosis, it is important that the physician listen carefully and obtain information from other professionals who have been involved in the case.

We are aware of one case that provides an example of how crucial such communication can be. A mother presented her 3-year-old child for consultation with a pediatric gastroenterologist due to reported chronic vomiting and diarrhea. In the course of providing the medical history, the mother claimed that the referring physician had diagnosed the child with a rare genetic disorder. Having no reason to doubt the diagnosis, and with no documents yet available from the referring physician, the consulting physician accepted this as part of the medical history and included it matter-of-factly in her consultation report. The mother returned to the referring physician and informed him, falsely, that the consulting physician had recommended surgery for her son. The referring physician was somewhat surprised by this conclusion and, not having worked with this particular consulting physician before, contacted her to discuss her recommendations. The two physicians ultimately uncovered many untruths perpetrated by this mother. Unfortunately, such communication does not always occur between physicians, especially when families do not seek follow-up care.

Most Munchausen by proxy syndrome cases involve lengthy and/or repeated hospitalizations. Even cases that are primarily conducted on an outpatient basis usually involve local hospital emergency facilities. The actual simulation or induction of symptoms appears to occur primarily in a hospital setting (Rosenberg, 1987). Thus the hospital is usually a central part of these cases and should be a central part of efforts to educate professionals. Therefore, the second step in education is to utilize local community and children's hospitals to provide continuing medical education for physicians, nurses, and technical staff. As we have noted, practitioners in many other disciplines will be involved in these cases (e.g., law enforcement personnel, hospital administrators, judges, attorneys, child protection workers, social workers) and will be asked to make decisions about how cases are handled. The hospital can take the lead by inviting these various practitioners to a multidisciplinary training and discussion forum.

Education can also occur through practitioners' reading of published MBPS case studies. Exposure to this literature is often helpful in breaking through the early denial experienced by all professionals who become involved with these cases. As we have noted, it is often difficult for those who have never seen such cases to comprehend what is being alleged, and their skepticism grows rather than diminishes as the mother-perpetrator and her family try to dispel the allegations. It can thus be extremely powerful for a professional to see a case unfolding exactly as other cases have been described in published articles. We are aware of one particular case, for example, in which a child-victim's guardian ad litem was initially quite skeptical regarding the allegations. However, prior to a crucial court hearing, the guardian spent several hours reviewing an expert's collection of published articles. Although his reading did not entirely convince him as to the validity of the MBPS allegations, he did form grave concerns about the safety of the child, saw many striking similarities in the current case to cases in the literature, and gained some appreciation of the difficulties these cases pose. As a result, the guardian was in a much better position to protect the child.

Physicians and others hoping to educate various professionals about Munchausen by proxy syndrome may find it useful to prepare a selected reading list to provide to those who come in contact with such cases. Such a list should include general review articles as well as specific case studies; the person offering the list can highlight those articles that describe cases similar to the case under suspicion.

## Conclusion

Medical personnel should take cases of suspected Munchausen by proxy syndrome very seriously, and should work hard to confirm or rule out any suspicion of this disorder. The perpetrators of MBPS abuse can be extremely bright and creative in their methods, and as protectors of children's well-being, physicians must be equally or more creative in their approaches to confirming the ultimate diagnosis. As we have discussed above, it may be necessary for physicians, working as part of a multidisciplinary team of professionals, to employ a combination of review of past history and current symptom patterns, video surveillance, and separation of the parent and child to build a case that will withstand legal scrutiny and protect the child. As with most forms of child abuse, a multidisciplinary team that includes medical personnel is best able to develop a case that will enable legal personnel to protect the well-being of the child.

# 5 Coordinated Case Management Through the Child Protection System

Teresa F. Parnell

> *While the medical profession plays a major role in the iden-*
> *tification of the battered child and will have a primary role*
> *in the alleviation of the consequences of parental abuse*
> *and the refamiliation of the abuser, and while welfare and*
> *social workers must play major roles in the resolution of*
> *the problem, ultimately the solution must be legal, in the*
> *form of legislation and judicial decisions, and the machin-*
> *ery of the state designed for the protection of the child.*
> —*A. H. McCoid, "The Battered Child and Other Assaults*
> *Upon the Family," 1965*

Protocols have been developed for the handling of child abuse cases nation-wide. Specifics vary from jurisdiction to jurisdiction, but these protocols provide guidance for the reporting, initial handling, and long-term management of such cases. As our understanding of various forms of neglect, physical abuse, and sexual abuse has grown, so has the unity of community response. The evolution of the handling of such cases can be described as follows: First, there was identification of cases, with no follow-up; then there was mandatory reporting of cases, with attempted follow-up; this was followed by broad-based response that ensured follow-up when cases were detected; and finally, rehabilitation of the family and a long-term management plan have become the goals. Munchausen by proxy syndrome represents a "new" form of abuse increasingly facing the child protection system, and MBPS cases are predictably following the trend seen in the handling of other types of abuse cases at their inception. However, we have the opportunity to apply what we have learned in handling other types of abuse to these cases.

Early MBPS case reports show that suspicious but sometimes ambivalent physicians confronted the mother-perpetrators, but without reporting their suspicions to child protection agencies (Guandolo, 1985; Mitchell, Brummitt, DeForest, & Fisher, 1993; Stone, 1989). The physicians, who appeared almost not to believe the allegations themselves, were, of course, met with denial by the alleged perpetrators. Although some case reports suggest that the mothers ceased their behavior after being confronted (Meadow, 1982a), most families were lost to follow-up (Mercer & Perdue, 1993; Orenstein & Wasserman, 1986; Smith & Killam, 1994; Sullivan, Francis, Bain, & Hartz, 1991) and had no known treatment intervention for the perpetrator (Leeder, 1990; Libow & Schreier, 1986). The next phase involved properly identifying these cases as a form of child abuse that must be reported to the appropriate authorities. However, mandatory reporting has not produced the swift, sure action necessary to protect children (Goss & McDougall, 1992; Kahan & Yorker, 1990; Kovacs & Toth, 1993; Lacey, Cooper, Runyan, & Azizkhan, 1993; Schreier & Libow, 1993a; Single & Henry, 1991; Waller, 1983), including many cases in which there has been no judicial intervention (Bools, Neale, & Meadow, 1993). When there is judicial intervention, cases are often determined to lack sufficient evidence to convict the alleged perpetrators (Halsey et al., 1983; Kahan & Yorker, 1990; Lacey et al., 1993), and even when abuse is confirmed, child-victims are returned home prematurely, often against medical advice (Goss & McDougall, 1992; Kahan & Yorker, 1991; Mills & Burke, 1990; Orenstein & Wasserman, 1986; Outwater, Lipnik, Luban, Ravenscroft, & Ruley, 1981; Turk, Hanrahan, & Weber, 1990). The major issue here is the believability of MBPS cases in the eyes of social service workers, state attorneys, and judges, all of whom are necessary to the implementation of protective actions and family services.

With increased identification and reporting of MBPS cases, we appear to be moving into a phase in which increasing numbers of institutions are developing acceptable response protocols. Abuse reports are now being followed by intervention, but, unfortunately, we are still lacking much of the information we need to understand this troublesome behavior. Skepticism remains regarding the diagnosis, the danger to the child, the potential for death of the victim, and the necessity of intensive long-term treatment for the perpetrator. As a result, even with the involvement of protective services and the judicial system, victims are continuing to be abused due to the level of perpetrator-victim contact being allowed (Bools et al., 1993; McGuire & Feldman, 1989). Mental health professionals are also often manipulated into believing in the innocence of mother-perpetrators or overestimating their progress in therapy. All members of the child protection system must be well educated and must understand their vital roles if treatment of MBPS cases is to evolve toward the goals of rehabilitation and long-term management.

## The Abuse Report

The first issue in the management of the Munchausen by proxy syndrome case is, of course, accurate identification (as has been discussed in Chapters 1-4 of this volume). Once a case is identified, the professionals involved should file an abuse report with the agency designated to receive mandatory reports of suspected child abuse cases in the state where the abuse occurred. Munchausen by proxy syndrome qualifies as abuse under the Child Abuse Prevention and Treatment Act of 1974, which sets the standard for state reporting laws. The act defines abuse and neglect as follows:

> The physical or mental injury, sexual abuse, negligent treatment, or maltreatment of a child under the age of 18 by a person who is responsible for the child's welfare under circumstances which indicate the child's health or welfare is harmed or threatened thereby as determined in accordance with regulations prescribed.

Although every state in the United States has mandatory reporting laws for human services and medical professionals, the thresholds for determining when abuse should be reported vary. Most professionals are guided by state laws using terminology such as "*reason to believe* or *having reasonable cause to suspect* abuse" (Kalichman, 1993, p. 30), but without further clarification. Definitions of *abuse, neglect,* and *maltreatment* vary among states, as do the conditions under which reporting is required. Professionals are often confused regarding what constitutes "suspicion" of child abuse (Kalichman, 1993). Further, research has shown that reports are filed in only about one-third of the cases of abuse suspected by various professionals (Finkelhor, 1984; Kim, 1986; U.S. Department of Health and Human Services, 1988). Professionals may fail to comply with mandatory reporting laws for numerous reasons, including lack of accurate knowledge concerning these laws, perceived conflict between reporting and the professional role, concern for the privacy rights of the client, the professional's belief that he or she can handle the situation more effectively without outside interference, concern regarding the consequences of reporting, and uncertainty regarding the accuracy of the suspicions (Kalichman, 1993).

The dilemma of what to report and when becomes even more pronounced in Munchausen by proxy syndrome cases, where the concrete evidence necessary to support an allegation is often unavailable. The data that arouse suspicion in the first place are usually nebulous, and the practitioner who suspects MBPS is also concerned with the need to protect the child by intervening rapidly, often before he or she can obtain solid evidence of the abuse. Gathering proof in MBPS cases is further complicated by the preverbal age of most victims, the cunning of the perpetrator, the very real physical symptoms that are often created, and the history of medical care already amassed. Additionally, as with general definitions of abuse, the definition of what constitutes Munchausen by proxy syndrome has been debated (see Parnell, Chapter 2, this volume), thus some professionals may be uncomfortable reporting what they consider to be "milder" forms of MBPS. When we add to all of this unsteady ground the disbelief that characterizes most professionals' responses to Munchausen by proxy syndrome, it is a wonder any cases have been reported at all.

When the proper authorities are notified of a case of child abuse, local child protective services and often law enforcement become immediately involved. Due to the uniqueness of MBPS cases, a child protection team should also play an immediate role when Munchausen by proxy is reported. Child protection teams exist in all states and most counties within the United States. Many child protection teams are affiliated with hospitals, and so are well situated to coordinate the response to MBPS cases, given the fact that MBPS abuse is most likely to occur within hospital settings. Certainly, the resources available to child protection teams are relatively limited in some communities, but all such teams have connections with various agencies and individuals (i.e., child protective services, law enforcement, hospital administration, hospital psychosocial services, and physicians) who can orchestrate effective intervention and investigation into MBPS cases. The involvement of the child protection team's consulting psychologist also allows for rapid intervention with the mother-perpetrator's extended family and the child-victim, if appropriate. Loss of contact between the perpetrator and the child generally occurs immediately and must be addressed within the rest of the family. (My colleagues at one hospital have developed a multidisciplinary protocol for rapid and comprehensive response to Munchausen by proxy syndrome cases that incorporates all the necessary individuals; for discussion of this protocol, see Whelan-Williams & Baker, Chapter 14, this volume.)

Once the abuse report has been made to the appropriate agency, the suspected perpetrator must be confronted. The multidimensional approach to the treatment of Munchausen by proxy syndrome has naturally led to some dispute about the most beneficial form for this confrontation. Mainly, the debate has concerned three alternatives: (a) medical confrontation by the physician, (b) a therapeutic type of intervention by a social worker, and (c) a confrontational investigative approach taken by a law enforcement officer. In a number of cases with which I am familiar, the law enforcement approach has resulted in partial or full acknowledgment by the perpetrator of her behavior. It appears that law enforcement confrontations may be able to break through the denial so often reported in the literature when confrontations are done by the treating physician and/or a social worker. Whatever form the confrontation takes, it should represent a preplanned, coordinated effort involving child protective services, the child protection team, law enforcement, the hospital, physicians, and a consulting psychologist (see Seibel & Parnell, Chapter 4, this volume; Whelan-Williams & Baker, Chapter 14, this volume).

The process of confrontation and the reporting of suspected abuse set into motion juvenile (or dependency) court and criminal actions, and, in some cases, later marital dissolution. Each of these legal arenas will deal with a multiplicity of issues involved in long-term management of the case. In this chapter I focus on the juvenile court, where most of the parameters for case management are established through the court's role of protecting the child.

## Juvenile Court

Child protective service agencies within each state maintain responsibility for investigating and handling an increasing array of abuses against children, and research has shown that many professionals have little knowledge of Munchausen by proxy syndrome (Kaufman, Coury, Pickrell, & McCleery, 1989; Stancin, 1990). The role of child protective services is vital in this potentially deadly arena, yet these agencies rarely have the resources to keep their workers on the cutting edge of information. Guidelines for effective child protective services response to suspected cases of Munchausen by proxy syndrome may be the most important tool to stop the abuse once it is identified. Given the unique nature of MBPS cases, it is beneficial if the child protective services workers assigned to these cases have some experience in this area; thus workers who have dealt with one Munchausen by proxy syndrome case should be considered for any new cases. (I am aware of one caseworker who has developed some expertise in these cases and as a result has been made available to assist caseworkers in a neighboring county.) Child protective services workers are the professionals with the most extensive, continuous contact with MBPS families; they coordinate services, monitor compliance, and evaluate progress. However, their effectiveness is significantly compromised if they receive no support from the juvenile or dependency judge to enforce the families' case plans.

Generally, an emergency motion must be filed with the court to place a child in protective custody. Often the child is still hospitalized, and the motion is filed to prevent the suspected mother-perpetrator, and possibly other family members, from having access to the child or removing the child. A petition is filed with the court setting forth the factual and legal basis for the allegations. The petition may indicate physical abuse, emotional abuse, other mental injury, and/or threatened harm, depending upon the actions of the perpetrator. The petition needs to outline specifically the actions taken by the mother, the consequences of those actions, and the resulting harm to the child. When the mother-perpetrator has induced illness, these issues will be readily apparent. In the case of exaggeration or fabrication, however, the petition needs to explain the harm caused by the unnecessary medical interventions received by the child as a result of the exaggeration or fabrication. Usually, allegations will also need to be articulated that the father of the child was unable or unwilling to protect the child or prevent the abuse (i.e., he knew about the mother's behavior and failed to take steps to prevent harm to the child). At the point of confrontation of the mother-perpetrator, the father will often staunchly support her, and therefore will be unwilling to follow the directives of the court to protect the child.

Any dependency petition filed with the court or case plan offered to the mother must include specific details of the Munchausen by proxy syndrome abuse. Offers made by the mother-perpetrator to cooperate voluntarily with protective services or to enter a consent to the dependency petition should not be accepted unless she acknowledges the Munchausen by proxy syndrome. I am aware of several cases in which perpetrators were willing to consent to the dependency and to participate in treatment, with the goal of reunification with the child, but without admitting the Munchausen by proxy syndrome, and I would advise extreme caution regarding such arrangements. Without an acknowledgment of the abusive behavior, the perpetrator cannot be held accountable for addressing that problem in the case plan and is obviously unwilling to do so anyway. Therefore, although there may be some control over the family with such a consent, the problems relating to the dangerous behavior will probably never be addressed. This places the child, his or her siblings, and any subsequent children at continued risk, despite any treatment the mother receives. MBPS perpetrators are generally masters of manipulation and deception, and mental health professionals are not immune to their talents.

I am aware of one case in which the mother-perpetrator was allowed to consent to dependency of the child-victim without acknowledging her Munchausen by proxy behavior. The consent included an agreement by the mother to seek psychotherapy, but because the consent did not include acknowledgment of the MBPS, the treatment was not directed toward that issue. In effect, the mother could complete treatment to the satisfaction of the consent decree and have her child returned to her care without ever acknowledging or addressing the Munchausen by proxy behavior. This is problem enough, but consider the other children who remained in the mother's care. A younger sibling began to exhibit the same symptoms as the child-victim and to implicate the mother, just as the original child-victim had. Child protective service workers felt paralyzed watching this happen. This child was not even part of the original dependency agreement, and therefore a new abuse report would need to be made. This would generate a new case with a new worker and a new judge; in other words, it meant starting all over.

As knowledge regarding Munchausen by proxy syndrome is becoming more widespread, some perpetrators and/or their attorneys have become sensitive to the label, even suggesting that to agree to it is tantamount to labeling the perpetrator a monster. If this is the case in a particular instance, I would concede that it is not so much the name of the disorder that must be included in the dependency (or criminal) action, but the specific behavior of the perpetrator and the impact on the child. It is important for the perpetrator to take responsibility for her behavior and for the authorities to identify clearly what must be addressed in treatment.

A major immediate issue for the child protective services worker in the MBPS case is how to ensure the physical safety of the child while minimizing the disruptive emotional trauma that separation from the family can cause. The ultimate goal of restoration of the family must always be considered, but this remains so far in the future in most of these cases that the main initial focus must be protection of the child, in conjunction with ensuring the cooperation of the family with the case plan. It is has been shown to be beneficial for the child to be removed from the home and placed in foster care, if only temporarily. Some children may require continued hospitalization or placement in medical foster homes. Placement with family members is certainly the least traumatic option for the child, but it is imperative that the caseworker understand the larger family system before making this determination. Munchausen by proxy syndrome is believed to be a disorder developed within a larger familial and societal context (see Robins & Sesan, 1991; Schreier & Libow, 1993a), and the caseworker should take this into account. Also warranted in MBPS cases is complete investigation of the medical histories of the child-victim's siblings, as well as any sibling deaths. In some cases, out-of-home placement is also needed for siblings.

Another important issue the caseworker must consider in placing the child-victim outside the home is whether the potential caretakers will follow the directives of the court designed to protect the child, even if the caretakers do not fully believe the allegations. Family members have been known to collude with the perpetrator and sabotage treatment (Libow & Schreier, 1986; Orenstein & Wasserman, 1986; Waller, 1983).

Complete psychological evaluations should be conducted immediately on the mother-perpetrator, the child-victim (if old enough), and the child-victim's father. Although psychological evaluations have not proven useful in isolation for diagnosing Munchausen by proxy syndrome (see Parnell, Chapter 7, this volume), careful review of educational, employment, and psychiatric records, when compared with information provided by the perpetrator, can sometimes uncover a pattern of fabrication about life events. Additionally, psychological evaluations provide the opportunity to obtain a full social history and to acquire data that identify individual psychodynamics, family dynamics, and treatment issues separate from the Munchausen by proxy behavior. The psychological evaluation should also include complete review of medical records and doctors' reports in order to be comprehensive and ensure an understanding of the situation. The diagnosis of MBPS is ultimately a medical diagnosis, and any mental health assessment must incorporate the medical findings.

Social histories taken from extended family members are also crucial for verifying information and for highlighting larger familial influences. This is especially important for family members who continue to have contact with the child-victim. A complete psychological evaluation may in fact be warranted for any family member whose home is being considered for placement of the child. The clinical interview/social history session with family members should also include some education of these individuals about Munchausen by proxy syndrome and exploration of their reactions to the allegations. This is an extremely emotional time for family members, and obviously it is quite difficult for them to accept these types of allegations. An assessment of each family member's willingness to support an appropriate case plan is important at this point. The family must be willing to acknowledge the Munchausen by proxy syndrome and to protect the child from the perpetrator, in the face of appeals to family loyalty. Family members will also have to make a substantial shift in perspective regarding the child, who was once perceived as quite ill and possibly fragile; they must learn to interact with the "well" child. Family members will also need assistance in developing appropriate, trusting relationships with mental health/medical professionals while fearing their scrutiny, given the circumstances.

Unfortunately, my colleagues and I have been involved with cases in which family members seeking placement of the child-victim initially vowed to do anything to protect the child and to follow the directives of the court, only to change their stance once they had physical custody of the child. In the initial shock of the allegations and the trauma of having the child removed from the entire family unit, there seems to be a desire to do anything to bring that child back into the family. Once the child is reclaimed and the reality of the allegations begins to seep through the shock, however, the family begins to resist. It is far too painful for family members to believe the accusations, and so they search for other explanations, sometimes adopting those being provided by the mother-perpetrator.

In addition to the denial that often pervades these families, it is difficult in the initial days after a confrontation to assess accurately the pathology within the family system. Deborah Day and I participated in a case in which a father initially displayed no overt psychopathology, only the expected distress after disclosure of his wife's behavior and her subsequent arrest. There was also no evidence to indicate that he had participated in the Munchausen by proxy abuse in any way. Placement of the child-victim and his siblings with the father was recommended, along with supportive family services. Unfortunately, over the next few months evidence emerged that he had also been abusive to his wife and children, but in different ways.

What is often most difficult for the family to accept is the restriction of contact between the child and mother. My colleagues and I recommend that there be no visitation between the perpetrating mother and the child-victim during this evaluation phase, nor until the perpetrator has acknowledged her behavior and is fully involved in psychotherapy. Our experience, as well as the limited psychotherapy literature (Day, 1994; Schreier & Libow, 1993a), suggests that these mothers generally become involved in therapy only to obtain visitation with their children. They are not considered to be insightful, nor are they psychologically inclined. Therefore, it is difficult for them to accept the need for therapeutic intervention.

Terminating contact between the mother and child is one of the most difficult issues in managing the MBPS case, not just for the family, but for child protective workers, judges, defense attorneys, and therapists. The above suggestions may appear to be unnecessarily restrictive, especially in so-called milder cases. The idea of developing a visitation plan based only on the severity of the mother's actions may appear enticing. However, I would strongly caution professionals to consider several issues before developing a visitation plan. First, MBPS abuse, no matter how seemingly mild, can lead to permanent injury or death, due not only to the mother's behavior but to what she allows physicians to do to the child because of her withholding of information. This point is often very difficult for various professionals to understand. Second, given the level of the deception in these cases, including even the acknowledging mother's initial tendency to admit to her behavior only partially, it is unlikely that everything that has endangered the child will be known. Finally, we return to the treatment issue. If the perpetrator is allowed to continue parenting, it is questionable whether the dangerous perpetrator dynamics will ever be addressed in treatment. Additionally, once visitation moves forward, it often becomes difficult in dependency cases to stop the momentum. Juvenile courts often must work within state-mandated time frames for restoration of the family. It is possible that visitation will proceed unencumbered due merely to the passage of time, and the mother is given the message that she need not ever acknowledge or address her behavior completely. Compare this situation with the current thinking regarding alleged child sexual abuse: We generally do not question a case plan that limits or prevents visitation between an alleged sexual offender and his or her child when the offender has yet to acknowledge his or her sexually deviant behavior with that child.

Some child-victims require placement in medical foster homes following discharge from the hospital. The MBPS child's progress following separation from the mother-perpetrator is often an important part of confirming the diagnosis. These children usually make incredible developmental and physical gains once this separation occurs, which may be the most striking evidence in cases where there is no confession by the perpetrator. Caseworkers must sometimes help even highly qualified, competent foster parents to understand that these cases are different, and that the foster parents' careful observations can be quite relevant to the child's future. Documentation of the child's physical condition and development should be maintained in pictures, videotapes, and journals. Specifically, the symptoms or concerns previously reported by the mother-perpetrator should be noted, if they occur and if they do not occur. Although the foster parents may usually take their foster children to a physician with whom they have developed a relationship, it is imperative that medical care of the MBPS child-victim continue with a physician who is familiar with the case. Foster parents must also be careful not to reveal information about the child to others or to develop relationships with the child's parents. My colleagues and I have been amazed at how MBPS parents seem to be able to access confidential information about their children's foster parents and their children's progress. Of course, these parents then will usually claim that the children are doing poorly or are experiencing the same medical problems as before. I am also aware of a case in which the mother-perpetrator was able to send messages to her child through visits with the child's siblings.

## Reunification

Reunification involves not only the ultimate return of the child to the mother as primary caretaker, but the contact preceding such an arrangement. As in other types of abuse cases, the visitation schedule should gradually move from no contact toward a less restrictive arrangement as appropriate. Only a few studies are available that address the physical and psychological conditions of the MBPS child-victim on long-term follow-up (Bools et al., 1993; McGuire & Feldman, 1989). Even less information is available on which case management techniques have had positive outcomes and which have not, including the issue of perpetrator-victim contact. Cases have been documented of continued Munchausen by proxy syndrome abuse while the mother was receiving psychiatric treatment (Croft & Jervis, 1989), after the involvement of protective services (McGuire & Feldman, 1989), during supervised visitation (Kinscherff & Famularo, 1991), and following reunification (Bools et al., 1993). We also know that the absence of fabrication alone does not mean the child will thrive psychologically and developmentally (Bools et al., 1993). The question for many clinicians, then, is not *when* the mother and child should be reunited, but *if* they should be reunited.

The perpetrator and family dynamics ascertained during the initial psychological evaluation and subsequent treatment should guide any reunification plan. As I have noted, no contact should occur between the child and the mother until the perpetrator is actively involved in treatment and can acknowledge the Munchausen by proxy syndrome behavior, even if complete understanding has not been accomplished. Part II of this volume is devoted to intervention and treatment in MBPS families, including the timing of resumed contact between perpetrator and victim. In this chapter, I will address the logistics of such contact in the context of case management.

In general, any contact between the child-victim and mother-perpetrator should be carefully planned and graduated to ensure the clinician adequate opportunity to observe parent-child dynamics and changes in the relationship. Contact should begin with therapeutic visitation, conducted with the child's therapist, the perpetrator's therapist, or both. The early sessions of therapeutic visitation should involve discussion of the allegations and the resulting separation between child and mother, depending on the child's age. An older child especially should be given an opportunity to articulate his or her knowledge of the fabrications and his or her feelings about the perpetrator's actions and about the separation. The child should be allowed to ask questions of the perpetrator as well. The perpetrator's therapist will already have worked with the perpetrator on appropriate responses to such inquiries.

Later therapeutic visitation sessions should focus on general parenting skills and parent-child interaction. Contact between mother and child should then follow a predictable pattern of increasing contact with decreasing supervision, as seen in other types of abuse cases:

1. Supervised visitation outside of the therapist's office
2. Unsupervised but videotaped visitation in the therapist's office that is initially monitored via one-way mirror by the therapist
3. Monitored access outside of the therapist's office
4. Unsupervised visitation outside of the therapist's office for short periods
5. Overnight visitation
6. Reunification

Most of these steps are self-explanatory for professionals who work with other types of abuse cases. Monitored access or visitation (Step 3) involves allowing the mother to have virtually unlimited access to the child within the child's home environment, which may include overnight stays on special occasions or holidays, with interactions less stringently monitored than previously. This step may not be possible in all situations, but it is more likely to occur if the child is placed with a relative (which, as discussed above, may have its own problems). Monitored access allows the mother to resume many aspects of the parenting role with significant opportunity for observation so that the clinician may assess how appropriately she can manage daily parenting tasks, school interaction, medical appointments, and so on. The therapist can obtain vital information from such monitoring regarding the mother's awareness of the child's needs, the mother's discipline skills, and the quality of the parent-child interaction.

Throughout the time when contact is gradually increasing between mother and child, a number of additional interventions should be occurring. First, the mother-perpetrator and the child-victim should continue to participate in individual and conjoint therapy. If the child is too young to engage in therapy, a clinician can still make office observations. Additionally, there will be a need to depend more on the observations made by the outside supervisor to assess progress in the mother-child relationship. As with placement issues, decisions regarding who should supervise contact must be carefully considered. In many respects, family members provide the most consistent environment for the child and are often more willing than others to cooperate with the many demands made upon them to meet all of the requirements of the case plan. However, the same potential problems as those related to placement should be considered. Other individuals who might supervise contact between the mother and child include the guardian ad litem, the child protective services worker, and professional supervisors.

Whoever is selected to supervise mother-child contacts must be familiar with Munchausen by proxy syndrome and with the details of the particular case. He or she should have the opportunity to provide continual feedback to the perpetrator's therapist regarding his or her observations. Proposed supervisors should each be interviewed by a therapist involved in the case to determine that individual's understanding of the allegations and his or her role as a supervisor. Initially, it is important that the supervisor be given explicit instructions regarding the parameters of supervised contact. In the early part of supervised contact, the mother-perpetrator should never be left alone with the child, even for a brief period. She should not accompany the child alone to the bathroom, nor should she bring candy, food, drinks, or medicines to the visits. Most mother-perpetrators accept these restrictions with little difficulty, especially if they understand that the rules can help to protect them from further allegations should their children become ill after their visits.

Also during the gradually increasing contacts between mother and child, it is helpful for the mother's therapist to hold periodic consultation sessions with the family members in order to obtain further family history and to gain insight regarding their observations of the parent-child interactions and perpetrator progress. Initially these may be individual sessions, although conjoint sessions that include the perpetrator are recommended as soon as this is therapeutically appropriate. Sessions with family members can be difficult at first, as the MBPS family system is often quite secretive. However, the therapist can gradually work with family members, who are concerned about the future of the child, to understand the need to be open with the therapist and confront the perpetrator with any concerns. The usefulness of these sessions will, of course, vary according to the pathology of the family system, especially when the mother-perpetrator has been a victim of abuse within the family.

The mother-perpetrator should also be reintegrated into the child's medical care during this period. All children require some level of medical and dental care throughout childhood, and the perpetrator must learn to manage this appropriately. Additionally, many child-victims have bona fide medical conditions separate from the fabricated symptoms or physical conditions acquired because of the fabricated illness. Preferably, the child should be followed medically by one physician, with as few specialists involved as possible. The identification of this physician should be incorporated into the case plan. In extreme cases, the case plan may indicate that the mother-perpetrator is not allowed to take the child to a physician without a court order. The physician must be someone who is knowledgeable about Munchausen by proxy syndrome. Sometimes, the primary physician who was treating the child at the time the allegations were made will wish to continue to follow the child, but many physicians who have been in this position simply want to terminate any involvement with these families.

Whoever chooses to follow the child, all health care professionals (including dentists, optometrists, and others) who see the child should be fully informed about the mother-perpetrator's abuse of the child. This may be done by the physician initially involved in the confrontation or by the perpetrator's therapist, with consent. During this informational contact, it will also be important to check the physician's comfort level with the case and any concerns he or she may have about interacting with the mother whenever she becomes involved in the child's appointments. The primary care physician should be a vital part of a system designed to intervene quickly if problems emerge with the mother's handling of the child's physical condition. The physician must be willing to confront the mother if he or she has any concerns about her presentation of symptoms, her interaction style, or misinterpretation of physician findings. The physician may want to provide brief, written notes to the mother at the conclusion of each visit, which are then signed by both the physician and the mother. Physician communication with the perpetrator's therapist regarding the mother's interaction is also important. The mother's attendance at the child's medical appointments should begin well before she is to have unsupervised contact with the child.

Cases in which the child-victim remains with the nonperpetrating parent and continues medical care with the same physician require some additional planning. The mother-perpetrator's behavior represents a major breach in the relationship between the physician and the mother that is likely to interfere with any future relationship. For the mother to manage her child's medical needs successfully in the future, the trust in this relationship must be re-established. A part of the mother-perpetrator's recovery can be her full disclosure of her actions to the physician, with assistance from her therapist. Reestablishing some level of trust and communication is important even if the mother-perpetrator is not actively involved in the child's medical appointments. When the mother is removed from the child's medical care, the physician must rely on the nonoffending parent for medical information, and this may be tainted by the spouse's anger. The nonoffending spouse and the physician may become aligned in their suspicion of the mother-perpetrator and hypersensitive to any changes in the child following contact with the mother. Actively working to reestablish an appropriate mother-physician relationship allows the physician to be comfortable in contacting and confronting the perpetrator directly with any concerns.

It is important to remember that a Munchausen by proxy syndrome case is likely to involve a lengthy supervised visitation schedule. Movement toward possible reunification is a laborious process. In one case in which the mother-perpetrator had administered laxatives to induce symptoms in her child, the mother and child had no contact for almost 12 months, and no unsupervised contact for an additional 9 months. Two years after identification of Munchausen by proxy syndrome, the child is still placed with a relative. It should be noted that this particular case involves an older child-victim who is capable of understanding and articulating what happened to her, as well as a mother who has made satisfactory progress in therapy.

How should the decision be made finally to reunite mother and child? Far too little empirical information is available to guide this critical decision. Meadow (1985) identifies several risk factors that may suggest that reunification is contraindicated. These include abuse involving suffocation or poisoning; a victim less than 5 years of age; previous unexplained death of a sibling of the child-victim; a lack of understanding by the mother of what is happening, as well as little feasibility of help for her and her family; a mother with Munchausen syndrome, drug abuse, or alcoholism; and fabrication that continues after confrontation. Schreier and Libow (1993a) propose specific criteria that should be met before reunification is considered seriously:

1. The victimized child does not also have any serious, bona fide medical problems that would require complex or extended contact with the medical system after reunification. This could seriously complicate the efforts of monitoring agents to determine if the Munchausen by Proxy Syndrome behavior has resolved.

2. The parent should have achieved some insight and a meaningful explanatory system for understanding the nature of her Munchausen by Proxy Syndrome behavior and the needs she was attempting to meet through use of the child as proxy.

3. The parent should have developed some alternative coping strategies to use when under stress and have demonstrated awareness of significant stress factors in her own life.

4. The parent's spouse, partner, or extended family should have accepted the reality of the abusing parent's Munchausen by Proxy Syndrome and demonstrated a sincere commitment to the future protection of the child(ren).

5. The parent's therapist as well as a more objective consulting psychologist/psychiatrist experienced with Munchausen by Proxy Syndrome patients should be in agreement that the parent has made progress during psychotherapy.

6. The parent should not also exhibit additional serious psychopathology such as a thought disorder, affective disorder, organicity, or the like.

7. There should be no evidence that the parent continues to claim that her child has unsubstantiated medical problems or that she is continuing to distort facts or somaticize her own problems.

8. The parent should be able to demonstrate adequate basic parenting skills, genuine warmth for the child, and increased empathic understanding of the child's experiences.

9. The court should mandate that the child's medical providers are kept to a minimum and coordinated by a single physician familiar with and committed to stopping the Munchausen by Proxy Syndrome behavior.

10. The social services arm of the court should provide long-term follow-up of the family's reunification over a period of several years rather than months. Follow-up does not simply mean periodic home visits and visual inspection of the child, but also regular communication with the child's pediatrician and school (to examine patterns of absence and medical utilization).

11. Provision should be made either for restrictions on the family's ability to move to new jurisdictions or at least a transfer of long-term follow-up responsibilities to educated authorities in new jurisdictions. (pp. 218-219)

Finally, Bools et al. (1993) provide some information about reunification in their report on the most complete assessment of child-victims' long-term adjustment to date: their study of 54 child-victims. Of these children, 30 were living in families with their biological mothers and 24 were with other families. Of the children residing with their mothers, adequate data on continued fabrications were available for 23. Of these, 10 suffered further fabrications and 8 experienced "other concerns" such as suspicious presentation of medical symptoms, lying by the mother, dependence on professionals, and concerns regarding the quality of the relationship with the mother. Of the children residing away from their biological mothers, there were no reports of further fabricated illness. However, Bools and his colleagues do report myriad emotional and behavioral problems among the children who resided with their mothers *and* the children who did not remain with their mothers. A more positive outcome rating was obtained by those children who had received short-term fostering before being returned to their mothers, as opposed to those who remained continuously with their mothers. Bools et al. conclude that the data available for their study were not consistent enough for them to comment on whether children fared better overall when they remained with their mothers or were separated from them. However, they state that long-term psychological morbidity of victims of fabricated illness is substantial, and that active, detailed, and early management that includes therapeutic intervention reduces the risk for child-victims.

Because there is virtually no information about nonperpetrating fathers in the literature, we have no data regarding child-victim outcomes after placement with the father. As I have noted above, however, placement with the father is not recommended until a full family assessment has been conducted and comprehensive psychological evaluations have been completed on all family members. Before the child-victim is placed with any family member, including the father, it is imperative that a clear understanding exists of each individual's role in the family system, and that a plan is in place. Placement or reunification of the child with the father should depend on the father's ability to acknowledge the Munchausen by proxy syndrome allegations, his understanding of the impact on his child, and the potential future risk to the child. Additional factors that must be considered include the father's parenting skills, his relationship with the child-victim and/or the child's siblings, his ability to protect the child from the mother-perpetrator if necessary, his willingness to follow the directives of the court, his involvement in treatment to understand his role in the family, and his willingness to address any issues raised in his psychological evaluation. Usually, because these fathers are not actively involved in the Munchausen by proxy abuse and they are available, even if they have been emotionally or physically absent, the courts lean toward placing children with their fathers rather swiftly.

### Termination of Parental Rights

In some MBPS families, rehabilitation of the perpetrator and reunification of child and mother may not be possible. The termination of parental rights is one potential outcome of involvement with child protective services in Munchausen by proxy cases. This may be a viable and necessary alternative in cases where the perpetrator maintains staunch denial of her behavior and thus is not amenable to treatment. This resistance places the child as well as the child's siblings at continued risk. In addition to treatment issues, Munchausen by proxy syndrome victimization can be seen as falling along a continuum, such that not all cases would require consideration of termination of parental rights (see Parnell, Chapter 2, this volume). A word of caution is in order, however. We cannot be certain, with our limited understanding of MBPS, whether mother-perpetrators engaging in "mild" forms of abuse may escalate their behavior, if not discovered, to more serious victimization. This certainly appears to be the case with serial Munchausen by proxy syndrome (Alexander, Smith, & Stevenson, 1990).

Many state authorities operate under the presumption that the ultimate goal of state intervention is to preserve the family unit, albeit with some improvements in the well-being of the children. Termination of parental rights strips a parent of all rights to communication with or access to the child for the remainder of the child's minor years; if both parents have their parental rights terminated, the child becomes available for adoption. This is a very serious deprivation, and some people view it as inexcusable interference in family integrity. However, sometimes family preservation is at odds with child protection. In order to terminate a person's parental rights, the court must generally find clear and convincing evidence that the parent is unfit to further the welfare and best interest of the child. In Munchausen by proxy syndrome cases, the child-victim's rights must be considered over parent rights when safety of the victim cannot be assured.

Kinscherff and Famularo (1991) suggest that termination of paternal rights should be considered immediately in cases of "extreme" Munchausen by proxy syndrome. They define the perpetrators of extreme Munchausen by proxy syndrome abuse as "parents who place their child victims at severe risk for death, disfigurement, invalidism, and massive impairment of psychological and social development by securing unnecessary medical interventions" (p. 41). They suggest that the argument for termination of parental rights is founded upon four issues:

1. The danger to the child is chronic and potentially lethal.
2. There are no known methods of reliably effective psychiatric intervention in the conduct of the perpetrator.
3. Children often continue to be victimized while the family is monitored and the perpetrator is in treatment.
4. Child protective services and juvenile courts are unable to provide adequate and reliable long-term planning and protection. (p. 45)

Kinscherff and Famularo raise viable concerns that must be considered. Bools et al. (1993), in a long-term follow-up of victims, found that even after discovery and intervention, mothers continued to fabricate illness in their children. However, these researchers also note the infrequent use of judicial intervention, commenting that "the management strategies used were not as strongly interventionist as may be required" (p. 629).

As I have noted above, the child protection system appears to be entering a phase in which comprehensive long-term case planning is beginning to be implemented in Munchausen by proxy syndrome cases. Progress has been made in some districts in Florida, where stringent controls on perpetrator-victim contact have been maintained over lengthy periods. A psychological treatment model has also proven effective (Day, 1994); in none of the cases to which it has been applied has continued victimization occurred. Realistically, even with termination of paternal rights, an MBPS perpetrator may still have contact with other children—those who remain in her home at the time of the termination and/or others born to her at later times. A perpetrator may easily establish residence elsewhere and begin her pathological behavior again. This would be of particular concern if termination of paternal rights were immediate, without any attempt at rehabilitation. It also must be considered that severity is not the only issue, because less extreme forms of MBPS may be equally intractable. As with other forms of abuse, some perpetrators will respond to treatment such that they can again care for the target child or other children, whereas others will not make such progress, even with "mild" abuse. Certainly we lack the knowledge at this time to make such distinctions in Munchausen by proxy syndrome cases. Schreier and Libow (1993a) articulate these issues clearly:

> The bottom line, however, is that we remain very far from having a comprehensive understanding of all the risk factors and individual determinants of a successful or unsuccessful reunification of child and parents. But given the severe and life-threatening extent to which some of these parents will go in their pursuit of a relationship with the medical system, we urge major caution on the part of the legal system in pressing forward with reunification. This is certainly a condition where in order to provide for physical and psychological safety, the parties charged with the task must suspend deeply held belief systems concerning the family and rely on the most current data and expertise available. (p. 220)

Although the focus of the long-term case management plan will be within the child protective services and juvenile court systems, the criminal and civil courts may also become involved in these cases. Ignoring these systems can result in problems, such as one judge ordering no contact between the perpetrator and child and another judge allowing such contact.

## Criminal Court

In their review of the literature, Schreier and Libow (1993a) found few MBPS cases with criminal follow-up. In the approximately 30 cases in which Deborah Day and I have been involved, one-third of the mother-perpetrators have faced criminal charges. However, of the 10 cases handled in our district, criminal charges were filed in 6. The charges have ranged from misdemeanor child abuse to first-degree murder. None of these cases has gone to trial, but a number have reached plea agreements (see Wilkinson & Parnell, Chapter 13, this volume). Those perpetrators who have been sentenced have received a combination of house arrest, probation, and therapy, with a recent case resulting in a significant prison term (see Table 13.1 in Chapter 13). Additionally, we have seen good cooperation between the juvenile and criminal courts in our local jurisdictions. This has enabled appropriate coordination regarding victim-perpetrator contact and psychotherapy services. This type of coordination is imperative to ensure the child's safety. Although the involvement of child protective services and the juvenile court strengthens the case management plan, the involvement of the criminal court provides even stronger assurance of family compliance. The various branches of the judicial system need to take responsibility for communicating with one another and for educating their respective judges. (I am aware of one case in which both the juvenile court and the criminal court appointed the same defense attorney for a client, due to the attorney's familiarity with Munchausen by proxy syndrome cases and to maintain continuity in the courts.)

As with other forms of abuse, questions arise as to whether Munchausen by proxy syndrome should be regarded as a mental disorder or a crime, and whether the focus should be on rehabilitation or punishment. These are, of course, not mutually exclusive. My colleagues and I recommend that authorities take a strong child-protective and prosecutorial stance while also making available treatment opportunities for alleged perpetrators and their families. As with other types of offenders, treatment goals include insight into the connection between psychological issues and behavior, accountability, and victim empathy. The literature on Munchausen by proxy syndrome cases thus far has not reported many favorable treatment outcomes or long-term prognoses (McGuire & Feldman, 1989; Schreier & Libow, 1993a; Zitelli, Seltman, & Shannon, 1987). However, it is unclear how many MBPS perpetrators actually acknowledge their behavior and receive treatment. A major obstacle, as with treating other offenders, involves the perpetrator's acknowledgment of her behavior. Without such acknowledgment, treatment cannot progress. Through careful management, as previously described, and using the treatment model that Deborah Day and I are developing (Day, 1994), we have seen treatment progress in our patient sample. Although we are certainly encouraged by this progress, this must be considered preliminary work due to the small sample size.

## Civil Court

In many cases of Munchausen by proxy syndrome, evidence of marital discord is uncovered at the time of suspicion. The stress inherent in removal of a child from the family, scrutiny by social service agencies, and involvement with the courts often places insurmountable strain on an unstable marriage. The perpetrator and spouse are then forced to acknowledge on some level the problems within the marital union. The spouse is also struggling with the deception of the perpetrator and her sometimes horrifying behavior. Additionally, separation from the perpetrator may be the only way for a father to regain custody of his child. In the population Deborah Day and I have studied, divorces have occurred in cases where the mother admitted the Munchausen by proxy allegations. The perpetrator's Munchausen by proxy syndrome behavior is likely to become an issue in the development of a parenting plan. For instance, Florida has a shared parenting assumption, but Munchausen by proxy syndrome may certainly create an exception.

MBPS cases have also been drawn into the civil courts through malpractice suits (Schreier & Libow, 1993a). As previously mentioned, alleged perpetrators only rarely acknowledge the behavior of which they are accused. Often the perpetrator, her family, and some professionals who have been involved in the victim's care respond to the allegations with indignation. These cases are often difficult to "prove," thus allowing the perpetrator to lodge a counterattack against the accusing physician. Additionally, such an attack seems to be a popular tactic of defense attorneys. Of course, some cases may be misidentified as Munchausen by proxy syndrome as we refine our understanding of this syndrome. Physicians will bear the most substantial risk, as they are on the forefront of identifying and reporting cases. How the judicial system will respond to the inevitable backlash of malpractice lawsuits is as yet unknown. In addition to physicians or hospitals being sued for erroneously identifying cases as MBPS, they may be sued for *failing* to identify MBPS, and thus continuing to provide medical care. I am familiar with one case in which a child-victim's father vehemently objected to his wife's being diagnosed with Munchausen by proxy syndrome, arguing, in part, that the primary physician had earlier considered and then rejected the diagnosis. Yet, when the diagnosis was affirmed by another professional, the father threatened to sue the primary doctor for failure to make the diagnosis. Interestingly, the father continued to deny the diagnosis for purposes of a defense in juvenile court.

Munchausen by proxy syndrome cases have profound emotional impacts on all the professionals involved, even those hardened to stories of horrendous physical and sexual abuse. It is difficult for many to fathom such direct, deliberate endangerment of infants, toddlers, and children, especially by mothers who are seemingly devoted to their children. It is important for professionals to remain cognizant of their personal reactions and biases to these very provocative cases. Further, it is important for them to remain open to input from other professionals and willing to participate in multidisciplinary dialogue, as in other cases of child abuse. The support of the judicial system is imperative if victims are to be safe and perpetrators are to participate in effective treatment programs.

# Part II

## Intervention With the Perpetrator and Family

# 6 Interviewing the Perpetrator After Medical Diagnosis

Deborah O. Day

> *We differ, too, in our capacity to detect deception and, more generally, in our ability to observe and name reality. We all repress, deny, project, distort, tune out, and get sleepy. Our knowledge and interpretation of "the truth" is, at best, partial, subjective, and incomplete. But we do have varying capacities for empathy, intuition, reflection, autonomy, objectivity, integrity, maturity, clarity, and courage—all of which enhance our ability to detect deception and incongruity in ourselves and in others.*
> *—Harriet Goldhor Lerner, The Dance of Deception, 1993*

As part of a multidisciplinary team investigating cases of Munchausen by proxy syndrome, psychologists and mental health professionals are asked to complete investigative interviews, including the initial confrontation interview, the investigative psychological evaluation interview, and second opinion interviews. Mental health professionals are rarely involved in the actual confrontation of a suspected MBPS mother-perpetrator, but they serve an important role in the education of the rest of the team on appropriate interviewing strategies. In this chapter I will discuss interviews in the context of the psychological evaluation, focusing primarily on second opinion interviews.

The primary purpose in conducting interviews with the alleged Munchausen by proxy perpetrator is to approach her in a manner that will help her to discuss what occurred with her child and make it possible for her to acknowledge her behavior. The secondary purpose of conducting interviews is to gather information (e.g., the mother's story of what is occurring, her marital history, her medical history, her medical knowledge and training, her mental status at the time of the confrontation, and any documentation the mother has kept regarding her child's hospitalization) so that other professionals involved in the case can continue their investigation; this can be accomplished even if the primary purpose of the interviews cannot. A skilled interviewer can obtain crucial information regarding the suspected perpetrator's interpersonal dynamics, marital history, and family of origin. Finally, second-opinion interviews are conducted in cases in which a firm medical diagnosis has been reached, but there is no admission by the mother concerning her behavior.[1] This chapter focuses on interviewing strategies; the discussion is based upon actual experiences my colleagues and I have had in interviewing suspected MBPS mother-perpetrators.

A review of the literature provides few insights into the interviewing process. Siegel (1990) presents an interview outline that gives guidance on how to obtain important background information, both past and present, relevant to confronting the Munchausen by proxy perpetrator. Siegel recommends the interviewing of third parties, such as physicians and family members, to obtain confirming information, and suggests that the suspected mother-perpetrator should be confronted when the medical diagnosis is confirmed. She further suggests that the hospital staff involved in the case should be involved in the process of developing an agenda for the confrontation meeting. Siegel recommends that at least one other family member and a neutral witness should be present when the suspected mother-perpetrator is confronted, and also notes that the confrontation interview is not the place to attempt to convince the mother or her family of the truth of the charges.

Teresa Parnell and I have had the opportunity to interview a number of mothers suspected of Munchausen by proxy syndrome abuse, in addition to mothers who have confessed to perpetrating such abuse. We have learned that the content of the mother-perpetrator's psychological evaluation interview differs greatly from that of the initial hospital interview or of law enforcement confrontations and interviews. This interview process is also significantly different from the process used by a consultant in a hospital when a case of Munchausen by proxy is suspected. On several occasions, we have interviewed suspected mother-perpetrators who have been interviewed previously as patients in psychiatric hospitals. (Such hospitalization may occur because of the mother's reaction at the time of the confrontation, or it may be part of a legal strategy that protects her from arrest.) As a routine part of a psychiatric hospitalization, mental health professionals become involved with the patient. Consultations and evaluations are requested by the admitting psychiatrist or are conducted at the request of the defense attorney. (Any requests made by a defense attorney should be coordinated with and ordered by the treating psychiatrist.) This situation does not change the fashion of the interview, but it may represent a less-than-ideal circumstance in which to gather the information necessary to assist with a diagnostic determination.

We have found that after the initial law enforcement confrontation, many suspected mother-perpetrators are not able to form attachments to mental health professionals. They withdraw and become self-defensive. Their denial, avoidance, and/or dissociation mechanisms make them unavailable to continue the interview process. One mother-perpetrator was arrested and then later, after she was bailed out of jail, psychiatrically hospitalized. She was shocked and depressed, and her attorney had instructed her not to speak to anyone about the charges pending against her. During the evaluation interview, she failed to reveal the traumatic experiences she had been exposed to in her life that formed the basis of her inability to trust authority figures or any other outsider. She was released from the hospital without having revealed any significant information. Her guarded presentation and avoidance of certain topics were clear cues that she was not forthcoming. Her psychological testing, although within normal limits (see Parnell, Chapter 7, this volume, for further discussion), provided valuable information. In her psychological testing and subsequent interviews, she revealed important information about her inability to trust others, especially males. Ultimately she revealed that she was the victim of multiple incestuous relationships. There was also other evidence suggesting that she was controlled by or fearful of her spouse. She based her identity solely on her skills as a mother, and she was dependent on others for her sense of well-being. While not revealing any information initially or acknowledging her behavior beyond the event she had been discovered perpetrating, she became increasingly dependent on the therapy sessions. This patient voluntarily participated in individual psychotherapy, and after 8 months of ongoing treatment, she began to tell her story. We were able to review retrospectively what information she had provided at the initial interview and evaluation, although she masked the information at the time of her psychiatric admission.

My role in the interview process has often been as part of the multidisciplinary team. Also, I have provided second opinions to social service agencies in cases in which the suspected perpetrators have not admitted to their Munchausen by proxy behavior. In the majority of these cases, the children have been placed outside their homes, either with extended family members or in the foster care system. The extended family members who become involved in foster care in these cases often do not understand or believe what child protection workers tell them. They are pressured by the accused parent or parents to believe that nothing occurred. The suspected mother-perpetrators try to buy time, knowing that social service agencies are under pressure to reunite families when there is a lack of confirming evidence that abuse has taken place. Child protection agencies seek second opinions in the hope of gathering additional information to help them with their decision making. Second-opinion interviewers can review the information already gathered by these agencies, which is often significant, to develop specific hypotheses and insights into a particular case prior to beginning actual interviews with the suspected MBPS perpetrator.

The second-opinion interviewer should be aware that the suspected mother-perpetrator is likely to be leery of the process and to have discussed the interview with her attorney. This is especially true if legal issues are pending before the court. At the beginning of the interview, it is important that the interviewer inform the suspected mother-perpetrator of the purpose of the interview. Before the interview begins, the interviewer should also discuss the limits of confidentiality and the evaluative process. At this time the interviewer may also share additional information, including why the interview was requested, what information was made available for him or her to review, and what additional information he or she may review in the future. (When I conduct an interview, I also offer to review any additional information the suspected perpetrator believes will be helpful to my understanding of what has occurred.) The interviewer should then describe the report for the suspected perpetrator and answer any questions she might have about the process (e.g., clarifying such issues as payment or scheduling of appointments). The interviewer should inform the suspected perpetrator that a medical diagnosis of MBPS has been made based predominantly on the medical information gathered. That is, the preponderance of the medical evidence has resulted in a physician's making a diagnosis of Munchausen by proxy syndrome. It is this medical diagnosis that has resulted in the abuse report made against her.

Evaluation interviews are typically more relaxed than are initial hospital confrontation interviews or law enforcement interviews. The evaluative interview process works best if the interviewer and suspected perpetrator can have the opportunity to meet on at least two separate occasions. The lengths of these appointments will vary, depending on the suspected mother-perpetrator's participation in the interview. The first session will generally last between 1½ and 2 hours, and the second session may be longer, depending on many factors. The interviews are conducted as any clinical interviews would be conducted, in the privacy of an office, without other parties present. Sometimes, attorneys or other professionals will ask that the sessions be video- or audiotaped, whether for legal, investigative, or educational purposes. The interviewer should deny such requests, as the recording of interviews is usually intrusive and inappropriate.

The interview generally proceeds as follows. The interviewer begins with an open-ended request for the suspected mother-perpetrator to describe what has occurred that led to her participation in this interview. The suspected mother-perpetrator uses this opportunity to detail what has happened to herself and her family. This initial part of the interview is typically a recounting of the course of hospitalization the child has experienced. Frequently, the suspected mother-perpetrator has kept a diary of the hospitalization. She may refer to her diary or even offer to let the interviewer read it. The mother's discussion is usually laden with medical terminology and names of procedures, most of which are unfamiliar to psychologists and other mental health professionals. The affect of the suspected mother-perpetrator is often inappropriate to the circumstances she is describing. For example, she may begin speaking in a monotone, displaying a flat affect, but as she starts to discuss the course of the child's hospitalization, some inflection may come into her voice and her affect may brighten. This almost excited presentation is in opposition to the trauma most parents would feel regarding a child's hospitalization or the prospect of being investigated for child abuse.

The initial part of the interview typically includes a recollection of the inadequate medical care the child received while a patient in the hospital. Frequently, the alleged perpetrator's first line of defense is to make allegations against the hospital, the nursing staff, and/or the attending physician who suspected MBPS abuse was occurring. It is important that the interviewer allow the suspected mother-perpetrator to tell her entire story, without a challenge. If interrupted with questions, she is likely to become distracted and unable to participate fully in the process. Little ground will be covered, as she is likely to bring the interview back to her story.

There are several important areas of which the interviewer should be aware at this point, as my own experience in interviewing Munchausen by proxy mothers has taught me. Clinicians learn to listen beyond what is being overtly said during a therapy session. This skill is like a third ear that allows the therapist to hear what others may miss. It is by using this skill that the therapist can sort out what is being said beyond the overt story being articulated by the suspected perpetrator. It becomes the interviewer's responsibility to listen to the suspected mother-perpetrator and formulate her emotional drive, while at the same time showing that he or she hears what the mother is saying. Ultimately, the interviewer has to communicate that he or she understands why the suspected perpetrator made the choices she did. It is important that the mother recount her explanation for the events, and that the interviewer listen with an intuitive ear. There is no need for the interviewer to challenge any information at this point; rather, he or she is simply gathering information and listening carefully.

From this point, the interview proceeds as any interview would in a mental health setting. Through questioning, the interviewer begins to piece together the clues of the case. The interviewer is responsible for being thoroughly familiar with the medical and investigative records of the case. He or she should note omissions and distortions, but confrontation is not recommended at this point in the process. It is often in gathering information about the suspected mother-perpetrator's family of origin that the interviewer begins asking questions. The interviewer should explore any history of abuse in the mother's family of origin, any presence of domestic violence, the emotional availability of both parents, the forms of discipline used, and parental expectations. The interviewer also needs to gather details of the physical health of family members, and should ask the suspected perpetrator if she recalls being sick as a child. When did she leave home and why? The interviewer should obtain her marital history, including a detailed history of the dating and courtship that led to the marriage, and should ascertain whether her partner is emotionally available to her. An interviewer can often obtain such information simply by listening rather than through direct questioning at this point. The suspected mother-perpetrator should describe her partner and also the children born into the marriage. Were the pregnancies planned? If so, by whom? The interviewer should also obtain a prenatal history regarding the child-victim, including the suspected mother-perpetrator's perception of the pregnancy. The woman's entire OB-GYN history is also important. Additional data gathered during this interview should include the suspected perpetrator's own medical history, information on her education and current employment, and any previous psychological, psychiatric, or therapy history.

As interviewers, Teresa Parnell and I have been able to gather information and clues that have led us to formulate a hypothesis regarding the intent of perpetrators of Munchausen by proxy behavior. We base the final part of the first interview on this hypothesis. The interview ends with the interviewer providing some direct information about the allegations, such as, "Your son/daughter told me that you told him/her not to tell the nurses about . . . ." This information may come from direct interviews the interviewer has had with the child-victim in the case or from credible sources if the child could not be interviewed. In a case in which the child-victim is too young to interview or to verbalize any information, the interviewer can phrase a similar statement about the most damaging medical information against the mother or an observation made about the induction occurring. The interviewer may make a series of such statements to the suspected mother-perpetrator. A common response is, "I don't have a good explanation for that," or the mother may attempt to make up an explanation on the spot, which might not agree with her previous stories. The interviewer ends the session by asking the mother, "What is the worst thing that would happen if you did do this?" The responses I have received to this question have varied, but they have all been very revealing. If dependency and abandonment fears are the mother's prevailing psychological issues, she is likely to reply that her husband or significant other will leave her. Others fear loss of family support (because they perceive conditional acceptance by their families) or worry about revealing family secrets. The responses are self-centered and immature.

If the suspected mother-perpetrator has previously been allowed contact with her child(ren), we recommend that the interviewer conduct a play observation that includes all family members before the next interview. This observation may generate additional insights that can be discussed in the second interview. If contact between the suspected mother-perpetrator and the child-victim has not been allowed, we do not recommend that contact be initiated only for purposes of this process.

The second interview should begin with a discussion of the marital issues and emotional milestones in the relationship of the mother-perpetrator and her spouse. As the woman describes issues of emotional distance or unavailability, the interviewer should reframe the responses. Often the suspected mother-perpetrator will recant a negative statement she has made about her husband in particular by later emphasizing that he is a "good father and husband." This is often an opening for the interviewer to remind the suspected mother-perpetrator that Munchausen by proxy behavior involves family dynamics, and she cannot be viewed in isolation from other family members. During one actual interview, the mother-perpetrator began to blame her husband for being unavailable to her and implied that she had unconsciously done these things to get his attention. It is at a point such as this in an interview that the interviewer may remind the suspected mother-perpetrator of her greatest fear. The interviewer should also begin telling the suspected mother-perpetrator about other information she has conveyed that is revealing. In this context, the interviewer should begin talking as if he or she knows it is true. This gives the suspected mother-perpetrator an opportunity to hear the interviewer's conclusions without the need to be confrontational. If the suspected mother-perpetrator becomes defensive, it is often useful for the interviewer to reflect back the information discussed by simply stating, "You told me . . . ," adding in the relevant information.

In an article on interviewing, Meadow (1985) suggests that the purpose of confrontation in the interview is not to prove that one is right and the other is wrong. As in the handling of mothers who perceive symptoms in their children that are not observable to others, the aim is to understand and respect the meaning of the symptoms in order to help the client. As Richtsmeier and Walters (1984) note, there is no point in explaining to the family what is really going on when clearly the family is unable to hear it; explanations seldom change behaviors that are illogically derived, and direct challenges of the defense will usually drive the patient away. The aim is not so much to get family members to look back on what was really happening as it is to get them to look forward to the future and feel good about the positive steps they are taking.

Mary Sanders (1995a, 1995b) refers to the "story of illness" that is developed by the Munchausen by proxy mother-perpetrator. She believes that using the story of illness as an informing technique is an effective treatment approach. This approach also has applications in the interview process described in this chapter. Sanders listens, forms hypotheses, and cocreates the story with the mother-perpetrator. The story is read back as it is created, and the mother-perpetrator is asked to modify or correct the story as treatment progresses. In this framework, the mother-perpetrator's spouse or significant other must also accept the Munchausen by proxy diagnosis and stop being the audience for the story of illness. (Sanders's technique is a variation of some of the therapeutic techniques suggested in later chapters of this volume.)

Frequently, the suspected MBPS mother-perpetrator will acknowledge some "bad" during the interviews, but will want to focus on the "good." The interviewer can describe some of the family dynamics that lead to Munchausen by proxy behavior and how these dynamics can lead individuals to make certain choices in their lives. Examples might include the need to be perfect within the family (the initial response to this dynamic may have been the development of an eating disorder), the desire to escape domestic violence, feelings of inadequacy as a parent, and the desire to be seen as extraordinary (mothers of sick children are viewed as distinctive and wondrous). As interviewers, we have learned to use the words of the suspected mother-perpetrator as we begin to tie the process together for her.

At this point, the interviewer can become more confrontational. He or she can suggest that the suspected mother-perpetrator has told at least a portion of why the Munchausen by proxy behavior might have happened. If the suspected mother-perpetrator remains attentive, the interviewer can reinforce that it is time for her to tell and begin to rebuild the lives of her family members. Similar techniques are used in psychotherapy. A therapist will often begin to reframe the information a patient has given him or her to help the patient draw conclusions from the information. Interviews in this context are very similar. If the interviewer has hypothesized, for example, that the husband is emotionally unavailable, he or she can use that information and state it back to the suspected perpetrator: "Your husband is emotionally unavailable to you." The interviewer can also point out that this is another piece of information consistent with Munchausen by proxy dynamics.

Restating what is said in therapy is consistently used as a therapeutic technique to assure the patient that the therapist is listening and understands what the client has said. If the interviewer is successful, the suspected perpetrator's defensive armor will be penetrated, and she will be telling herself something like, "This person knows who I am." The suspected mother-perpetrator's emotional vulnerability at this point will allow her to acknowledge some of what may have occurred. An admission will usually be only partial and superficial, but will often contain enough information to begin to build upon in a therapeutic relationship. In my experience, full acknowledgment of the Munchausen by proxy behavior will not occur for a significant time. Obtaining additional information or admissions should not be the goal of this interview. That becomes the goal of an ongoing, safe, therapeutic relationship.

If an admission does occur and the spouse is available, we strongly recommend that the interviewer hold a joint meeting with both spouses immediately, at the conclusion of the interview. In this meeting, the mother-perpetrator should inform her spouse of her acknowledgment to the interviewer. This is often an unexpected outcome for the spouse, who has likely supported the mother-perpetrator throughout the investigation, and the interviewer should expect shock, anger, and disbelief. (In one case I know of, in which an admission occurred and a joint meeting followed, the husband responded to his wife's disclosure by stating that he had thought the interviews were a waste of time and money, but now he "guessed" he had been wrong.) Holding this joint session can also deter the mother-perpetrator from leaving the interview and recanting her admission. Even with the joint meeting, the interviewer might later hear that the mother-perpetrator has reported that she was coached or coerced during the interview.

The mother-perpetrator is likely to revert to her manipulative skills and attempt to protect herself, and the interviewer must understand her needs and allow her to continue to justify or blame others. This is also the reason the goal of the interview is not to uncover every behavior perpetrated. The accused mother-perpetrator is too vulnerable to approach the picture in its entirety. Total responsibility is a treatment issue, and should be respected as such. Through treatment, the mother-perpetrator will begin to accept responsibility for her horrendous behavior. She will experience her own pain as well as the pain she has caused her child.

Because of the vulnerable psychological position in which an admission places the mother-perpetrator, the interviewer must take care to ensure that she has immediate support and that a plan is in place for therapy to begin. It can be quite interesting to watch the family dynamics unfold after an admission. The mother-perpetrator may begin to discuss her partial admission to select individuals, while continuing to deny her behavior to others. Little is known about the exact elements of this type of interview that might or might not facilitate disclosure. Teresa Parnell and I have speculated that our being "out-of-town experts" has at times facilitated admissions. Our successes, although very limited, have occurred when we have traveled out of town to complete second-opinion interviews. The number of admissions we have obtained during these interviews, however, is still fewer than the disclosures I have obtained during psychotherapy with Munchausen by proxy mother-perpetrators.

## Note

1. I want to make it clear that when I am asked to conduct a second-opinion interview, a set of medical facts has been amassed that has resulted in a firm medical case pending against the suspected perpetrator, and a medical diagnosis has resulted. I am not suggesting that every suspected MBPS perpetrator is one, nor have I affirmed every case I have seen with this diagnosis.

# 7  The Use of Psychological Evaluation

## Teresa F. Parnell

> *Our experience, similar to Waller's (1983), is that sometimes professionals have been misled by continuing deception and the ability of the mothers to compartmentalize problems, possibly using dissociative mechanisms. Our findings indicate that difficulties for most of these mothers continue with little moderation over time and that a single interview to assess the mother's mental state has limited value in assessment.*
> *—C. N. Bools, B. A. Neale, and S. R. Meadow, "Munchausen Syndrome by Proxy: A Study of Psychopathology," 1994*

Psychological testing is used broadly by mental health professionals in diagnosis, personality description, and treatment planning. Psychological testing has long been utilized in a forensic context, including the evaluation of abuse perpetrators. Many attempts have been made to identify abuse perpetrator personality types in order to establish a baseline with which to compare sample cases (Levin & Stava, 1987; Milner & Chilamkurti, 1991; Murphy & Peters, 1992; Quinsey, Arnold, & Pruesse, 1980; Wolfe, 1987). Researchers and clinicians hope that by identifying personality types or profiles, they will be better able to determine the likelihood that given individuals may promulgate abuse; the ability to predict the future behavior of clients would clearly be extremely useful to therapists for case planning.

Therapists must view any categorization of personality types based on testing with caution, however, because research has shown that no test is foolproof; no test has been devised that is strong enough to evade false positives or false negatives (Murphy, Rau, & Worley, 1994). For instance, among sexual offenders, "normal" profiles on the Minnesota Multiphasic Personality Inventory (MMPI) (Hathaway & McKinley, 1983) are not uncommon (McCreary, 1975; Scott & Stone, 1986). Additionally, there is tremendous variability in these profiles such that no specific profile can be reliably associated with a particular type of sexual offender (Erickson, Luxenburg, Walbek, & Seely, 1987; Friedrich, 1988; Hall, Maiuro, Vitaliano, & Proctor, 1986).

No personality profile has been established thus far for the Munchausen by proxy syndrome perpetrator. The literature alludes to some psychiatric interviews (Bools, Neale, & Meadow, 1992; Nicol & Eccles, 1985) and/or psychological evaluations (Palmer & Yoshimura, 1984), but the data available on the perpetrators are generally incomplete. Diagnostic comments, usually referring to personality disorders, appear often in the literature, but without sufficient information for readers to understand how these diagnoses were reached (Atoynatan, O'Reilly, & Loin, 1988; Black, 1981; Chan, Salcedo, Atkins, & Ruley, 1986; Epstein, Markowitz, Gallo, Holmes, & Gryboski, 1987; Griffith, 1988; Hodge, Schwartz, Sargent, Bodurtha, & Starr, 1982; Pickford, Buchanan, & McLaughlin, 1988; Rogers et al., 1976; Sigal, Gelkopf, & Meadow, 1989; Stankler, 1977; Stone, 1989; Woollcott, Aceto, Rutt, Bloom, & Glick, 1982). Only a few researchers have included perpetrator psychological testing data in their published reports (Griffith, 1988; Rosen et al., 1983; Schreier & Libow, 1993a).

Additionally, the information that is available often suggests completely normal protocols or interviews, sometimes leading mental health professionals to state that there is no way a particular mother could have perpetrated such abuse. Considering how the perpetrator has fooled family, friends, and physicians, often for a very long time, regarding her "normalcy," it only makes sense that she will likely be able to fool a mental health professional (Ravenscroft & Hochheiser, 1980; Waller, 1983), especially if the professional depends on a single clinical interview in making his or her determination. The most common presentation of the MBPS mother-perpetrator is of an individual who displays no overt indications of psychopathology or disturbed parent-child relationship.

Psychological testing data cannot in and of themselves lead to definitive diagnosis of Munchausen by proxy syndrome. This diagnosis is first and foremost a medical diagnosis. However, the psychological evaluation can supplement the medical information with social, intrapsychic, and familial information. It is imperative, however, that the psychologist not conduct the evaluation in isolation. He or she must review and understand all of the medical records of the mother-perpetrator as well as the child-victim.[1] In addition to supplementing the medical diagnosis, the psychological evaluation is vital for identifying personality characteristics and assessing the perpetrator's general functioning and level of psychopathology. The therapist can then use this information, along with data on familial and intrapsychic dynamics, to establish a treatment plan and outline a long-term plan for the family.

There is no one battery of psychological tests typically used with alleged Munchausen by proxy syndrome perpetrators. As in any competent forensic evaluation, the clinician should utilize those instruments with which he or she is familiar that are the most psychometrically sound and that may have utility in the particular case. When we conduct an evaluation of a suspected MBPS mother-perpetrator, Deborah Day and I employ a combination of objective and projective personality instruments as well as assessments of parent-child interaction. Additionally, we have found that a cognitive screening (or, preferably, a complete intelligence test) is beneficial for two reasons. First, the individual's cognitive functioning will influence the interpretation of many of the personality instruments. Second, a suspected mother-perpetrator may claim that she did not understand certain instructions or conclusions communicated to her by a physician. Intellectual assessment and sometimes specific assessment of learning abilities and language skills may help the clinician to determine whether this claim has any merit.

In addition to the psychological testing, the evaluator should obtain a typical comprehensive mental status and social history, including information on the suspected mother-perpetrator's family of origin and current family, personal and family medical history, psychological/psychiatric history, education, employment, social history, childhood abuse history, spouse abuse history, and current and past stressors. (See Day, Chapter 6, this volume, for further discussion of the interview portion of the evaluation.) An observation of the mother-perpetrator's interaction with the child-victim should also be conducted unless contact between them is prohibited at the time of the evaluation.

The evaluator should also contact (with consent of the suspected mother-perpetrator) such external information sources as family members, friends, neighbors, coworkers or employers, teachers, and day-care workers. Additionally, it is important that the evaluator conduct a careful review of the suspected perpetrator's educational, employment, medical, and psychiatric records. Sometimes a pattern of fabrication about life events is revealed when the evaluator compares information from these sources with that provided by the suspected perpetrator.

As is noted throughout this book, there is evidence of severe family dysfunction in Munchausen by proxy cases; thus the evaluator should attempt to understand the entire family system in a suspected case. I strongly recommend that evaluators conduct assessments with *all* family members. In my jurisdiction, although there has been good overall response by the judicial system to the handling of suspected cases of Munchausen by proxy, with psychological evaluations of alleged mother-perpetrators now routinely ordered by the courts, my colleagues and I are just now managing to persuade the courts to order evaluations for the family members, including any members with whom the child may be placed. Therefore, the data available on psychological testing of child-victims, siblings, fathers, and extended family are extremely limited. In this chapter I focus on the use of psychological evaluation with mother-perpetrators.

## Review of the Literature

Schreier and Libow (1993a) obtained psychological testing protocols on 12 mother-perpetrators. Although theirs is the largest sample of such protocols discussed in the literature, the sample is too small to generalize from. However, the descriptive information that Schreier and Libow provide constitutes a useful beginning.

Of the 12 subjects in Schreier and Libow's sample, intelligence test scores (Wechsler Adult Intelligence Scale–Revised, or WAIS-R) were available for 7. Most results were in the borderline to low-average range of intellectual functioning (FSIQ = 74, 71, 78, 79, 85, 89, 92). Schreier and Libow comment that these findings cannot be generalized because their sample includes individuals who either willingly submitted to psychological testing or were ordered by the court to do so. Thus they speculate that "mothers of higher intellectual functioning and/or social class may not be caught as readily, may be less cooperative, or have access to legal representation that helps them to avoid court-ordered psychological assessment" (p. 173). Schreier and Libow analyzed the WAIS-R subtests; they conclude that these mother-perpetrators had a poor fund of general information and a superficial level of social adeptness, and lacked comprehension of the more abstract concepts underlying the social world.

Of Schreier and Libow's 12 subjects, 9 had completed the Minnesota Multiphasic Personality Inventory (two of these had completed the MMPI-2). Except for one protocol, very few clinical scale elevations were obtained by this group. However, a high negative F-K index (average of −14)—

suggesting a lack of personal insight, defensiveness, and a possible attempt to fake good—may have suppressed the clinical scale scores. Schreier and Libow analyzed the profiles in depth, including their differences. They suggest the following consistent themes among the protocols: a rigid defensive style with underlying suspiciousness; marked immaturity; rebelliousness; lack of social conformity or outwardly conforming behavior; repressed hostile and aggressive features; an outgoing style of shallow, superficial relationships; a proclivity to cover over negative feelings with a rigidly positive veneer; self-centered, narcissistic inclinations; and impaired capacities for intimacy and reciprocity with others.

The Thematic Apperception Test (TAT) was conducted with eight of Schreier and Libow's subjects. Schreier and Libow describe generally brief, constricted stories with an undertone of dysphoric feeling, mainly about loss. A child's passive resistance of parental expectations of which he or she is aware can result in guilt, shame, frustration, and anger in the child. Some protocols described passive helplessness, whereas half of the protocols included stories of murderous or suicidal impulses that got out of control and resulted in unintentional deaths. There was a marked absence of warmth and relatedness between characters described for several protocols. Some protocols had very little in the way of nurturing figures, whereas some stories suggested a perception of men as more nurturing and supportive than women.

Schreier and Libow presented five of the TAT protocols in their sample to an expert in TAT interpretation, psychologist Dr. Drew Westen, director of psychology at the Cambridge Hospital in Massachusetts. Without knowledge of the Munchausen by proxy allegations, he summarized the protocols as follows:

> By and large, the records suggest minimal capacity to invest in other people, minimal complexity to representations of people, minimally developed sense of causality in the social realm and a rather bleak (though not always grossly malevolent) object world. Themes of badness, loss and deformation (or sexualized aggression) are prominent. Defensively, most of the responses are "shut down," as the subjects appear to be clamping down on associations to painful experiences, perhaps of abuse, and to their internal lives more generally. Denial is prominent, and many of the protocols have a childish quality, although it is difficult to know how much this may reflect age or intellectual factors as much as psychopathology or emotional issues. (quoted in Schreier & Libow, 1993a, p. 182)

Schreier and Libow also analyzed Rorschach inkblot test protocols for subjects in their sample, although only four were available. They also presented these protocols to an expert blind to the Munchausen by proxy diagnosis, Dr. Carl Gacono from Atascadero State Hospital in California. He reportedly gave the following impressions:

These are mainly protocols of patients with chronic problems, although Patients 2 and 4 may have some situationally induced problems. All of them have low self-esteem and all have cognitive slippage as well as depression and aggression problems. Rather than pathological narcissism, egocentricity may manifest in passive dependent or demanding behavior. Affect is particularly problematic for this group. Problems modulating strong affect such as depression and anger are indicated. Poor affect modulation contributes to cognitive slippage and scores indicate moderate to severe thought disorder. As a group they attempt to manage affect through avoidance and distancing. These subjects rely on primitive defenses that are only marginally successful. All use devaluation typical of character disorders. Interpersonal difficulties are apparent. . . . The women's responses to Card IV ("father card") may in part offer hypotheses concerning their disturbed object relations. Poor reality testing, primitive defenses, and unusual content elaboration on Card IV are consistent with patterns of women who have been molested, abused, or could be a partner in a battering relationship. (quoted in Schreier & Libow, 1993a, p. 184)[2]

Schreier and Libow reach the following conclusion:

While no single or simple psychological test profile yet emerges of the "classic" MBPS mother, we do feel an impressive consistency in the patterns of these mothers' limited store of information (with the exception of medical knowledge), poor abstract conceptual abilities, superficial social skills, and outgoing behavior. This is coupled with a rigid, denying defensive style masking an underlying rebelliousness, emotional immaturity, self-centeredness, lack of social conformity, and intense passive resentment. This is the profile of a patient who is likely to be very resistive to psychotherapy and therefore very challenging to treat. (p. 185)

Bools, Neale, and Meadow (1992, 1993, 1994) have published a series of studies regarding 56 Munchausen by proxy families. In their 1994 article, they report on how they evaluated the individual psychopathology of the mother-perpetrators by assessing their current psychiatric statuses and psychiatric histories. They were able to obtain complete psychiatric histories for 47 of the mothers and to conduct follow-up interviews with 19 of the 47. The interviews, which followed a semistructured format, concerned the mother's childhood, education, and current life situation. Additionally, Bools et al. administered two standard psychiatric interviews: the Clinical Interview Schedule (CIS) to assess current mental state and the Personality Assessment Schedule (PAS) to investigate personality and to apply *DSM-III-R* (American Psychiatric Association, 1987) criteria for diagnosis of personality disorders. Also, in 10 cases they conducted parallel interviews with informants, one in each case, usually the mother's spouse or one of her parents. Bools et al. thus had a very detailed history and/or personal interview available on each mother, the depth of which contrasts with the usually limited personal histories available during psychiatric evaluations of these women.

Bools et al. note that their sample likely represents more severe cases along the continuum of Munchausen by proxy abuse, with a high proportion of repetitive smothering, poisoning, and/or other direct harm to the child-victims. Within the larger sample of 47 mother-perpetrators, 41 had histories of one or more of the following: "somatizing disorder," self-harm, and substance misuse. Specifically, 10 had histories of alcohol/drug misuse, 26 had histories of self-harm, and 34 had histories of a somatizing disorder. (Bools et al. use the term *somatizing disorder* to describe either a somato-form disorder or a factitious disorder, because they had difficulty retrospectively assigning a more precise diagnosis.) Nine of the mothers had known forensic histories, including four convictions for theft, one for fraud, and three for arson. One mother received a probation order, but her offense was unknown. Bools et al. also indicate that one mother was strongly suspected of having committed arson at a psychiatric hospital where she had been a patient.

Of the 19 mothers Bools et al. interviewed, 15 had histories of somatizing disorder, 12 had histories of self-harm, 7 had histories of substance misuse, and 5 had histories of learning difficulties. None displayed evidence of psychotic illness at the time of discovery of the Munchausen by proxy behavior. At the time they were interviewed, 3 of the mothers had well-defined disorders (excluding personality disorders): an eating disorder, a possible psychotic illness with mainly affective symptoms but possible symptoms of schizophrenia, and hypochondriasis. Another mother suffered from a chronic state of irritability and epilepsy, 3 other mothers displayed somatic complaints with a substantial psychological component, and 4 other mothers had ill-defined disorders with a range of neurotic symptoms.

From the PAS ratings, 14 of the 19 mothers met the criteria for a number of coexistent personality disorders, more than four disorders in one-half of the cases. The categories achieving raised scores most frequently were antisocial, histrionic, borderline, avoidant, narcissistic, schizotypal, dependent, and paranoid. Predominant categories were selected, and 17 of the 19 mothers ultimately received diagnoses of personality disorder. The most common diagnoses were histrionic and borderline; Bools et al. note that these were particularly prominent diagnoses among the mothers who actively induced symptoms in their children. Dependent and avoidant personality disorders were also identified. Bools et al. further state that although antisocial behavior was evident, they were unable to conclude that any of the subjects met the criteria for antisocial personality disorder. In terms of the mothers' histories, it is important to note that 4 of the 19 reported physical abuse in childhood, 4 reported sexual abuse, and three-quarters had histories of emotional abuse or neglect.

## Mother-Perpetrator MMPI-2 Protocols

For analysis in this chapter, I considered 28 evaluation protocols from suspected Munchausen by proxy cases on which Deborah Day and I were consulted; from these, I selected a sample of 15, none of which has previously appeared in the literature.[3] I excluded the remaining 13 cases for several reasons. For example, the MMPI was not administered to two mother-perpetrators because of these women's severe reading disabilities and limited intellectual functioning. Further, several evaluations involved second opinions in which Deborah Day and I did not conduct the psychological testing, and the original raw test data were not available. Additionally, I excluded those cases in which the diagnosis of MBPS remained unclear for any reason. The 15 remaining protocols include 9 mother-perpetrators who acknowledged the abuse. In the remaining 6 cases there was substantial evidence supporting the Munchausen by proxy syndrome diagnosis, and this diagnosis was made by medical and psychological evaluators.

Of these 15 cases, 13 involved court-ordered evaluations; the remaining 2 evaluations were conducted at the request of the mother-perpetrator's attorney. All of the evaluations were conducted from a private practice setting, although 2 were conducted while the subjects were hospitalized in a psychiatric facility. Five of the mothers had victimized more than one of their children, and two of these siblings had died of complications from the same type of illness as that fabricated in the current target child.

For each of the cases in this sample, we administered multiple personality test instruments, objective and projective. However, the specific instruments administered varied from case to case. Early in our work with MBPS perpetrators, we certainly did not anticipate the number of cases in which we would eventually be involved. We selected instruments for evaluation independently for each specific case, and not with research in mind. Although now we are attempting, when circumstances permit, to increase the consistency of tests administered among cases, I do not believe there are sufficient data available to warrant analysis of each test at this time. Therefore, I present only the MMPI-2 results in this chapter. Table 7.1 provides demographic data for each of the 15 cases discussed, as well as the MMPI-2 K-corrected T scores. Figure 7.1 displays the mean MMPI-2 profile for all 15 cases; Figures 7.2 and 7.3 display the mean MMPI-2 profiles for the mother-perpetrators admitting the abuse and the mother-perpetrators denying the abuse, respectively.

Although these protocols can be considered only as preliminary data, it is interesting to note that they reveal no particular pattern or profile concerning the mother-perpetrators as a group. Only minor differences can be seen when the perpetrators are separated according to whether or not they admitted the abusive behavior. These individual protocols present a diverse group compared with other offender populations. Consistent with the literature described previously in this volume that indicates these mothers often appear quite "normal" to mental health professionals, there are very few clinical scale elevations individually, and none when a mean T score is computed.

Some tentative observations from the mean profiles are noteworthy, however, and in fact are consistent with some of the conclusions drawn by Schreier and Libow (1993a). As a whole, these protocols can best be considered subtly defensive profiles, with slight to moderate elevations on the validity scales of L and K. The average F-K score is −14, the same as that obtained by Schreier and Libow. Some protocols suggest more overt attempts on the part of the mothers to present in a positive light. This finding is not unexpected given the reasons for their referrals and the referral sources. Similar findings have been obtained from other court-ordered individuals who are dealing with issues related to child custody and/or abuse allegations. Although there are no scale elevations on the basic clinical scales when mean profiles are computed, low or moderately low scores worth consideration appear on the Social-Introversion (Si or 0) and Schizophrenia (Sc or 8)

*(Text continues on p. 143)*

**TABLE 7.1  MBPS Mothers' Test Data**

| # | M Age | C Age | C Sex | Mode of Abuse | A | M/S | Psych History | Abuse or Neglect History | Spouse Abuse | Diagnosis | IQ |
|---|---|---|---|---|---|---|---|---|---|---|---|
| 1 | 26 yrs. | 9 mos. | M | induced vomiting with ipecac | yes | Ma | IP/OP | none | yes | panic attacks | 103W |
| 2 | 20 yrs. | 8 mos. | F | simulated bloody vomiting | yes | Si | IP/OP | physical | yes | borderline personality disorder; personality disorder-NOS; dysthymia; adjustment disorder | 80W |
| 3 | 30 yrs. | 20 mos. | M | induced infection in line via injection of feces | yes | Ma | none | sexual, emotional | yes | none | NA |
| 4 | 26 yrs. | 6 mos. | F | induced vomiting with ipecac | yes | Ma | IP/OP | sexual | yes | anorexia; dependent personality disorder; major depression; personality disorder-NOS; anxiety | NA |
| 5 | 35 yrs. | 6 yrs. | M | induced infection in line via injection of feces | yes | Ma | OP | none | no | anorexia; dysthymia | NA |
| 6 | 32 yrs. | 6 yrs. | F | induced diarrhea with laxative | yes | D | IP/OP | sexual | yes | major depression; anxiety-NOS; personality disorder-NOS | 123S |
| 7 | 38 yrs. | 3 yrs. 20 mos. | F M | fabricated sexual abuse allegations; fabricated/ simulated medical symptom | yes | D | OP | sexual | no | bipolar disorder | 123S |
| 8 | 25 yrs. | 3 yrs. | M | induced coma with insulin injection | yes | Si | none | emotional, physical | no | personality disorder-NOS | NA |
| 9 | 25 yrs. | 4 yrs. | M | exaggerated symptoms; induced vomiting with ipecac; smothering | yes | Ma | OP | emotional | no | major depression; personality disorder-NOS; dysthymia | 102S |
| 10 | 25 yrs. | 2 yrs. | F | induced vomiting with ipecac | no | Ma | none | none | no | none | NA |
| 11 | 50 yrs. | 10 yrs. | F | exaggerated/fabricated/simulated asthma, allergies | no | D | OP (disability) | none | yes | personality disorder-NOS | 105S |
| 12 | 28 yrs. | 4 yrs. | F | induced cyanosis | no | D | none | none | no | none | 98S |
| 13 | 29 yrs. | 5 yrs. | M | fabricated/exaggerated/induced psychogenic vomiting | no | D | none | none | no | none | 81S |
| 14 | 38 yrs. | 7 yrs. 14 yrs. | M F | overmedicated; false sexual abuse allegations | no | D | OP | sexual | yes | post-traumatic stress disorder; bipolar disorder | NA |
| 15 | 34 yrs. | 6 yrs. | M | induction of line infections; exaggeration | no | Ma | IP/OP | none | no | dysthymia; major depression; eating disorder-NOS; alcohol abuse | NA |

**MMPI-2 T Scores (K Corrected)**

| # | Scores | | | | | | | | | | | | | | |
|---|---|---|---|---|---|---|---|---|---|---|---|---|---|---|---|
| 1 | 66/L | 51/F | 65/K | 80/Hs | 75/D | 82/Hy | 60/Pd | 50/Mf | 67/Pa | 62/Pt | 55/Sc | 39/Ma | 46/Si | 78/R | 59/O-H |
| 2 | 62/L | 41/F | 56/K | 46/Hs | 47/D | 47/Hy | 53/Pd | 38/Mf | 34/Pa | 44/Pt | 41/Sc | 45/Ma | 38/Si | 52/R | 66/O-H |
| 3 | 57/L | 51/F | 35/K | 33/Hs | 44/D | 34/Hy | 39/Pd | 50/Mf | 52/Pa | 34/Pt | 32/Sc | 53/Ma | 61/Si | 46/R | 16/O-H |
| 4 | 62/L | 44/F | 63/K | 71/Hs | 68/D | 65/Hy | 51/Pd | 47/Mf | 56/Pa | 55/Pt | 42/Sc | 37/Ma | 55/Si | 67/R | 66/O-H |
| 5 | 62/L | 37/F | 59/K | 46/Hs | 38/D | 56/Hy | 45/Pd | 67/Mf | 42/Pa | 37/Pt | 37/Sc | 43/Ma | 42/Si | 54/R | 55/O-H |
| 6 | 52/L | 41/F | 52/K | 46/Hs | 47/D | 47/Hy | 55/Pd | 47/Mf | 56/Pa | 47/Pt | 42/Sc | 45/Ma | 40/Si | 46/R | 59/O-H |
| 7 | 62/L | 41/F | 70/K | 54/Hs | 42/D | 58/Hy | 55/Pd | 47/Mf | 45/Pa | 49/Pt | 50/Sc | 71/Ma | 36/Si | 52/R | 63/O-H |
| 8 | 76/L | 61/F | 46/K | 49/Hs | 55/D | 47/Hy | 55/Pd | 43/Mf | 67/Pa | 39/Pt | 53/Sc | 56/Ma | 46/Si | 52/R | 55/O-H |
| 9 | 47/L | 55/F | 37/K | 65/Hs | 47/D | 56/Hy | 68/Pd | 43/Mf | 63/Pa | 53/Pt | 57/Sc | 74/Ma | 41/Si | 33/R | 41/O-H |
| 10 | 43/L | 44/F | 61/K | 43/Hs | 36/D | 51/Hy | 49/Pd | 69/Mf | 39/Pa | 40/Pt | 39/Sc | 47/Ma | 37/Si | 62/R | 70/O-H |
| 11 | 81/L | 41/F | 70/K | 61/Hs | 51/D | 61/Hy | 51/Pd | 47/Mf | 63/Pa | 51/Pt | 50/Sc | 47/Ma | 43/Si | 62/R | 70/O-H |
| 12 | 62/L | 37/F | 70/K | 51/Hs | 44/D | 61/Hy | 53/Pd | 65/Mf | 45/Pa | 47/Pt | 48/Sc | 47/Ma | 41/Si | 54/R | 74/O-H |
| 13 | 71/L | 55/F | 50/K | 38/Hs | 51/D | 43/Hy | 55/Pd | 40/Mf | 56/Pa | 53/Pt | 44/Sc | 59/Ma | 46/Si | 60/R | 66/O-H |
| 14 | 57/L | 41/F | 61/K | 51/Hs | 42/D | 54/Hy | 51/Pd | 57/Mf | 52/Pa | 44/Pt | 48/Sc | 71/Ma | 36/Si | 54/R | 70/O-H |
| 15 | 38/L | 55/F | 37/K | 49/Hs | 66/D | 49/Hy | 66/Pd | 47/Mf | 63/Pa | 64/Pt | 62/Sc | 43/Ma | 76/Si | 57/R | 37/O-H |

NOTES: M = mother; C = child; A = admitted MBPS abuse; M/S = marital status; IP = inpatient; OP = outpatient; W = Wechsler Adult Intelligence Scale–Revised; S = Slosson Intelligence Test–Revised; NA = not administered; M = male; F = female; Si = single; Ma = married; D = divorced.

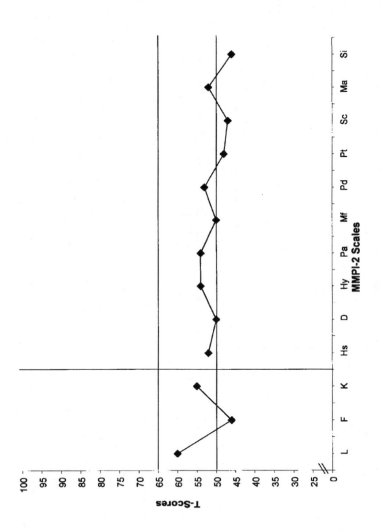

**Figure 7.1.** Mean MMPI-2 Profile for 15 Cases

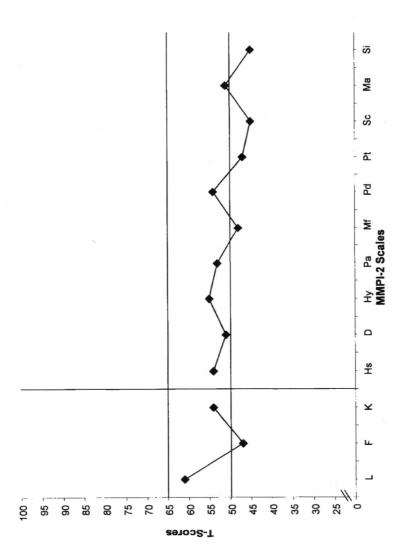

**Figure 7.2.** Mean MMPI-2 Profiles for the Mother-Perpetrators Admitting Abuse

SOURCE: Minnesota Multiphasic Personality Inventory-2 (MMPI-2) Profile for Basic Scales. Copyright © 1989, the Regents of the University of Minnesota. All rights reserved. "MMPI-2" and "Minnesota Multiphasic Personality Inventory-2" are trademarks owned by the University of Minnesota.

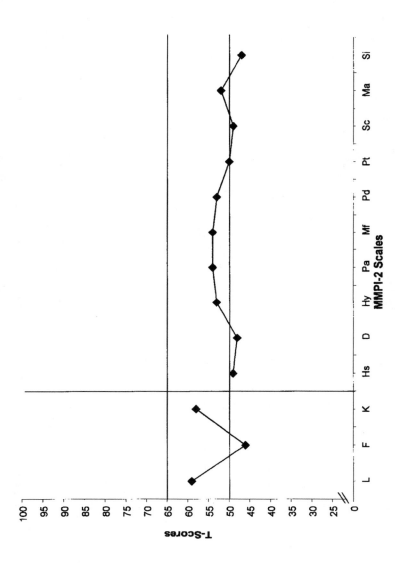

**Figure 7.3.** Mean MMPI-2 Profiles for Mother-Perpetrators Denying Abuse

SOURCE: Minnesota Multiphasic Personality Inventory-2 (MMPI-2) Profile for Basic Scales. Copyright © 1989, the Regents of the University of Minnesota. All rights reserved. "MMPI-2" and "Minnesota Multiphasic Personality Inventory-2" are trademarks owned by the University of Minnesota.

scales, and a mild elevation appears on the Paranoia (Pa or 6) scale. Elevations are present for many subjects on the content scale Overcontrolled Hostility (O-H), and the mean O-H scale for the nonadmitters approaches the clinical range. No profiles suggest a psychotic disorder, and very few suggest an antisocial personality disorder.

If the mean profile were considered as an individual profile, the interpretation might be something like the following:

The validity scales suggest an individual who needs to present a positive veneer in the testing situation as well as in life. She is likely to be outwardly conforming and concerned with social approval. Thus she may appear conventional and moralistic to the point of rigidity. She may be considered quite dependable, responsible, and capable in many areas of her life. She is likely to be concrete in her thinking, to have little insight into her own motives, and to depend upon simplistic defense mechanisms of denial and repression. Further, this self-centered individual may lack awareness of the impact or consequences of her behavior on others. Although fragile, adequate ego strength and psychological resources allow this individual to maintain an appearance of being well-adjusted.

The resulting clinical profile is probably an underestimate of problems, symptoms, and psychopathology, but the protocol is not invalid or uninterpretable. However, with all clinical scales below a T score of 60, the profile does not provide much useful clinical information. A generally sociable, gregarious, and friendly individual, she may be quite verbally fluent and persuasive. However, her social relationships are in fact superficial, shallow, and even insincere. Rather suspicious of others, she sees the environment as demanding and unsupportive. Therefore, in spite of her apparent social adeptness, she is actually restrained in relationships, avoiding deep emotional involvements. Her sensitivity to what others think of her and her perception of a negative environment may have given rise to hostility, anger, and resentment. Yet, as previously described, this individual espouses self-control, inhibition, and compliance, especially with authority. She may also be interested in recognition and status. Immaturity, self-indulgence, and problems with impulse control may also be present. (Particularly in the group of nonadmitters, unacknowledged hostility may be present that emerges impulsively and periodically.)

In terms of treatment, this individual likely has adequate ego strength and psychological resources to participate in psychotherapy. However, it will be difficult to penetrate her rigidly positive veneer and the unreproachable self-perception she needs to maintain. Candid therapeutic communication will be minimal, at least initially. Further, this individual's lack of inward scrutiny and denial of symptoms or problems suggest little motivation for treatment.

It should be noted that on a case-by-case basis, in my clinical experience with these mother-perpetrators, those with MMPI-2 protocols that are slightly to moderately defensive and have no clinical scale elevations are more likely to acknowledge all or some of the MBPS abuse and to participate in treatment. These are the mothers who have made the most substantial treatment progress. Again, this may be considered consistent with MMPI-2 patient data indicating that those individuals who have stronger defensive structures and better functioning across many life spheres are likely to demonstrate more progress in mental health treatment.

Also interesting are the MMPI-2 protocols obtained during the course of the mother-perpetrators' therapy to assess treatment progress. The retest MMPI-2 data generally show the individual perpetrator's psychopathology along with the anxiety and depression that emerge during the uncovering therapeutic process. A protocol obtained even later in therapy usually shows less defensiveness than the first protocol and has lower clinical scales than the second protocol, with perhaps a more realistic picture of the perpetrator's personality structure. Figure 7.4 reflects Subject 3's MMPI-2 protocols at different points in the evaluation/therapy process: the initial evaluation protocol; a protocol obtained to assess treatment progress after approximately a year of intensive therapy; a protocol obtained 2 years later, at the beginning of a lengthy termination phase of therapy; and a final protocol obtained almost 1½ years later, at about the time of termination.

Subject 3 was hospitalized for evaluation when the first MMPI-2 was administered. Interestingly, a computerized interpretation or a basic "cookbook" approach to interpretation of this protocol would indicate that this is a valid profile from an individual who cooperated with the administration. The resulting within-normal-limits profile would be viewed as an adequate indication of her personality functioning at that time. Characteristics of her thought patterns suggest obsessiveness and indecision. Interpersonally, she would be described as somewhat hypersensitive, inhibited, and shy. However, clinically she presented as anxious, depressed, withdrawn, secretive, and barely communicative. The MMPI-2 protocol actually revealed very

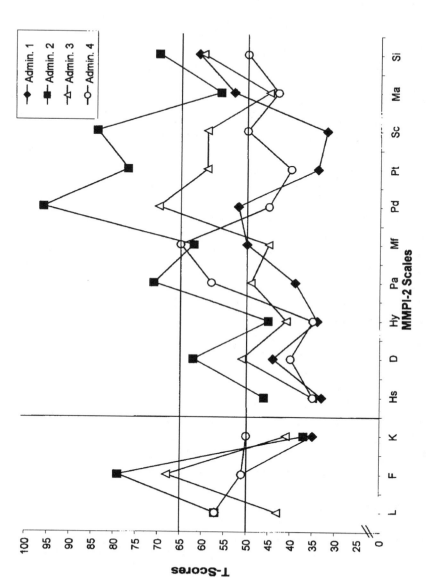

**Figure 7.4.** Subject 3's MMPI-2 Protocols

little about who this woman was. It did reflect the repression that allowed her to present a "life is fine, I just want to go home and bake cookies for my family" facade at that time. Although she admitted nothing at the time of her arrest, within months she provided a partial admission to the evaluating psychologist. This of course allowed psychotherapy to begin without the impediment of the subject's obsession with convincing the therapist of her innocence.

As therapy progressed (following the format outlined in Day, Chapters 9-11, this volume), the subject revealed a childhood history of sexual abuse by multiple perpetrators and an adult history of spouse abuse (denied by her husband). She also gradually revealed multiple episodes of induction of illness in her infant over a 2-year period. During the time in which she was revealing this information, she presented clinically as extremely depressed with suicidal ideation, emotionally unstable, and extremely hypersensitive and hypervigilant. She was also intensely needy and dependent on the therapist. She began to have contact with the child-victim, but in a therapeutic, supervised setting. Her MMPI-2 protocol from this stage is vastly different from that produced by the previous administration. This protocol, obtained within the safety of a therapeutic relationship, shows the personality decompensation seen during the course of treatment. At this point the mother-perpetrator trusted the therapist enough to let her know who she truly was, with some exaggeration just to make sure she was "heard." The clinical presentation at this time was one of anxiety, posttrauma symptomatology, and disturbed interpersonal relations with hypersensitivity, social inadequacy, and introversion.

The third protocol was obtained when termination of therapy was first being considered, owing to the mother-perpetrator's progress, which included her ability to take responsibility for her abusive actions, her empathic understanding of the child-victim's suffering, her realistic and appropriate views of all of her children and their needs, her ability to maintain unsupervised contact with all of her children without incident, her ability to engage in meaningful adult relationships, her stable self-concept and vastly improved self-esteem, and her stable employment with significant success. The MMPI-2 protocol from this stage also reflects an individual who is pulling herself back together with decreased depression and anxiety, no suicidal ideation, improved coping skills, and increased insight into herself and others. Interpersonal hypersensitivity remains as part of her character but is manifested moderately. Additionally, fears related to the alleged abuse by her former spouse continue to be prominent at this point.

The final protocol is consistent with this mother-perpetrator's presentation at termination. She was energetic, much more independent, open to new experiences, confident, and self-expressive. Interpersonally, she was far more comfortable in social settings than she had been when therapy began, and she was not socially isolated. There was an absence of clinical symptoms.

Another interesting example of changes in MMPI-2 protocols over administrations is provided by Subject 4. This subject was alleged to be responsible for the death of a previous child-victim who had died after a similar clinical presentation as the victim identified in the current case. This subject completed at least five MMPIs over the course of 7 years of contact with mental health professionals and forensic experts. Four of these protocols are represented in Figure 7.5.

The first known protocol, an MMPI rather than an MMPI-2, was obtained during a medical hospitalization the subject underwent for abdominal pain and nausea that occurred several months after the first alleged victim was born. Whether Munchausen by proxy behavior was occurring at this time is unknown. However, it was determined that the subject's own medical presentation was affected by psychological factors. She was also diagnosed with anorexia, but denied inducing her own vomiting at that time. The MMPI is described as a code type of 1-2-3, with $T$ scores of 91, 82, and 79, respectively.

Two years later, this subject was evaluated, including an MMPI-2, while psychiatrically hospitalized due to allegations of Munchausen by proxy syndrome. The alleged victim was her then 3-month-old second child. Her first child had died approximately $1\frac{1}{2}$ years earlier. The subject made no admission to law enforcement, but gave a partial admission to the evaluating psychologist. Her perpetration with her second child had begun immediately after the child was born. This protocol is a relatively benign 1-2-3 code type. Although consistent with her features of histrionic, dependent, and depressed, the clinical presentation was far more troubling. The subject presented with a psychotic depression and an eating disorder with severe bingeing. She was also incredibly dependent, which quickly transferred to her relationship with the therapist. This protocol and the first protocol for Subject 3 reflect these perpetrators' uncanny ability to manipulate their presentation to the world.

Following hospitalization, Subject 4 participated in outpatient therapy for more than a year before the death of her first child was investigated. She was jailed and awaiting trial when the second MMPI-2 was administered by her treating therapist. By this time, she had begun to reveal the depth of her

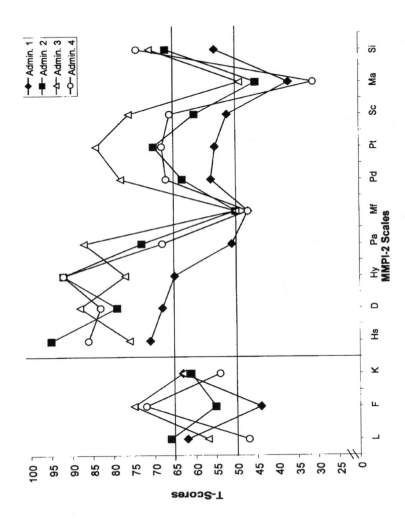

**Figure 7.5.** Subject 4's MMPI-2 Protocols

SOURCE: Minnesota Multiphasic Personality Inventory-2 (MMPI-2) Profile for Basic Scales. Copyright © 1989, the Regents of the University of Minnesota. All rights reserved. "MMPI-2" and "Minnesota Multiphasic Personality Inventory-2" are trademarks owned by the University of Minnesota.

thought processes regarding the perpetration of abuse. She was finally able to let go of her terrible secret.

The third MMPI-2 was administered under the same conditions as the second by an independent evaluator for the defense. This was during the height of the trial preparation. The subject was jailed in a county some distance from her treating therapist and thus had no consistent therapeutic intervention. Her eating disorder was out of control, and her thought processes were near delusional.

The subject ultimately pled guilty to second-degree murder in the first child's death. During her incarceration, her eating disorder became so debilitating that she was hospitalized for 10 months. Shortly after this hospitalization, the fourth MMPI-2 was administered by her treating therapist. Although hospitalized, she had received individual therapy of questionable usefulness. This mother-perpetrator's antisocial and narcissistic personality traits led her to mock and manipulate most mental health professionals with whom she had contact.

At this time, evaluators of Munchausen by proxy abusers can best employ MMPI-2 data, as well as data gathered using other projective and objective test instruments, to understand individual subjects' intrapsychic dynamics, to guide treatment, and to assess treatment progress. Considerable research is needed before we can determine the possible utility of psychological testing profiles for individual cases. Additionally, there is virtually no information yet available regarding psychological evaluation of child-victims and other MBPS family members.

## Notes

1. The psychologist should never assume that all medical records have been obtained and reviewed by the physicians involved. Deborah Day and I have been involved in cases where a diagnosis of Munchausen by proxy has been made, but the diagnosing physician never bothered to review all pertinent medical data. It is the psychologist's job to conduct as thorough an evaluation as he or she would in any other case, without relying solely on information provided by others.

2. Schreier and Libow (1993a) remark that although both outside experts speculated that the subjects might be victims of sexual abuse or spousal battering, only two of these patients revealed such histories. Additionally, they note that abuse histories are not identified in most case reports on Munchausen by proxy mothers. After reviewing the literature, Deborah Day and I have concluded that very few case studies indicate the presence or absence of such a history, which suggests that these important questions may not even have been asked. Further, in our experience,

mother-perpetrators rarely reveal childhood or marital histories of abuse during initial evaluation; this information emerges in therapy.

3. Specific tests that Deborah Day and I have commonly utilized include the Slosson Intelligence Test–Revised or the Kaufman Brief Intelligence Test, Minnesota Multiphasic Personality Inventory–2, Millon Clinical Multiaxial Inventory–III, Thematic Apperception Test, Rotter Incomplete Sentence Blank–Adult Form, the House-Tree-Person/Kinetic Family Drawing, and the Parenting Stress Index. Additional instruments may include the Wechsler Adult Intelligence Scale–Revised, Sentence Completion-Parenting Series, and Rorschach inkblot test. We may also use other tests as appropriate, such as the Symptom Checklist-90–Revised, the Beck Depression Inventory, or similar specific instruments.

# 8 Setting the Treatment Framework

Deborah O. Day
Teresa F. Parnell

The dynamics of psychotherapy with Munchausen by proxy syndrome per-petrators have been elusive for mental health professionals. The published literature has consisted of case reports that reflect clinicians' conceptualiza-tions of singular cases and often their frustration in dealing with Munchausen by proxy patients (Chan, Salcedo, Atkins, & Ruley, 1986; Leeder, 1990; Mayo & Haggerty, 1984; Nicol & Eccles, 1985; Taylor & Hyler, 1993). Perpetrators have usually terminated psychotherapy prematurely, without a true understanding or resolution of their psychopathology. Thus there has been no place for mental health professionals to turn for guidance in treating these baffling patients. This chapter as well as Chapters 9-11 focus on a psychotherapy approach used with Munchausen by proxy mothers who have confessed and then willingly participated in the treatment process.

Setting a framework for psychotherapy is necessary to establish an appropriate and effective therapy process with Munchausen by proxy pa-tients. These patients often flee when confronted (Atoynatan, O'Reilly, & Loin, 1988; Leeder, 1990; Sullivan, Francis, Bain, & Hartz, 1990), and even when they participate in therapy, they are considered treatment failures (Janofsky, 1986; Kinscherff & Famularo, 1991; Mayo & Haggerty, 1984; Stone, 1989). This is largely due to the level of denial, manipulation, and deception inherent in their pathology. Further, many of these patients have personality disorders, a category of diagnoses that are notoriously resistant to therapeutic change. The lack of support from other professionals involved in these cases also contributes to the failure rate. Establishing a clear, specific framework in which the perpetrator's individual therapy is to be conducted can help to reduce these obstacles. Mental health professionals must also begin to insist on appropriate child protective services and judicial support if therapy is to be considered an option with these patients (see the chapters in Part III of this volume for discussions of multidisciplinary collaborations). Skepticism and disbelief have been common reactions within the legal system, as lawyers and judges struggle to understand how a parent could simultaneously make her child appear ill and seek the best possible medical care for that child (Waller, 1983). The parameters discussed below represent ideal conditions under which all Munchausen by proxy syndrome cases should begin treatment. Realistically, some components may be difficult to arrange.

**Referrals**

An MBPS case is usually referred to therapy by child protective services, a judge, or a defense attorney after an abuse report has been made and the perpetrator has been confronted. If there is no support for the referral from the perpetrator's attorney, it is advisable that a court order for evaluation and treatment be obtained. Competent interviews with the mother-perpetrator and complete psychological evaluation are vital components preceding the therapy process. In some MBPS cases in which we have been involved, we have completed the initial interviews and evaluation, and then have also provided therapy. The unique components of Munchausen by proxy limit the availability of mental health professionals who are willing and qualified to provide services. In a therapeutic relationship in which the professional assumes more than one role, it is important that he or she establish the boundaries of each role (objective evaluator or treating therapist) immediately with the referral source and the patient. If the mental health professional first evaluates and then treats the mother-perpetrator, he or she should avoid playing an evaluative role later in the case (see the discussion in Day, Chapter 9, this volume).

In small communities it may be particularly difficult for therapists to avoid such dual-role relationships. Moreover, some communities will have no "experts" available to provide any interventions. In these situations, the evaluator and therapist should have at least a strong understanding of family systems and childhood histories of sexual, physical, and emotional abuse, as well as experience dealing with perpetrators of abuse. These professionals should also arrange for supervision, by telephone if necessary, with an individual who is experienced in MBPS cases.

## Financial Issues

Before proceeding further in an MBPS case, the therapist must be prepared to make a long-term commitment to the patient. Treatment may be expected to take between 3 and 4 years. Realistically, few individuals have the financial resources to pay for long-term treatment in a private practice setting. With managed health care, sessions are limited in frequency and number. The therapist should clarify, in a written contract with the patient, all fees, patient payment requirements, and services charged in addition to therapy time (e.g., daytime telephone calls, emergency calls, summary letters).

Community-based, state-funded mental health service clinics are also available in most communities. State agencies usually provide services on a sliding fee scale. Unfortunately, these agencies will rarely be able to provide the long-term commitment needed. In our experience, perpetrators often use financial limitations as an excuse for not initiating therapy or for disengaging from the therapeutic process.

## Use of a Cotherapist

Although there are cost limitations, we recommend the use of a cotherapist. The cotherapist should be familiar with the case and able to serve as a backup for the primary therapist. Especially in the early stages of treatment, the needs of the patient may be overwhelming for a single therapist. The primary therapist should introduce the cotherapist concept to the Munchausen by proxy mother-perpetrator in the first session of psychotherapy, clarifying the role of the cotherapist, especially how, when, and why this therapist might be used in the case. For example, multiple telephone emergencies are often generated in a single case, and the treating therapist is not always available. Specific coverage is needed so that the mother-perpetrator does not have to "tell her story" repeatedly to other therapists. Additionally, mother-perpetrators are known to have recurrent suicidal thoughts. If the primary therapist is not available, the cotherapist is more likely than someone unfamiliar with the case to respond to the patient in a manner consistent with the treatment plan. The primary therapist's leaving for a vacation can be the precipitating event for a patient crisis; the cotherapist, again, can handle such a crisis within the treatment plan.

As in treatment with other complex families, multiple family members may be participating in therapy with multiple therapists, preferably within the same office. Often it is possible for one of these therapists to serve as the cotherapist for the mother-perpetrator. This will, of course, depend on the specific status of the case and the dynamics within the family. Once again, all therapists involved must clearly articulate the boundaries of the various therapeutic roles.

In addition to multiple therapists, many other professionals remain actively involved in these cases, such as physicians, child protection workers, and attorneys. The mother-perpetrator's therapist may need to assume the role of the primary therapist and take steps to maintain regular, appropriate contact with these individuals. The therapists involved in a case in particular should hold case staffings at regular intervals. This opportunity for communication will help them to maintain a reality-based and clear-cut treatment plan and also reduce the possibility that the mother-perpetrator will be able to create any split among the professionals. Of course, the therapists should obtain proper authorization for such contact from all the clients involved. Furthermore, the mother-perpetrator and other family members should be informed of these contacts when they occur and should be provided with a synopsis of the information shared.

## Legal Issues

When a patient is referred, the therapist needs to understand the case in terms not only of the therapy process but also of the legal process. The Munchausen by proxy mother-perpetrator is often confronted in the hospital setting where the child-victim is a patient. She is often arrested, or at least threatened with arrest. She may feel legally pressured to confess, and has probably had the child-victim, and possibly her other children, removed and placed in the care of relatives or a foster family. These events can lead to confusion and fear, complicated by the mother-perpetrator's intense need to deny what is being alleged. This crisis stage often sends the perpetrator deeper into her denial. It is our opinion that removing the child-victim from contact with his or her parent at this stage ensures the child's protection (see Parnell, Chapter 5, this volume). A dynamic has emerged with Munchausen by proxy mother-perpetrators who have admitted to their behavior. They report an initial compulsion to prove they did not hurt their children. They want access to the children, and, by again inducing symptoms to create illness, they hope to create the perception that the allegations against them are false, and that the children are really ill. This distorted, irrational behavior is a core treatment issue and has consistently reinforced for us the need to separate the child and the perpetrator.

The therapist needs to clarify for the mother-perpetrator the limits of confidentiality. Because Munchausen by proxy behavior is both child abuse and a crime, there may be serious ramifications to disclosure. This may be especially relevant as treatment progresses and the patient is encouraged to acknowledge and assume responsibility for all of her abusive actions. As a result, she may admit to behaviors that she did not initially acknowledge and that possibly were not even suspected. The status of the case within the criminal and dependency courts will influence how the therapist handles such information. In our cases, we have addressed this issue directly with the attorneys involved. Thus far, there has been no concern that sanctions would be imposed if disclosures were made in therapy regarding past abuse.

## Psychiatric Hospitalization

Due to the initial disorientation of the perpetrator, a brief psychiatric inpatient hospitalization may be recommended. This short-term psychiatric stay removes the Munchausen by proxy mother-perpetrator from the pressure of outside influences. The interviewing and treating mental health professionals can address several crucial issues while the perpetrator is in a safe environment. Psychiatric hospitals, however, are not the ideal setting for investigative interviews (see Day, Chapter 6, this volume). It is during this hospitalization that the initial psychological evaluation can be completed, including a comprehensive history and mental status examination (see Parnell, Chapter 7, this volume). Because the patient's state of mind may become an issue later in the legal proceedings, the assessment must include observations regarding the presence of hallucinations, delusions, paranoia, and/or suicidal ideation, as well as mood and affect. Other important information that should not be omitted includes any patient reports of spouse abuse and the patient's childhood history of abuse. (In our treatment cases, we have found a significant amount of domestic violence and childhood abuse to be present.) The history gathered at this time also becomes a foundation for assessment of the patient's general honesty. Some perpetrators are known to fabricate about all aspects of their lives (Kinscherff & Famularo, 1991; Schreier & Libow, 1993a), which we believe reflects more serious pathology.

## The Treatment Plan

After the initial evaluation has been completed, the next task is to establish the treatment plan. The main focus of the plan will be the mother-perpetrator taking responsibility for all of her perpetration and gaining victim empathy. This will include understanding the dynamics leading to the Munchausen by proxy behavior. At the beginning of therapy these may not be clearly understood, although hypotheses will have been generated by the evaluator's or therapist's formulation during the interviews. For example, fear of abandonment, excessive dependency, escape from domestic violence, empowerment through ego enhancement, and increased feelings of self-worth through the challenge of fooling doctors are all motivators that have to be explored as the treatment begins. The psychological testing will also highlight issues for focus in therapy. Identification of the major psychological dynamics will be the foundation for beginning treatment. The negative consequences of missing some of these issues can include placing the child-victim at risk for reabuse and reinforcing the Munchausen by proxy mother-perpetrator's ability to be deceptive in the therapeutic relationship.

It is not uncommon for a therapist to find him- or herself caught up in the crisis of the moment with a Munchausen by proxy mother-perpetrator and her family, deviating from the treatment plan to rescue them from crisis. The therapist can use the case history and treatment plan to assist him or her to remain focused on the abuse that was perpetrated. With a mother-perpetrator who has not admitted responsibility, the therapist may need to return to this information repeatedly to counter his or her own doubts about the mother's responsibility. Because of the significant risk factors present in these cases, the clinician should not deviate from the predetermined treatment plan.The complexity of the psychological issues in Munchausen by proxy syndrome suggests that treatment in these cases must be equally intricate. However, only individual therapy should occur during the first stage of treatment. Other modalities of therapy can be added later in treatment, once the dynamics of the case are understood and treatment progress warrants a change. Meanwhile, the other family members should be following the treatment plans indicated for them. Later-stage treatment strategies should include not only individual psychotherapy but also family, group, and joint sessions with other significant individuals. These individuals are important in the development of an effective resolution of the psychopathology that has led to Munchausen by proxy syndrome; they may include the child-victim's pediatrician, consulting physicians, the child's guardian ad litem, and family members who do not have current involvement with the

Munchausen by proxy mother-perpetrator but have had significant impact on the shaping of her early family dynamics.

Treatment passes through distinct stages and evolves at multiple levels simultaneously. As therapists, we are required to use all the skills available to us in treating MBPS cases, and we still often feel inadequate when faced with the challenge of treatment. Other mental health professionals have also recognized the need for an integrated treatment framework. Sanders (1995b) suggests that a team approach must be used in the management of these cases, and notes that the management efforts should last throughout the lifetime of the child-victim.

## Review of the Literature

There are very few discussions of the therapy process with Munchausen by proxy mother-perpetrators in the published literature. There is more information regarding therapy with factitious illness when the perpetrator victimizes their own body, although this information is not encouraging. Mayo and Haggerty (1984) present a somewhat more positive perspective. These authors report on the long-term treatment of Munchausen syndrome; although they do not address Munchausen by proxy, they clearly articulate the difficult and treatment-resistant nature of factitious disorders. They state, "Recent experience indicates that, contrary to traditional wisdom, patients with chronic factitious illness do seek out psychiatric treatment, and on occasion are capable of forming at least rudimentary treatment alliances" (p. 571). In their review of the literature, Mayo and Haggerty found 37 reported cases in which patients agreed to some sort of extensive evaluation or treatment. Of these patients, 22 continued in outpatient psychotherapy for months to a year or more, and 10 were said to improve.

In an attempt to make factitious behavior "more comprehensible," Mayo and Haggerty examined the behavior in the context of "a developing object relationship." They suggest the following. First, they observe that the "factitious symptoms and other fabrications are comprehensible as metaphorical communications relating to the state of the patient's current object relationships." Second, current abandonment experiences are important in the activation of factitious behavior. Mayo and Haggerty believe that factitious symptoms may "serve the purpose of *maintaining* an object relationship by splitting off threatening, rageful impulses." Finally, their experiences support the idea that "factitious illness is an attempt to ward off ego disintegration" (p. 575).

Waller (1983) notes that although the features of Munchausen by proxy syndrome have been delineated and the psychodynamics are increasingly understood, there remain important obstacles to appropriate treatment of these cases, including continuing risk to the child's life, the symbiotic tie between parent and child, the persuasive denial of the parents when con-fronted, and the skepticism of legal authorities. According to Waller, the consulting psychiatrist has an important role to play in ensuring that the children and parents involved in these cases receive appropriate medical and psychological care. Further, he suggests that the consulting psychiatrist is in the optimal position to function as the ongoing liaison among the family, legal representatives, child protective agencies, mental health professionals, and physicians. The psychiatrist in this role should strive to maintain alli-ances with all the individuals involved and should be charged with educating all professionals concerned with the case. As Waller notes, professionals do not yet know the long-term outcomes of cases in which parents have received apparently successful courses of psychological treatment. Therefore, he recommends that child-victims receive periodic monitoring of their physical and psychological functioning following the termination of treatment.

Nicol and Eccles (1985) describe the chronic hospitalization of a toddler for salt poisoning. She had been subjected to two computed tomograms of the head, two blood transfusions, three radiographs, one electroencephalo-graph, 51 stool specimens, and 83 venepunctures. Her mother and father were confronted in a meeting with the pediatrician in charge of the case.

A child psychiatrist completed an assessment of the family. Nicol and Eccles do not provide the details of this assessment, but note that during the assessment the mother vehemently denied the allegations. She also mini-mized two psychiatric problems: her depression at the time of her daughter's birth and her father's alcoholism. The mother later confessed to the abuse when she was told that a decision had been made to place her child in foster care. Once the mother confessed, it was decided that treatment was now a possibility. The case was taken before the court, and the child remained in the home under very strict supervision. As an essential part of the case planning, psychotherapy was attempted. The initial goal was to assess whether the mother could benefit from long-term supportive therapy that would "fulfill her dependency needs" and discourage further inappropriate seeking of medical care.

After a few sessions, the mother demonstrated a strong wish to under-stand herself. Nicol and Eccles describe her as intelligent, with the capacity to bring active and painful feelings to the therapy sessions. For these reasons, a more active and deeper form of interpretive therapy was undertaken. Nicol and Eccles (1985) describe the general themes of the therapy as follows:

> Mother came to therapy sessions looking well and attractive. She was always on time and seemed glad to see the therapist. The sessions were often emotionally charged and there were very few silences. The patient often brought the outcome of thoughts during the week, "I've been working out . . . " indicating that the sessions continued in her mind for many hours outside their formal time. (p. 346)

As treatment in this case continued, the reasons the abuse had occurred emerged. Nicol and Eccles report that these complex reasons included the mother's superficial desire for attention, the pleasure she got from contact with doctors, and the fact that she had found the doctors "dithering and took considerable pleasure in having outwitted them for so long" (p. 346). Full realization of the danger in which she had put her child emerged gradually for this mother-perpetrator. Nicol and Eccles describe the emotional experience of therapy as most important, with the affective states of remorse and depression of particular significance in this case. Remorse was intense in the early stage of treatment and resurfaced throughout the year. The woman also frequently complained of an unpleasant mood state, different from her remorse, which she called depression. This was not clinical depression, but it played a major role in the origin of the abuse. Nicol and Eccles state that "it was a dangerous affect, which seemed to have infantile rage as a central component, together with a crushingly low self esteem" (p. 347). The connection was made to dominant family members' rage, and it became clear that the patient's father played a key part in her early dysfunctional upbringing. The therapeutic relationship was central to her recovery process, as the therapist was "a consistent figure in an otherwise unreliable world" (p. 348).

Nicol and Eccles (1985) report the following changes achieved in therapy:

> (1) Further abuse had not occurred and mother's care of all her children had not given rise to concern over a 15 month period from confession. (2) There had been a cessation of her abnormal illness behavior. (3) There were changes in her attitude to religion. Less censorious and severe and more informed by her own humanity. (4) During therapy, she was able to become firm in her management of

her father. (5) While never a very demonstrative person, she felt that she became warmer and more spontaneous socially. (6) Despite the pain of the events, the mother said she was glad that she had been found out and that she could get the help she needed. (p. 348)

Nicol and Eccles conclude that individual interpretative psychotherapy may have a place in a minority of MBPS cases, when the patient is reasonably well motivated to confront her difficulties, is of average intelligence, and is not beset with family and social problems.

Chan et al. (1986) describe the course of the hospitalization of a 5-year-old who presented with psychogenic aspects of chronic cyclical vomiting. This child had been diagnosed at age 4 with Bartter's syndrome, a genetic condition characterized by dehydration, low potassium and sodium levels, polyuria, and alkaline blood pH. The cyclical vomiting began more than 2 years prior to the reported admission. The hospital staff began to suspect that the mother may have been surreptitiously administering diuretics to her child, and a psychological assessment of the mother and child was begun. Mental status evaluation of the child found him alert and oriented. Speech, thought organization, and memory were within normal limits. He was weak from dehydration, but he separated easily and played appropriately. The psychological intervention intensified after the mother was confronted with the staff's suspicions. She reacted across four stages: disbelief, denial, anger, and depression. A search warrant was executed for the home, and bottles of the medication furosemide were found, along with syringes, in the mother's bureau drawer. She requested immediate psychiatric hospitalization.

Chan et al. (1986) note: "The long-term efficacy of inpatient hospitalization of the Munchausen by proxy parent is unclear. The patient's denial is often so strong that even with clear evidence, no admittance of the act is ever obtained" (p. 77). In this case, the mother maintained her denial. Chan et al. emphasize the importance of the psychologist, noting that it is crucial for the psychologist to work closely with the physicians and the nursing staff in such cases. The psychologist may become involved in teaching, liaison work, and psychotherapy with family or medical staff.

Leeder (1990) takes a feminist perspective in her discussion of treatment approaches that might be used in handling Munchausen by proxy cases. She describes the beginning stage of therapy with the mother-perpetrator, in which early sessions are consumed by the mother's recounting of all the professionals who have failed to find a cause for her child's illness. Once trust is established, Leeder recommends beginning to explore the mother-perpetrator's own family history as well as her medical background. She has found that these mothers present themselves within normal limits psychologically, have no psychosis, and use denial as their primary defense. In the initial stage of therapy, Leeder also gathers information about the dynamics of the mother-perpetrator's marriage. Only after trust and rapport are established can the in-depth family systems work be completed. Resolution occurs as the patient gathers competence and self-confidence. According to Leeder, the mother-perpetrator should be helped to understand the deep emotional needs that were unmet in her own childhood and why she has developed this method of having those needs met. Couples treatment occurs at this stage and focuses on communication, the partners' understanding of each other's emotional needs, and how the couple might better take care of those needs in the future. Leeder notes that the criteria for termination of these cases are unclear. She suggests that the patient needs to come to an understanding of the nature of the problem and to feel confident, and the couple, if there is one, needs to be communicating and attempting to recognize and fulfill needs of their own.

## The Role of Lying

No discussion of therapy with Munchausen by proxy perpetrators would be complete without specific mention of the issue of deception. Deception and denial are the threads that weave together the story of illness, and sometimes the perpetrator's entire life.

Lies have been postulated to be mechanisms that facilitate repression and/or denial. Ford, King, and Hollender (1988) comment that an untruth told over time may become increasingly believable and acceptable as fact to both the people who tell the lie and the people to whom it is told. The need for lies may serve to displace or disguise conscious awareness of conflict. Munchausen by proxy perpetrators develop systems of deceit that can include their personal histories and the histories of their families of origin. At the time they begin to fabricate or induce illness in their children, they have already perfected the ability to repress and deny their behavior. According to Ford et al., "The most obvious reason for lying is its external effect: to have an impact on the environment by influencing others" (p. 557). This attempt to influence the environment is the basis for the patient's induction or feigning of illness in her child. These patients have the ability to present historical information that they control and provide at their discretion. Munchausen by proxy perpetrators have discussed the satisfaction they feel when they have stumped the most experienced doctors. For some, it seems to be a bizarre game in which they match themselves against the best specialists and hospitals they can find (Meadow, 1982a). For others, the lying assists them in continuously presenting a facade they believe will be acceptable to the receivers.

Lying has a compulsive feature to it that is consistent with the compulsive quality of Munchausen by proxy behavior. MBPS perpetrators who have entered treatment and have begun to describe the induction of illness have also noted that they recognized what they were doing was wrong but were unable to stop themselves. Munchausen by proxy perpetrators have discussed many obsessive thinking patterns consistent with obsessive-compulsive disorder and other addictive patterns. They bargain with themselves and calculate the ending of their behavior. At times, they are successful at stopping their behavior, only to have it return. They attempt to regulate their self-esteem and to master an overwhelming need to feel in control. Pathological lying represents a core ego deficit, according to Ford et al. (1988).

Lying as a focus of psychotherapy has been explored (Ekstein & Caruth, 1972; Lerner, 1983), although not specifically with Munchausen by proxy until Feldman's 1994 article. The pervasive issue of denial has been discussed, including several hypotheses that may be useful for suggesting methods to break through denial. One of these hypotheses holds that, in deceiving health care professionals, the Munchausen by proxy mother unconsciously accomplishes the primary task of deceiving herself into believing that the sympathy and attention she receives are warranted. A second hypothesis involves projective identification. Through this defense mechanism, the mother projects onto her child her unconscious longing for nurturance, then ensures, through her own indefatigable attention as well as that of caregivers and others, that the child receives the nurturance she herself so desperately craves. Third, in cases involving conscious deception, perpetrators may be emphatic in their denial in an effort to block disclosure of such motivations as manipulating or exacting retribution from others.

Although Feldman admits he is unaware of consistently effective specific treatment programs for Munchausen by proxy perpetrators, especially if they refuse to acknowledge their involvement, he asserts that psychotherapy (individual and/or family) would seem to offer the best, and perhaps only, hope for treatment. The basic aim of this psychotherapy would be to teach the Munchausen by proxy parent adaptive ways to get her needs met, including expressing painful affect with words rather than abusive actions. Feldman also believes this same goal is central in the treatment of patients with severe personality disorders. This view supports the concept that treatment success will be limited unless the therapist can find a way to break through the patient's denial.

Feldman (1994) proposes modifications of Eisendrath's (1989) strategies for ending factitious behavior without mandating a confession:

> Sample strategies include: 1) inexact interpretations of psychological defenses (i.e., offering psychodynamic hypotheses to the patient that encourage a change in behavior without declaring the disorder factitious), and 2) therapeutic use of a double bind (e.g., telling the patient that if the next therapeutic intervention fails, a diagnosis of factitious disorder will be proved.) (p. 126)

## Gender Issues

Certain theories about the psychology of women may help to explain why women are more vulnerable than men to developing Munchausen by proxy syndrome. The chronic powerlessness related to female sex roles often contributes to psychological distress in women, and can lead to a higher prevalence of certain psychological disorders. Women develop a sense of identity in a context of connection to and caring for others; a relational mode of development thus ensues. Men, on the other hand, develop a sense of identity based on experiences of separation and competition. For women, a risk lies in the overdevelopment of that aspect of caring for others. Although many women find adaptive ways of coping, some turn to medical professionals as a socially sanctioned way of receiving care.

The ultimate role of caretaker is that of the mother figure. Women are expected to be the primary nurturing figures for their children and to attach to them protectively. However, MBPS mother-perpetrators clearly display a disorder of empathy and attachment with their children. They harm their children without feeling the children's pain. The children become objects used horribly by the mother-perpetrators in order to have their own needs met. The reasons attachment fails to develop are diverse, but they grow from disturbed object relationships beginning in childhood with experiences of physical, sexual, and emotional abuse.

Society provides many stereotypes of femininity and expectations for women. Vulnerability to development of Munchausen by proxy syndrome may reflect a woman's perceived relationship with the world. The MBPS mother has taken to an excessive level the socially prescribed roles of nurturer and caregiver. Her needs are met primarily through her caring for others, especially her children, but she must have a sick child to present to medical professionals to continue receiving validation for this role. Furthermore, Munchausen by proxy is a mechanism that disguises the lack of attachment that exists between the mother and child. The mother-perpetrator strives to cover up her lack of attachment with a perfect caricature of mothering while simultaneously receiving approval and support for her mothering and nurturing skills from powerful figures: medical professionals. When the mother-perpetrator can fool doctors and receive praise for exceptional parenting at the same time she is hurting her child, her behavior is reinforced, and therefore it continues.

Treatment conceptualization also has to take into account the broader aspects of women's lives. Munchausen by proxy syndrome develops for many reasons, most simply because of the adaptive and protective mechanisms the behavior provides for the mother-perpetrator. Although the issue of gender cannot be ignored, understanding women's vulnerability to development of this syndrome does not explain why the abuse occurs, particularly in a given individual. We must consider a combination of core factors, including gender, the role of deception, the influence of victimization history on identity development, lack of empathy, the disorder of attachment, and the role of medicine in our society. All of this, however, must be assessed in the context of each mother-perpetrator's unique life experiences.

In a thought-provoking article, Robins and Sesan (1991) consider many gender-related issues in the development of Munchausen by proxy syndrome by exploring three etiological perspectives: family systems theory, theory of women's psychological development, and child abuse theory. Although these authors acknowledge that MBPS is a complicated syndrome with multifaceted causative factors, they assert that the occurrence of this disorder primarily in women is related to gender role and power imbalances within the family, difficulties with self-care in the service of caring for others, and unresolved victimization histories. They further suggest that women are more vulnerable than men to using children to satisfy unmet needs and to seeking out medical professionals to meet socially sanctioned self-needs. Robins and Sesan present a multimodal treatment approach utilizing individual, family, marital, and/or group psychotherapy that incorporates feminist therapy theory, a sociocultural perspective, and treatment models that have been developed for working with adult survivors of abuse. They refer specifically to the use of feminist therapy—as outlined by Lerman (1986), Butler (1985), and Gilbert (1980)—as a guide to treatment.

Robins and Sesan (1991) comment that the therapist may engage the mother-perpetrator in therapy by approaching treatment from the perspective of helping the child. Specific mental health interventions may include "(a) supportive therapy for the mother, allowing her to discuss the stress of having such an ill child; (b) support groups for mothers of chronically symptomatic children; (c) educational workshops or classes for parents; and (d) couples therapy, using a family systems approach" (p. 288). They also assert that Munchausen by proxy mothers rarely need inpatient treatment, and that therapy should be conducted within a supportive, nurturing, therapeutic relationship in order to allow the perpetrator to deal ultimately with such issues as past victimization, rigid adherence to traditional sex roles, imbalances of power, imbalances of self-care versus other care, denial of own needs, unmet dependency needs, reliance on male authority, and devaluation of female authority.

Another contribution to the therapy literature that considers the development of Munchausen by proxy syndrome in multiple contexts is Schreier and Libow's book *Hurting for Love* (1993a), which provides a rich exploration of perpetrator dynamics, although it does not add greatly to our understanding of psychotherapy. In their postulation of etiology, Schreier and Libow consider individual perpetrator dynamics, the doctor-perpetrator dyad, and the larger patriarchal society's influence on women's development. They place the individual dynamics within the framework of a female form of perversion, and postulate that an "impostor mother" seeks to sustain a relationship with a powerfully parental image of physician, using her child, the fetishistic object, as a means of connection. The mother, desperate for recognition and nurturance, seeks a relationship with the physician to repair early experienced trauma.

In their review of psychotherapeutic work with MBPS mothers, Schreier and Libow (1993a) discuss therapy with Munchausen syndrome patients and then present psychotherapists' recollections of their work with two different MBPS mothers. Schreier and Libow suggest that the mother-perpetrator patient needs to explore her early and current feelings of neglect, abandonment, and deprivation. They also indicate the importance of the therapist's helping the mother-perpetrator to articulate her feelings and express her needs for support and recognition to her family, noting that this may help her to forgo her destructive reliance on her child as a means of keeping the physician close. According to Schreier and Libow, the mother-perpetrator's success in therapy, which may be court ordered, will ultimately depend on four factors: the individual dynamics of the patient, her willingness to acknowledge her fabricating behavior and its destructiveness, the responsiveness of other family members to the need for change in the family system, and the therapist's ability to work supportively with the patient without being deceived.

Schreier and Libow also add some important cautions for therapists. They note that MBPS patients are "masterful at evoking the sympathy, doubt, and narcissism of their caretakers" (p. 162). They recommend that, in order to manage the countertransference issues that will arise, the therapist should read extensively about the syndrome prior to beginning treatment, have access to ongoing consultation or supervision, and establish collaborative relationships with other therapists involved in the case. Finally, they mention the difficult balancing act the therapist faces, between providing input to the court regarding the patient's progress and jeopardizing the trust and confidentiality established within the therapeutic relationship.

In our practice we have developed a treatment strategy for the mother-perpetrator that is focused on simultaneously understanding her personality development and the origins of the abuse for which she is responsible. This approach incorporates cognitive-behavioral techniques and object relations theory. The treating therapist must believe that Munchausen by proxy syndrome behavior does exist and that the mother-perpetrator is still worthy of treatment. We are aware that strict treatment guidelines must be adhered to, or the child-victim may be placed at substantial risk. As we have followed treatment cases, we have been amazed at the consistency of Munchausen by proxy mother-perpetrators' responses to the treatment process. We have also been pleased with the positive treatment outcomes obtained using the treatment model detailed in Chapters 9-11 of this volume.

# 9 The Initial Therapeutic Stage

## ⌘ Trust

Deborah O. Day

> *I understand your desire to have a special relationship with me, one that meets your needs for connectedness, rescue, protection, even love. But our relationship isn't for those things. It's better, because it's based on you and your continued learning and growth—not on a fantasy that could be blown away in a second (as undoubtedly it has many times in your past). Because it is real, you can count on it, on me. The good news is that although I am not your fantasized savior/parent/lover, this relationship is a place where you can feel safe, supported, and optimistic, and where you can examine things that you otherwise might not. All of these things are based upon what is actually present, right now, right here.*
> —*John N. Briere,* **Child Abuse Trauma: Theory and Treatment of the Lasting Effects,** *1992*

Most mental health professionals will receive one referral of a Munchausen by proxy syndrome perpetrator in their careers. As the preceding chapters in this volume have made clear, these cases are complicated by pending legal issues, by crises, and by the needs of young children. Therapy is most successful when it begins with a level of acknowledgment on the part of the mother-perpetrator—at least a partial admission or acknowledgment that she exaggerated the illness or symptoms in her child. As later chapters will show, this has been found to be only the surface of what will eventually be uncovered.

## Defining the Therapist's Role

The treatment process with Munchausen by proxy mothers starts with a clear role definition from the therapist, expressed not only to the patient, but to the other professionals involved in the case. Too often, mental health professionals are asked to engage in dual relationships in MBPS cases, most often motivated by their lack of knowledge regarding these types of cases. Evaluators should maintain their ability to provide objective opinions to the courts and child protective agencies. Therapists must focus on maintaining the therapeutic relationship. As therapists will learn, maintaining the relationship will be difficult even under the best of conditions. Trust is the primary therapeutic goal as treatment begins. Any perceived violation of that trust on the part of the patient will result in the disintegration of the therapeutic relationship.

In a Munchausen by proxy syndrome case, several different legal systems may require the treating therapist's opinions, by way of summaries of treatment progress. These systems may include the dependency court; family (civil) court, if a divorce is pending; and the criminal court, if the perpetrator is charged with a criminal act. Child protective agencies may be providing family supervision, or the child-victim may be in foster care. If disclosures of information will be required, the therapist must obtain the customary written releases from the patient. When the patient is asked to sign a release, it is essential for the maintenance of therapeutic trust that the therapist discuss with the patient the meaning and effects of the therapist's providing the information to others. This discussion should include the content of the information to be revealed.

It is critical that trust be established between therapist and patient. The only way this will happen is if the clinician establishes the guidelines for trust and models the expectation of trust. Therapists should not become advocates for their patients or become involved in their legal difficulties. The mother-perpetrator's therapist in an MBPS case should provide only basic information to authorities as required, with full disclosure to the patient. It is not the role of the treating therapist to provide recommendations for contact between mother and child, although many therapists have found themselves in this role. It is the job of the court-appointed evaluator to provide this type of recommendation, using the therapist's information, without damaging the therapeutic relationship. Information on the patient's continued need for treatment and any progress made by the patient in therapy is appropriately contained in the evaluator's report.

## Understanding Initial Clinical Issues

Due to the initial disorientation of the MBPS patient, a brief psychiatric hospitalization may be recommended. Often, the mental health professional involved in the case will have little information upon which to make this decision. This short-term psychiatric stay removes the mother-perpetrator from the pressures of outside influences and allows the treating mental health professional to address several critical issues while the patient is in a safe environment. The patient may have made statements alluding to suicidal thoughts, or may have made some type of threat that is of concern to other professionals involved in the case.

The initial evaluation, whether conducted on an inpatient or outpatient basis, should address the mental status of the mother-perpetrator, including suicidal ideation, family dynamics, spouse abuse, and delusional or paranoid mental processes. The history gathered at this time also becomes a foundation for the assessment of the patient's general honesty. Some patients fabricate about all aspects of their lives (Schreier, 1992). The patient's tendency to lie or fabricate plays a role in the planning of initial and long-term treatment. Patients who do not fabricate about all aspects of their lives have been found to have less pathology and a higher likelihood of engaging in the treatment process. However, these patients may still be very dangerous.

The first striking clinical impression reported by many mental health professionals working with Munchausen by proxy mothers is the predictable nature of the patient's response once she enters treatment. This patient never has enough time to tell her story. Telling her story can involve telling of the mistakes made by the doctors, nurses, lawyers, and law enforcement personnel. With pride, she discusses her knowledge of medical procedures and the medical staff's reliance on her to help with her child's treatment. Even when she acknowledges her behavior, she is not willing to let go of the blame she places on others. This "blaming" dynamic can be expected to continue for months, sometimes years, into treatment. As trust is developed, the patient will begin to decrease her need to prove other professionals or persons involved wrong.

Beyond the noticeable and confusing emotional presentation these patients have, they also fall into distinct physical classifications. Some patients are shy and reserved upon presentation, appropriate in dress and grooming; these are the patients who are most believable. They have the ability to fit in and to take on characteristics of the people around them. Their documentation of the events of their cases is relatively organized and sensible. They have often befriended hospital staff members and may, paradoxically, even be the shoulders that the nursing staff lean upon when frustrated with their children's cases. A second group of patients present with severe deficits in their personal hygiene that also seems to correlate with the severity of their personality disorganization. They do not take pride in their appearance— poor grooming, weight issues, and lack of personal pride are all present. Several patients I have seen had an unusual appearance, particularly in their modes of dress. There were also collateral reports that their homes were cluttered and unclean. The paper documentation they kept was unorganized and as disheveled as they were. These were also the cases with more pervasive life fabrication and more overt hostility; generally, they were the most challenging to engage appropriately. Interestingly, they also seemed to keep their interactions medically related.

I treated one such women who had kept the baby shoes and leg braces that had belonged to her now adolescent child, reporting she had done so "just in case" she needed to prove her daughter had worn them as a toddler. She brought these leg braces and shoes to me as evidence that her child had indeed had multiple medical problems since her birth. Her proof was that her daughter's doctor had prescribed the braces. However, available documentation was not able to verify this mother's story. I was left wondering if this was part of her extensive fabrication, which in this instance included props.

As the therapist begins the therapy relationship with a Munchausen by proxy syndrome patient, he or she may find it useful to rely on previous experience working with severe personality disordered patients. Borderline, dependent, and narcissistic personality disorders, post-traumatic stress disorder, and adult sexual abuse survivor dynamics are, in one form or another, likely present with Munchausen by proxy patients. A fundamental working knowledge of the works of major contributors to the literature on abuse survivor therapy and therapy with personality disorders (e.g., Briere, 1989, 1992; Courtois, 1988, 1991; Hersen, Kazdin, & Bellack, 1983; Kernberg, 1989; Kernberg, Selzer, Koenigsberg, Carr, & Appelbaum; 1989; Kohut & Wolf, 1978; Masterson, 1981; Meichenbaum, 1992; Turner, Calhoun, & Adams, 1981) can be of great benefit to the therapist tackling a Munchausen by proxy case. Courtois (1991) describes the preliminary phase of treatment with adult sexual abuse survivors:

Of foremost importance at this stage is the development of a consistent, reliable and stable therapeutic relationship. Survivors often have great disillusionment and mistrust of authority figures: Therapists are no exception and are tested throughout the course of treatment. They must expect this and try to provide the conditions within which to develop trust right from the start. (p. 54)

These observations are consistent with the treatment issues seen with Munchausen by proxy perpetrators.

Without a doubt, MBPS patients have poor boundaries. These mothers have been observed in therapists' waiting rooms engaging other patients in inappropriate conversations. They violate the privacy of other patients without any overt awareness of what they are doing. Other mother-perpetrators are so full of shame that sitting in the waiting room is intolerable. Still others are angry; these are the patients who have not acknowledged any aspect of their behavior and are attending therapy appointments only to "prove" their innocence. These patients' poor boundaries are also evident in the therapeutic relationship. There is lack of respect for the time limits of the sessions and disregard for the clinician's available telephone time. One patient continuously commented on the beauty of the office building and my clothes, with particular attention paid to my shoes.

The literature to date (Kinscherff & Famularo, 1991; Manthei, Pierce, Rothbaum, Manthei, & Keating, 1988; Sigal, Gelkopf, & Meadow, 1989) and my own clinical experience are convincing regarding significant, preexisting psychopathology in the Munchausen by proxy mother. This pathology does not represent a consistent, specific *DSM-IV* diagnosis, but certain personality characteristics have been repeatedly identified. Hysterical personalities, serious depressions, antisocial beliefs, relationship difficulties, obsessive-compulsive behaviors, narcissism, and dependence have been described consistently (Folks & Freeman, 1986; Schreier, 1992; Sheridan, 1989; Waller, 1983).

Beyond the well-documented and recognizable personality characteristics, a "secret" thought process has been identified in Munchausen by proxy patients. Simply put, their focus is on themselves, and they are able to dehumanize (Schreier, 1992) their children to meet their own needs. In one case, a mother I saw in treatment admitted to injecting her toddler with insulin, causing a life-threatening reaction. Her behavior was identified after the second episode, and she admitted what she had done. As we explored the dynamics of her behavior, it was clear she had felt that her child had taken attention and focus away from her. She had been desperate to gain her parents' attention, and she quickly lost that attention when her child was born. Her Munchausen by proxy behavior was reinforced when immediate attention and support were forthcoming, not only from her own parents but from the hospital staff and the father of the toddler, who had abandoned the mother before the birth. The patient had injected her own mother's insulin into her child. The obvious anger she had toward her mother for the lack of attention and nurturance throughout her life was symbolically played out through the use of her mother's insulin.

My colleagues and I have found the presence of domestic violence to be prevalent in our clinical population of Munchausen by proxy perpetrators; this issue has been underaddressed in the published treatment articles. The therapist working with an MBPS patient must address domestic violence through multiple individual sessions. Without further exploration of this issue, the potential of the patient's beginning couple therapy or family therapy with an abusive spouse severely inhibits the early progress that can potentially be accomplished in these cases. The domestic violence issue is consistent with many dynamics seen in mother-perpetrators (i.e., dependency, low self-esteem, lack of ability to form plans of escape) and is consistent with the number of mother-perpetrators who were victims of child abuse.

The clinician's understanding of the dynamics of the patient's family of origin is essential in the early stages of therapy. Family of origin dysfunction among the MBPS patients with whom I have worked has taken the forms of incest, early emotional abandonment by a parent, and family members with Munchausen syndrome. I have also seen at least one mother-perpetrator who was the victim of Munchausen by proxy by her mother. These issues facilitate patients' beliefs that as children they were unloved, unwanted, or somehow otherwise different from their siblings and peers.

Family issues will form the basis for psychotherapeutic understanding of the patient's behavior. As a therapist, I have been consistently amazed at the number of perpetrator family members who are passive-aggressive with my patients in their attempts to sabotage treatment. Sabotage becomes a recurrent theme, and can take the form of financial manipulation (threats to remove available funds for treatment), limits on the number or length of appointments, and undermining of the trust the patient has begun to develop with the therapist. This becomes clear when the abilities of the therapist are repeatedly questioned. These dynamics are designed to undermine the confidence the patient is developing in the therapy and cause a split in the relationship.

In several of my cases, the mothers of the MBPS mother-perpetrators became very aggressive in their attempts to undermine treatment. One mother, who was believed to have been a Munchausen by proxy perpetrator herself, continually questioned my treatment recommendations, reinforced the mother-perpetrator's perception that she was unable to function independently, and did her best to establish distrust. Her goal was to keep the family dynamics "secret." In this family, there were many secrets to be uncovered. As treatment progressed and secrets were revealed, the patient's mother became more vigorous in her attempts to control her daughter. The patient was a married adult who had been out of her parents' home for many years. The primary role this patient's mother had maintained with her daughter after she left home was to reinforce with the patient how physically fragile she, the daughter, was. When the patient resisted her mother's ideas, the mother quickly regressed to the role of a hurt child, which induced pain and guilt in the patient. She would eventually give in to escape the emotional pain. At times, this patient's mother was successful at causing a split in the therapeutic relationship. Although this patient was unable to discuss when her mother's verbal messages caused mistrust in the therapeutic relationship, she did express herself through her nonverbal body language. She would arrive late for her appointment and enter the treatment room with her head down. She would avoid eye contact, and her arms would be folded across her chest or she would close off her body in other ways. Her tone of voice would change. These cues allowed me to confront her gently about her changed presentation. She learned how she changed when she felt pressured to give in to her mother's desire to recapture control over her. She was then able to relay what her mother had said, either about me or about her treatment, and we were able to work through the issue successfully and reestablish trust. This patient was vulnerable to cognitive distortions, and the issues with her mother were fertile therapeutic ground for dealing with these distortions.

Current research on the issue of gender and Munchausen by proxy syndrome discusses the socialization process of women and their vulnerability to early childhood victimization (Leeder, 1990; Robins & Sesan, 1991). The cycle of abuse and the learning patterns of the perpetrator are directly correlated to the ultimate manifestation of abuse through fabrication or induction of illness in the child. Understanding the perpetrator's early family history and her socialization/learning process is the therapist's foundation for helping the perpetrator begin to understand her level of functioning.

Another essential dynamic that the therapist needs to understand is the bonding that exists between the perpetrator and her primary attachment figures. Perpetrators lack bonding and/or attachment to their children

(Schreier, 1992). Leeder (1990) addresses this issue through a discussion of a particular case. She begins:

> Why would a mother do such a thing to her child? Most of the evidence indicates that this is a mother who is well trained and competent at mothering. She is nurturing, loving and caring, and has been well socialized into the role of motherhood. In fact, she is so well socialized that her main identity comes from caring for an ill child and receiving praise and confirmation for herself as a person from highly respected social authorities, for example, the medical establishment. It appears to me that this syndrome is actually a predictable outgrowth of the dominant patriarchal social order and its training of women. If a woman feels that she has little means to gain selfhood beyond that inherently in the role of mother, then this syndrome could be the consequence. (p. 77)

This identity crisis may become a causative factor in the development of a parent-child role reversal. In cases of moderate-to-severe role reversals, the parent envies the love or attention given to or by the child. She may want to be the child. The parent may feel overwhelmed or intolerant of the child's neediness. These factors, combined in one form or another, can lead to lack of attachment and the inability to feel empathy for the child. Any history that may help explain the lack of the parent-child attachment is vitally important.

It is also important that the therapist rule out the existence of a delusional disorder within the mother-child relationship. This delusion may be the basis of the lack of attachment. The literature suggests that few patients with Munchausen by proxy syndrome are delusional (Waller, 1983). It has been my clinical experience that this is likely to be true. Of all the cases assessed in our practice, only one case appeared to meet the criteria for a fixed delusion. In this case, the perpetrator reported a belief that the child was truly ill, and that inducing the illness would hasten the doctors' belief that there was a medical problem. Therefore, the child would receive the treatment needed. This belief has been identified in other MBPS cases, and is not unusual in itself. This case was different, however, because of the mother-perpetrator's history and the impact this history had on the mother-perpetrator. Her belief system was embedded in the experience she had following the death of her first child to sudden infant death syndrome. It was discovered, with careful research, that this mother was a victim of Munchausen by proxy when she was a child. As an adult, she maintained a relationship with her mother, although the focus of the relationship was her illnesses. Even after the patient began to understand this dynamic, her mother maintained a strong, negative influence on the patient's self-esteem, self-confidence, and ability to think independently.

Ravenscroft and Hochheiser (1980) have perhaps best described certain patients' thinking as quasi-delusional, although there is an absence of a formal thought disorder. They suggest that the disturbance in thought content and behavior may be a dissociative phenomenon, a form of pseudologia fantastica, or pathological lying, in which the parent comes to believe at least intermittently the fantasy that the child has an illness, rather than factitious illness. The initial assessment of the Munchausen by proxy perpetrator should establish whether a delusional and/or paranoid system is at work that is potentially contributing to the ultimate abuse of inducing or feigning illness in the child.

In an MBPS case, the therapist's understanding of the immediate family is crucial for establishing the safety of the children. Multiple pathologies have been found to exist with the fathers in these families (Griffith, 1988). Certain psychological characteristics are often present, such as rigidity, lack of emotional closeness, and a desire to maintain a closed family system. Although the father may not have overt knowledge that his child is being abused, his need to maintain the status quo in his family system renders him unwilling to recognize the abuse. When the therapist begins to explore these issues, the perpetrator's spouse often becomes defensive and emotionally aloof. The therapist is seen as intrusive and demanding. Revealing family information is contrary to the father/spouse's desire to operate in a closed family unit. It has been my experience also that the father/spouse is usually supportive of his partner, and he may vehemently deny that any abuse could have been perpetrated. If he is emotionally strong and/or domineering, his initial attempt to preserve the family unit may take the form of threats against the hospital. He focuses blame on the hospital, and his anger dominates session after session. If the patient is fearful of her spouse, she must collude with him to ensure her safety and protection. This is also a patient dynamic when the partner is absent. She becomes her own best advocate, spending countless sessions proving that the doctors and the hospital are at fault.

The Munchausen by proxy mother-perpetrator is notorious for documenting, in diary form, the course of her child's hospitalizations. She also will use her diaries initially to prove she did not perpetrate the behavior of which she is accused, or that she only "did it once," which happens to be also the occasion on which she was caught. The treating therapist should use this information to address the patterns within the family system, especially the level of denial that places all the perpetrator's children at risk for further abuse. Simply because the father/spouse was not the actual perpetrator does not mean that children are not at risk in his care. It has even been suggested that the nonperpetrating father may encourage symptom production to prove that the mother, now separated from the child, could not have produced the symptoms.

The placement of MBPS child-victims with extended family members raises the same important questions. Although family members (e.g., aunts, uncles, grandparents) may initially be in agreement with efforts to protect the child-victim and support no contact between the perpetrator and the child, the dynamics often shift, primarily due to the closed family system and the inability to acknowledge the possibility that their loved one perpetrated this unthinkable behavior. In an extension of the family dynamics discussed previously, as the shock of the disclosure subsides, the family regroups and seeks to protect the family secrets. Minimization, denial, and anger become prominent emotional responses among family members. If the code of silence is broken within the family system, family members often turn on each other, and it is at this time that the therapist can uncover family secrets.

It is also at this time that the father/spouse will increase his control over the mother-perpetrator through both overt and covert methods. Nonperpetrating spouses have been known to threaten mother-perpetrators in a variety of ways to keep them from disclosing family secrets. The emphasis for the nonoffending spouse at this point is often not on the perpetrator's behavior, but on maintaining the family system. The therapist's involvement in this process can be seen as intrusive, and the anger that the nonperpetrating parent feels toward the legal and child protective systems can easily be turned on the therapist, who becomes the perceived threat.

## Beginning the Therapeutic Process

In initiating therapy with a Munchausen by proxy perpetrator, it is important that the therapist identify her primary coping strategies. Often, denial, blocking, dissociation, and manipulation are the most easily identified defensive mechanisms. Blocking allows the perpetrator to maintain her quasi-delusion or fantasy of helping her child, and denial maintains distance between her and the legal system. Manipulation has become a survival strategy for many perpetrators, who have been deceitful regarding many aspects of their lives. Their manipulative skills do not falter in the initial stages of therapy, and therapists often wonder whether these perpetrators may actually be innocent. These skills allow the perpetrators to disconnect their thoughts, feelings, and behaviors. During psychotherapy sessions, perpetrators have described how they have seen themselves floating above their victims, or how they have been watching from a distance as they perpetrated abuse against their children. As therapy progresses, they begin to connect their behaviors with their feelings. Often they are flooded with overwhelming guilt for what they have done. These feelings, when genuine, place them at risk for self-destructive behavior, including suicide.

The Munchausen by proxy mother-perpetrator has likely remained resistant to treatment, and has not acknowledged the amount of abuse in the family system. Her disclosure of abuse has created chaos and has separated her from family members who have often protected her from the outside world. Trust is not established easily with such a patient; the therapist can hope to build trust only by employing the most basic of therapeutic techniques. Trust begins when the perpetrator feels the therapist is listening, is nonjudgmental, and is available to her. The perpetrator may begin to show trust by becoming too dependent on the therapist. Fear of being abandoned by the therapist and transference become early therapeutic issues. During this initial stage of psychotherapy, the therapist needs to set clear and specific boundaries while considering the additional needs of a patient who may be in significant distress. Arrangements for telephone support, additional therapy sessions, and a backup therapist are important for maintaining the patient through multiple crises. The therapist needs to set explicit guidelines and rules because of the manipulative skills of this patient and her continued belief that rules do not apply to her. The perpetrator will often attempt to invoke sympathy and to gain support beyond the boundaries of the psychotherapeutic relationship. The clinicians should be cautious of this issue and should provide an appropriate role model to the patient by setting clear boundaries and maintaining them.

After trust begins to be established and the complications of transference and boundaries have been addressed, the therapist can employ cognitive therapeutic techniques to deal with the distortions or quasi-delusions that exist in the perpetrator-child relationship. The distortions within the MBPS mother-child system are overwhelming. While dealing with these distorted perceptions, the therapist will discover that the perpetrator has also distorted the facts of other aspects of her life—her daily living relationships, accomplishments, and goals. The mother-perpetrator will often describe a life for herself that is in direct contrast to reality. Her belief in this life gives her comfort, and she will not easily or willingly give up the distortions. These distortions have also served as survival mechanisms. This is especially true in cases where family violence has been occurring between the perpetrator and her spouse. These distortions serve to provide safety from abuse; they often function as the perpetrator's built-in escape mechanism. Having a medically ill child allows the perpetrator to escape to a safer existence in the hospital. While in the hospital, the perpetrator plays the role of a loving, concerned mother and is given praise and support for her behavior. Returning home means being dominated, attacked, and often abused. Although case histories have shown that some MBPS mothers distort this abuse, reporting it beyond its actual level, the perception of severe abuse is present. It is also important to note that the domestic abuse was not the beginning of the deteriorating personality of these perpetrators, but rather a continuation of a cycle of abuse.

Partial disclosures are the initial focus of the therapeutic relationship. It is essential for the maintenance of therapeutic trust that the therapist refrain from judgmental statements while gently probing these incidents. If a perpetrator perceives any negativism or lack of acceptance from the therapist, the treatment relationship will not continue. When the therapist makes judgmental statements, this serves to reinforce the perpetrator's distortion that others cannot be trusted and will not understand, sending her further into her manipulative survival skills. The perpetrator is hypersensitive to every word, behavior, and response of the therapist. For this reason, the therapist would be wise to begin each session by recounting the previous session and encouraging the patient to ask for clarification of any issues or statements that are unclear. The therapist may find him- or herself clarifying simple issues that had hidden meanings to the patient.

## Therapeutic Techniques

Some techniques that can be extremely helpful in the beginning stages of treatment with the Munchausen by proxy syndrome mother-perpetrator include having her keep a journal, the use of relaxation techniques, the videotaping of sessions, and the use of family photos.

### Keeping a Journal

Having a mother-perpetrator keep a journal during therapy has been found to be an exceptionally productive technique. In my own clinical practice, journals have laid the foundation for major breakthroughs in denial, thereby strengthening the patient's trust relationship with the therapist. The therapist's instructions to the patient regarding how to keep a journal can be very nonspecific initially. The technique is intended to help the patient in connecting thoughts and behaviors. Because keeping a journal does require the patient to "work" outside the sessions, initial resistance can be expected. The patient maintains the journal on a daily basis and brings the journal to each therapy session. The therapist may also ask the patient to drop off her journal before her therapy session, so the therapist can review the material in advance.

MBPS mother-perpetrators' journals have been found to provide fruitful leads concerning the thought processes of these patients that can then form a basis for moving forward in therapy. Patients have also used their journals to test their therapists' sincerity. Patients can write in their journals about issues they cannot speak about in sessions. They can use their journals as a safe way of telling information they may feel is too shameful to report aloud. Patients then become sensitive to the influence their journals have on the patient-therapist relationship. Also through patients' journals, therapists begin to receive clues about issues that may not have initially been revealed, such as abuses perpetrated against the patient or that the patient has perpetrated against others.

## Videotaping

Because of the rich material initially disguised in therapy as either clues or metaphors, it may be beneficial for the therapist to videotape the first sessions with the patient and other family members. The clues revealed in these tapes can provide productive therapeutic material. Videotaping is also an invaluable tool for monitoring a patient's progress; the therapist can obtain feedback from the patient as she watches herself on tape, and can gather material to use in addressing the subtleties in the patient's relationship with her child.

## Family Photos

Reviewing her family photos with the therapist can help the patient to look at her own life from a historical perspective. Initially, the patient will paint her family as functional. With the use of photos, the patient can recapture specific events, and dysfunction can begin to emerge. Family photos can be used throughout the therapy process; each time they are used, additional material is uncovered.

## Audiotaping

Patients often experience significant distress in the initial phases of therapy. They do not trust themselves, do not trust others, and often feel alone in their pain. One technique that has been found to be useful in alleviating these feelings is for the therapist to tape-record sessions so that the patient can later review the therapeutic work accomplished in a particular session. Audiotapes can also provide a way for the patient to hear the therapist's voice when she feels the need, without violating the boundaries of the patient-therapist relationship. This has been found to be an alternative to the patient's overutilizing the support of the therapist through telephone contact.

## Relaxation Tapes

In some cases, instead of providing patients with generic relaxation tapes, therapists can help patients to make their own. Such tapes give patients an anchor to the therapeutic process and provide a suggestion of safety. As treatment progresses with the Munchausen by proxy perpetrator, she often feels that the therapist is the only one who understands, and the actual physical location where therapy occurs becomes a safe haven.

## Some Concluding Remarks

The therapist working with an MBPS perpetrator should take care not to become too involved with the distress of the patient. This distress typically comes after a period of resistance to the therapeutic process. The patient may be late for appointments, may claim she had no time to complete her home-work assignments, and may not bring therapeutic materials to the sessions. She may use her distress as a way of avoiding responsibility or confrontation. When trust is established, the patient's overdependence on the therapeutic process can become emotionally draining for the therapist. Maintaining clear boundaries and appropriate emotional distance from the patient decreases therapeutic work later in treatment.

Based on my clinical experience, working through the first stage of the therapeutic process with a Munchausen by proxy perpetrator typically occurs over a period of about a year. The sessions vary in length and time, but typically occur twice per week. A significant issue regarding the length of treatment has to do with the patient's ability to work through denial and establish therapeutic trust. This depends on outside influences that are potentially unknown to the therapist. Even the known sources can weigh on the patient to maintain status quo in the family. I recommend that the therapist make collateral contacts with family members during the initial stage of therapy. These may take place with or without the patient present, although individual interviews with family members may be more productive. It is important that the therapist interview those family members who have frequent and regular contact with the patient. As new issues unfold, they can be incorporated into the treatment plan in the middle stage of the process.

Throughout the early stage of treatment, the therapist may often feel pressured to reestablish contact between the perpetrator and the child-victim. This pressure can come from the perpetrator, from family members (e.g., the perpetrator's spouse), or from a defense attorney. My experience suggests that some time without contact between the perpetrator and child-victim is best in the long term for the child and the patient. As I have noted previously, the patient is often driven by an obsessional need to prove her innocence, and is at risk for reoffending until the compulsion is controlled. Several patients whom my colleagues and I have treated have talked about their overwhelming desire to reoffend. That desire diminished only after they felt safe and had been out of contact with their child-victims. To my knowledge, this urge has not been acted out with other family members or other children with whom these patients have come in contact. A caution is in order, however. The therapist must thoroughly assess the perpetrator's level of psychopathology before he or she can make a generalized statement regarding the safety of other children. All professionals involved with Munchausen by proxy mothers should avoid making such generalized statements.

When the patient has acknowledged her behavior and is engaging in the therapeutic process, limited, supervised, in-office visits with her nonvictim children should begin first. These visits should be held in addition to the regular therapy sessions. The information gained in these play observation sessions can provide prolific material for the individual therapy sessions. The connection between treatment progress and contact with the child-victim is extremely important. Patients who have been given access to their child-victims before they have engaged in the therapeutic process have been significantly less motivated to begin the necessary therapeutic process and significantly more resistant to acknowledging their behavior. Contact with her child-victim should be a reward for the patient's reaching her therapeutic goals. Once contact between mother and child has been reestablished, there is decreased motivation for the patient to work therapeutically. Several patients with whom I have worked have found it convenient to maintain the role of part-time mother, allowing responsibility for caring for their children to fall to others.

This is not true in all cases, however. Patients who maintain a degree of denial see contact with their children as proof that they are not perpetrators. The therapist should be prepared for the likelihood of the patient's becoming stuck at this stage of treatment, and should repeatedly confront the perpetrator regarding her lack of motivation. It is also important that the therapist be aware that other family members or child protective agencies may not approve of therapeutic contact between the patient and the child-victim. A guardian ad litem or a similar individual may have been appointed by the court to represent the best interest of the child-victim. The therapist should maintain some contact with this individual to ensure that the best interest of the child includes appropriate understanding of the therapeutic goals for the mother-perpetrator.

Finally, as the goals of the initial phase of treatment are reached, therapist and patient should consider additional psychotherapeutic services. If it has been discovered that the patient has been a victim of childhood sexual abuse or domestic violence, the therapist should encourage her to begin participating in a specific treatment group that focuses on the identified issue. It is at this point that the middle stage of treatment begins.

# 10 The Middle Therapeutic Stage

## ⌗ The Secrets

Deborah O. Day

Entering the second stage of psychotherapy with the Munchausen by proxy mother-perpetrator means that the patient has acknowledged her abusive behavior. In my experience, this means that she has likely disclosed abusive incidents in addition to those for which she has been forced to seek therapy. These disclosures have occurred only because of the therapist's ability to maintain a nonjudgmental and supportive stance while hearing the details of abuse. Therapists may find this stage of treatment to be personally difficult, because the abuse these patients have perpetrated is often unimaginable. During this stage, the crisis interventions needed in the first stage of therapy have decreased in their overt presentation. Because progress has been made, the treating therapist will naturally be inclined to believe that the patient is more open and trustworthy. Patients who still want excessive contact with the treating therapist may, during this stage of treatment, revert to covert manipulative behavior to maintain the symbiotic relationship they are attempting to replicate. Manipulation can occur as the patient makes demands for additional time, creates crises and attempts to draw the therapist into them, or engages in other behavior designed to dominate, control, or orchestrate the therapeutic relationship. The high level of dependency the patient has on the therapist is often still present, re-creating the same dynamics seen in the relationship the patient had developed with the medical staff and physicians who were treating her child-victim.

As the second stage of treatment begins, the patient's journal becomes a great source of information for the therapist to use in addressing continued treatment goals and monitoring the internal dialogue of the patient. The patient is likely to begin revealing more of her secrets as she feels safe in the relationship, and the depth of her journal entries will increase. With this depth also come tactics to test the sincerity of the therapist. Metaphors and hidden meanings will be more apparent, although deeply embedded messages will continue.

Trust continues to be the primary focus of treatment. Without trust, the patient is likely to avoid certain topics. The therapist's knowledge of the patient's nonverbal expressions will allow him or her to confront any avoidance behavior. Decreased eye contact and changes in typical body posture are examples of nonverbal communications associated with avoidance (see Day, Chapter 9, this volume). With several patients, I have observed dramatic changes in body language when sensitive subjects are approached.

The therapist should also monitor the patient's attitudes and general openness. One patient with whom I have been working for several years is particularly hypersensitive to my responses to her, both verbal and nonverbal, even on what I would consider relatively benign topics. To avoid what she perceived as my disapproval or potential rejection, she would begin a session by rejecting me. Minimizing her responses and responding with a negative tone of voice are examples of maneuvers she would use, but some of her other behaviors were much more subtle and indirect. When I confronted her with her inappropriate presentation, her ability to respond became much more appropriate. The most important aspect of this confrontation was her ability to acknowledge her behavior as a manipulation similar to her pattern of behavior with other professionals. She could recall and discuss the similarity of her response with me to the behavior she engaged in with medical and hospital personnel. As the hospital staff began to notice issues she interpreted as threatening to her role as the mother of a chronically ill child, her manipulations increased. The confrontational style used in treatment was helpful to the therapeutic process. This intervention served to reinforce the issue of trust in the therapeutic relationship while also setting the treatment boundaries by modeling appropriate interpersonal interactions and responses. If this behavior had not been addressed in treatment, a destructive pattern could have been reactivated that may have ultimately reinforced the patient's manipulative behavior.

Patients at this stage of therapy are now ready to explore their own histories of victimization, which may include childhood sexual, physical, emotional, and verbal abuse. Knowing the literature on the treatment of abuse victims (Briere, 1992; Courtois, 1988; Sgroi, 1989) will allow the clinician to incorporate known abuse treatment with the treatment for Munchausen by proxy behavior. This is the stage of treatment where patients can look at parental relationships in terms of the abuse they endured rather than maintain the superficial "perfect" family presentation. Patients who can expose family secrets are amazed at what they learn about their family dynamics. So often, they have been told that they were the problem, either because they were physically ill or because their attempts at questioning the family system were met with lies, distortions, and verbal assaults. The patients learned to stop trying to make sense of their families and joined the dysfunctional system. Joining meant becoming either a passive victim or a participant in the abuse.

If they were victims of Munchausen by proxy, they often joined the abuse by developing medical problems on their own. In one case that Teresa Parnell and I had the opportunity to evaluate, the mother had been reporting medical symptoms in both of her daughters since their birth. At the time the evaluation was completed, the mother was exclusively focused on her younger daughter. The mother in this case had gone so far as to relocate the family to Florida, to live in a warmer climate to help her ill daughters. When this family came to the attention of child protective authorities, the youngest daughter was placed in shelter care. The child then began reporting a list of various symptoms to her foster parents. Separating her from her mother did not reduce her symptoms—she simply began reporting the symptoms on her own. This mother never acknowledged her role in her child's severe emotional problems, and eventually the child was returned to the mother. After this child was returned home, other professionals involved with the family made similar abuse reports. The child has now been removed from her mother's care on multiple occasions, but each time she has been returned home. This case illustrates well the judicial system's frustration with symptom fabrication cases of Munchausen by proxy.

## Therapeutic Techniques

As the patient begins to understand her family of origin, two therapeutic techniques may prove helpful: the construction of a genogram and the use of photographs.

## Genograms

The use of genograms with dysfunctional families has been recommended by several authors (e.g., Karpel & Strauss, 1983; Love, 1990). Constructing a genogram provides the patient and therapist a glimpse into the family from a point of objectivity. This work encourages the patient to visualize the family along with the secrets kept. This technique enables the patient to see that she is part of a system, and that changing the system means more than just changing her own abusive behavior. The genogram lays out the generational component of abuse in black and white and encourages the patient to let go of the secrets and to recognize the family dynamics.

## Photographs

The genogram can be expanded upon by photographs. The photos that are generally most helpful for uncovering family dynamics are early childhood photos, particularly those taken during periods for which the patient has few if any memories. Photos can also serve as validation of events or dynamics the patient can recall but about which she does not trust her memories. Often, specific events are not discussed in the family, so the patient has been left to question her recall.

Family photographs have often been used in the treatment of adult sex offenders, and have been found to be quite appropriate to use with Munchausen by proxy mothers. In several cases in which I have been involved, siblings of patients have provided photos forgotten by or unknown to the patients. In one case, a male sibling provided his sister with a family photo that she had been unaware existed. It was extremely telling about the incest that had occurred in her family and served to validate her. The photo, shocking in its depiction of a child's anguish shortly after being raped by her father, was actually taken to represent the happy and perfect family the world was allowed to see.

## Coping Mechanisms

Through years of dysfunctional coping, patients begin to develop what I have called *underground coping mechanisms*. Although patients are aware when they use these techniques, they are not able to verbalize what they are doing, only that at that moment they can meet their own needs. Examples in treatment of Munchausen by proxy perpetrators include the same behaviors other people in the patient's life might label as manipulative. These are the passive-aggressive or passive-dependent behaviors of the patients: following people without their knowledge; calling and hanging up on individuals with whom they want to speak; canceling others' electrical, telephone, or water services without their knowledge; and, in more general terms, reverting to behaviors that simulate what they did in the hospital to control the situation. Excessive compliments are another example. These can be in overt form, such as admiring someone's dress or hair, or may manifest in the more covert pathology of copying the style of dress or mannerisms of an individual upon whom the patient has become dependent. If the therapist confronts such behavior directly, the problem can be processed. These behaviors represent survival strategies; in time, if they are not addressed, they will replace the patient's own individual identity. It is much easier for a Munchausen by proxy patient to imitate another individual than to begin to develop her own identity and be rejected.

A word of caution is in order here. Clinicians should not reveal personal information about themselves for several reasons. Most obvious among these is the need for therapeutic boundaries, but more important in these cases is the fact that MBPS patients are capable of using personal information in an unhealthy and, on occasion, destructive manner. Further, it is not exclusively the patient who may demonstrate pathological behaviors. The therapist should remember that a patient's spouse will often go to great lengths to keep the family together and to maintain control of every situation.

Recently, I saw a patient who was referred for marital therapy. As part of gathering background information, we began to discuss her mother and their relationship. This patient described herself as a sickly child who averaged one doctor visit a month from birth until her late teens. As we explored this pattern further, the patient could not recall feeling ill or reporting her illnesses to anyone. In fact, what she recalled was her mother repeatedly telling her she was ill. This patient remembered feeling guilty for her illnesses, which reinforced the symbiotic relationship that existed. Today, this patient is an adult with an ongoing relationship with her mother that continues to center on the patient's health. I suspect that as treatment continues and further exploration is accomplished, an adult survivor of Munchausen by proxy may be discovered (see Libow, 1994, for a preliminary study of adult survivors of Munchausen by proxy).

As the patient develops her identity and her feelings of safety increase, the therapist should reduce phone contact with her. (As I noted in Chapter 9 of this volume, a patient may need extensive phone contact at the beginning of therapy.) The number of sessions may still be twice weekly, with the additional support of group psychotherapy. The group therapy is designed to address other specific issues the patient has experienced. Individual weekly sessions can be reduced at this point (it is wise for the therapist to contract with the patient ahead of time regarding when the number of sessions per week will be reduced), but the therapist should be aware that this may precipitate a crisis for the patient.

The therapist may want to encourage the patient to audiotape certain sessions so that she can play them back at times when she is experiencing distress. Such tapes can help the patient in two ways. First, they remind her that the issues about which she is concerned or distressed have been discussed in treatment, and that there are solutions and problem-solving strategies available to her. Second, they allow the patient to visualize herself in the therapeutic setting. This has a calming effect and increases the patient's feelings of safety. Also, as I have mentioned in Chapter 9, the therapist may encourage the patient to make her own relaxation tapes while in the therapist's office. This technique helps with the obvious issue of relaxation, and also reinforces feelings of safety. Finally, the therapist may want to encourage the patient to talk into a tape recorder during times of crisis and distress. Patients have consistently reported that this technique has been very helpful in decreasing the distress they were experiencing at that moment. One of the therapist's goals is to promote autonomy in the patient, and these self-help techniques reinforce the patient's positive abilities and serve to decrease her dependency on the therapist.

## Rebuilding the Mother-Child Relationship

The most important issue in treatment during this stage is the rebuilding of the relationship between the patient and her child, if this option is available. When the patient has confessed to abusing her child, and she begins to understand the extent of what she has done, shame plays a part in keeping parent and child apart. This provides the patient with the distance she needs to explore fully what she has done to her child. Supervised contact between patient and child is still highly recommended. Education regarding attachment is the first part of the process.

Many patients find this self-exploration extremely painful, and sometimes they will sabotage the therapist's attempts to get them to deal with the issues in a comprehensive manner. In such a case, it can be effective for the therapist to confront the patient regarding her resistance. The patient is required to discuss many secrets and to acknowledge that she was abusive and threatened the life and psychological well-being of her own child. As the issues of bonding and attachment between the patient and victim are explored, the therapist must keep in mind that there may be other siblings in the home (or who have been removed from the perpetrator but have or will have contact with her) who are not attached to their mother. This is the appropriate time to begin exploring the perpetration of abuse on other children. Even if actual abuse is not found, thoughts of such behavior may have been present, but not acted upon. A progression of decreased bonding and attachment may be observed from the oldest to the youngest child, and may be the reason the youngest child is most likely to be the victim of Munchausen by proxy behavior. The youngest child may also represent the patient's desire to maintain her role as a caretaker and to ensure that someone is dependent on her. Munchausen by proxy mothers rarely have an identity except for the mother caretaking role.

The patient's development of an empathy bond to her child begins with the therapist's guiding the patient through the child's thoughts and feelings as the child experienced the pain of the abusive behavior. This includes putting words to the child's thoughts and feelings, given that most child-victims are too young or developmentally delayed to make verbal statements. This therapeutic technique will be used throughout the remainder of treatment as a marker of progress. Each time it is utilized, new, painful material will surface. As the patient begins to develop this insight, the issue of death and her unconscious desire for her child to die can be addressed. Most patients are unwilling to acknowledge that their children could have died as a result of their own abusive behavior. At this stage, the patient can begin to connect her personal experiences with death. It might be that she experienced a positive change in her life after the death of a family member. The patient brings together her motivation to abuse her child and her previous experiences with death. There may be a link between the two.

If a patient has experienced the death of an abusive parent, she may link death with a way of ending abuse. Because the patient has not attached to her child, for a variety of reasons, the child may represent a problem to the parent. A variety of explanations for this have been suggested. For example, a patient who suffers from spouse abuse may see the child as the cause of the abusive behavior by a spouse who verbally batters the patient for her lack of parenting skills. The thoughts of the patient can develop in two directions: One is the desire to remove the child through hospitalization or death so that the spouse abuse will no longer occur; the other is the desire to prove she is a good mother. Proving she is a good mother may begin with her performing some rescue with the child as a way of showing she is fit and competent. The attention she receives temporarily proves her worth as a parent and provides her with a respite from the abusive spouse. Unfortunately, due to the compulsive nature of this behavior and the reinforcements attached to it, the actual incidents of harm to the child increases in frequency, as well as in severity.

For a patient who is immature and self-centered, the motivation can be as simple as a desire to remove the "object" that has taken attention away from her. The patient loses the favored position within the family unit when the infant fills that position. When the child's grandmother is a significantly domineering and critical figure, the distortions in the patient can lead her to attempt to remove the object that has captured the attention of her own elusive mother. Therapeutically, the important issue becomes separating the mother and daughter (patient) as an unhealthy dyad and encouraging the patient to establish herself as an individual with self-worth. This becomes a very difficult task for the patient who now faces an environment void of family support systems that can appropriately meet her needs.

The dynamics discussed above may take up to a year to resolve themselves fully. The patient may begin to discuss the "rebirth" of her child. When the therapist believes the attachment and bonding issues are being resolved, more creative contacts can begin. As discussed elsewhere in this volume (see Parnell, Chapter 5), unsupervised visits may begin in a playroom with a video camera recording the interaction. The therapist can review the tapes and use the information to work with the patient on improving her skills as a mother and to continue the attachment education process. If unsupervised visits are being discussed, an evaluator should complete a reevaluation of the patient. The therapist provides input to the evaluator about the treatment the mother has completed as well as the treatment goals. The evaluator can provide an objective opinion regarding the progress that has occurred. The process of reuniting patient and child-victim can also be part of the updated evaluation. The final stages of treatment will begin the process of reunification if the objective data support this decision. The specifics of what reunification means and the legal implications should become part of the treatment process. Often court orders will preclude any contact between mother and child or specify that any change in the status of contact cannot take place without the consent of the court. Obtaining this consent is the responsibility of the patient.

The therapist should discuss with the patient continually the original fear the patient had about reabusing her child due to the compulsive nature of the behavior. The patient should not express any fear of reabusing at this stage of treatment. Objective measures for determining this fact are few. Objective changes in psychological test scores are one measure of change. The therapist should also see a difference in the patient's thinking. An example of this change is the decreased need to tell her story. The patient's overt and covert manipulations should have decreased, and the therapist should not feel overwhelmed by the patient's needs and demands.

## Partner Issues

If the patient's marriage has survived, it is during this stage of treatment that the patient must prepare to address and ultimately begin to deal with marital issues. The patient should be able to confront the absent spouse and begin to find other ways to make sure her emotional needs are met, whether by him or by other friends and loved ones. If the patient does not have a partner, she may not have anyone to turn to for assistance in parenting or for support in her attempt to develop a healthy self-concept and personality (Leeder, 1990). If that is the case, the patient must be responsible for developing an external support system of friends.

At this stage of treatment, the patient no longer needs to prove her story. She has begun to decrease their blaming, focusing instead more on herself and the pain she is experiencing. The therapeutic relationship is the basis for the patient's giving up blaming others. She is able to experience unconditional acceptance, which is a relationship component she is unlikely to have experienced previously. Because the therapeutic relationship is unconditional, she can be herself, and does not have to blame others.

During this stage of treatment, other psychological problems will be identified. In my own experience, I have seen a significant number of patients with eating disorders. The dynamics of eating disorders clearly fit with the family systems issues addressed above. Specialized referrals and psychiatric assistance may be needed. This is also true for patients who are in need of psychopharmacological treatment for depression and anxiety. These concurrent issues may require specialized treatment. The treating therapist should refer the patient to a professional who is competent in the particular area identified. The adjunct treatment will then become part of the treatment plan, and the treating therapist will be part of the team involved with the patient and her family. If the specialty therapist has no previous experience with Munchausen by proxy patients (which is likely, given that few therapists have such experience), he or she should work closely with the primary therapist, in addition to educating him- or herself about the personality dynamics of these patients.

During the middle stage of treatment, traumatic memories resurface and appropriate therapeutic work is accomplished. The final phase of this treatment stage includes identification of the remaining goals of treatment and the final goals to be accomplished.

# 11 Later Therapeutic Stage

## ⊠ Identity Reformation

Deborah O. Day

> *Success in therapy will ultimately depend on the individual*
> *dynamics of the patient, her willingness to acknowledge*
> *her fabricating behavior and its destructiveness, the*
> *responsiveness of other family members to the need for*
> *change in the family system, and the therapist's ability to*
> *work supportively with the patient without being deceived*
> *by her cheerful surface presentation.*
> —*Herbert A. Schreier and Judith A. Libow,* **Hurting for**
> **Love: Munchausen by Proxy Syndrome,** *1993*

This is, by far, the most difficult chapter to write, because of the lack of successful treatment case outcomes to report. The literature struggles to define treatment perimeters, and specific criteria for successful treatment outcome have not been established (Leeder, 1990). In this chapter I will attempt to provide an overview of the projected criteria for successful termination of Munchausen by proxy cases. The most important issue in measuring successful treatment outcome is the safety of the child-victim and the other children with whom the perpetrator will have contact.

## Acknowledgment, Empathy, and Attachment

The patient's acknowledgment of the abuse has taken place in the early stages of treatment. Additional disclosures are likely to have followed—not always, as mentioned in Chapter 10, from the perpetrator; they can come through an articulate child-victim. I had the opportunity to treat a victim who was 4 at the time the Munchausen by proxy-induced illness was discovered. The child was placed with relatives, and she had no physical contact with her mother for approximately a year. As the mother progressed in treatment, the decision was made to begin joint therapy sessions with the mother and daughter. Both the child and mother were prepared and ready to begin the sessions. The sessions went well, and their relationship progressed to the point of supervised visitations (outside of the therapy office). The daughter continued in her individual treatment. When the child was 6 years old, she disclosed another prior incident of induced illness perpetrated by her mother. The joint sessions had progressed to the point that the disclosure could be brought directly into the joint session. A mother-perpetrator who had continued her denial and minimization would have distorted this new information, become defensive, and provided confusing reasons why what the child had said was not true. In this case, however, the patient had made substantial progress in treatment and, although she denied any recollection of perpetrating the specific incident, was able to be empathic and supportive of her child. The patient made no attempt to cover up or explain away what the child was reporting. Additional self-exploration followed in her individual treatment.

In this final stage of treatment, the mother-perpetrator can correctly identify and acknowledge the physical and psychological impact her behavior has had on the child-victim. She can acknowledge the life-threatening nature of her behavior. The affects she displays are consistent with the types of issues with which she is confronted. At this stage, the mother-perpetrator reacts to the issue of her child's potential death in the same manner a nonabusive parent would react to the potential loss of her child. She also displays an appropriate empathy reaction to the child. A notable change is evident in the interaction and attachment between the parent and child. This change represents secure attachment, consistent with attachment described by Ainsworth (1985) and Bowlby (1988).

The mother-perpetrator goes through the grieving process regarding many issues uncovered in the course of therapy. She mourns incest, divorce, termination of parental rights, spouse abuse, and the loss of daily contact with her children. At this point, she will have successfully negotiated the grieving necessary to move forward psychologically. The later stage of therapy will see the end of the grief and resolution work done around any early abuses uncovered during the course of treatment. This grieving reaction and the patient's acknowledgment of the abuse she perpetrated will positively influence her ability to attach to her children. The attachment is not self-serving or pathological, but rather will reflect the ability of the parent to meet the child's needs before meeting her own. As Leeder (1990) notes: "Unfortunately, there is no guarantee that the symptoms may not recur. Of course, this is often the case with other forms of therapy as well; we never know for sure" (p. 86).

In one case I know of, treatment termination became the goal when the patient explicitly verbalized the new relationship she had with her child. The mother-child relationship felt new to the patient; it was something she had not experienced before. She was able to feel empathy for her child's pain. This empathy included the recognition that her child had almost died. The patient recognized what the loss of her child would have meant to her, and this recognition was different from the narcissistic, attention-seeking way she had first viewed the possibility of that loss.

Fisher, Mitchell, and Murdoch (1993) describe a therapeutic breakthrough that occurred 9 months into treatment with a Munchausen by proxy mother-perpetrator. After the breakthrough, "her grandiose presentation and facades significantly decreased and she was able to relate affectively in a more appropriate manner. She no longer focuses on her children as problematic and has almost given up the belief that her son's allergies were the cause of all his problems" (p. 702). The need for a therapeutic breakthrough in treatment that specifically demonstrates the development of attachment and the resolution of the mother-patient's narcissism has been repeatedly described in successful psychotherapy cases. In a follow-up of Munchausen by proxy parents in treatment, Bools, Neale, and Meadow (1994) discuss two mothers who were classified initially as predominantly borderline personalities:

> Objective evidence for one mother confirmed substantial improvement and both had been able to talk freely of their previous behavior. Both mothers had received lengthy psychiatric treatment and both changed their partners and had greatly altered life situations. The later ratings were such that a diagnosis of personality disorder could not be made. (p. 788)

In large part, the safety of the child-victim remains the focus of treatment. Without clear evidence that the child will be safe, treatment cannot be considered successful. Through the course of treatment, it is often revealed that the patient has perpetrated abuse on more than one of her children. If a mother-perpetrator is being considered for termination of therapy and these issues have not been discussed and acknowledged, significant risk factors continue to exist. The mother-perpetrator must be able to acknowledge the significant level of physical and psychological trauma she has inflicted on her child. The emotional absence of the mother-perpetrator as she inflicted or exaggerated the illness in her child has left the child feeling insecure and unsafe in his or her environment. The safe person, mother, abandoned the child to meet her own needs. The mother-perpetrator must acknowledge this dynamic. Actual grieving can be expected from the patient as her recognition reaches true levels of understanding.

## Identity Reformation

The later phases of treatment center on the reformation of the patient's identity. This includes the development of support systems that include functional relationships, the setting of vocational goals, and appropriate separation from therapy.

### Support Systems

A goal worked on throughout the therapy process is the development of appropriate support systems. The patient identifies support systems (groups, organizations, friendships, and so on) and learns to use them appropriately. As has been noted throughout this volume, the Munchausen by proxy syndrome patient is often the product of a dysfunctional family of origin, and subsequently marries or forms relationships with dysfunctional partners. We also know that at the time the accusations of Munchausen by proxy are made, the mother-perpetrator returns to her family for support. The family protects the perpetrator and minimizes her behavior, presenting alternate hypotheses for the Munchausen by proxy behavior.

As the patient works through the treatment process, she must recognize her dysfunctional relationships. She may choose to maintain the relationships, but she should show that she can recognize and establish relationships that do not replicate previous ones. The foundation of this ability has been laid throughout the treatment process. Yet the patient must also recognize that she will make poor choices as she attempts to form new relationships; she should learn to accept these mistakes and learn from her experiences.

This is particularly important considering the history of spouse abuse found in many MBPS cases. The patient's understanding and ability to recognize and maintain personal boundaries will be the hallmark of her recovery. Group therapy will provide the patient with real-life experience in relationships that she can use as she establishes herself as an independent individual.

My experience has shown that the formation of functional relationships is very difficult for the Munchausen by proxy mother. Such relationships represent her ability to engage in mutually satisfying interpersonal inter-action without using the manipulations and self-centered approaches she has used in the past. The patient finds herself in the position of attempting to replicate the therapeutic relationship.

### Vocational Goals

Many patients begin treatment without the ability to support themselves. By the time therapy with the MBPS mother-perpetrator is terminated, voca-tional goals should be in place. Although many of these patients are inter-ested in careers in the medical field, few, if any, have ever actually pursued a medical career.

### Ending the Therapeutic Relationship

As termination of treatment is explored, the patient's lack of therapeutic dependence will be clear. During this stage of treatment, either the therapist or the patient can cancel a session without needing to reschedule the appoint-ment immediately and without the therapist needing to be concerned about the safety of the patient. This will have a distinct clinical meaning, in contrast to the reluctance to participate or the clingy dependence seen in earlier stages of treatment.

The therapist's first move toward termination is to space sessions further apart and to set limits on additional contact. If the patient is comfortably able to accept a greater time lapse between sessions, the therapist can begin to introduce the topic of termination into the sessions. Termination, like the other stages of treatment, should move slowly. There is no established time frame therapists can refer to and compare their patients and their progress. This lack of guidance can create uncertainty for the therapist who is dealing with a patient who is potentially harmful to others.

The therapist can review the chart progress notes with the patient to assure her of the progress she has made. Because the mother-perpetrator is now dealing with other life situations, she may find it difficult to reflect objectively on her progress in therapy. By making this information available to her, the therapist can provide her with the kind of objective data that have been absent in her life. Many patients are surprised at the progress they have made. With this information, the patient can begin to make sense of her own life, developing insights and connecting thoughts and feelings she was not aware existed before she began treatment.

## Psychological Testing

Identity formation can be measured through the same psychological test instruments previously used to evaluate the patient. Psychological testing is of significant value at this point in treatment; the scores serve as an objective measure of the mother-perpetrator's therapeutic gains. Psychological testing can also be continued as part of the mother-perpetrator's routine measure of treatment progress. The MMPI-2, administered at different intervals in treatment, provides the patient with feedback regarding her progress and the treating therapist with additional information to use in measuring change.

For a patient who is nearing the termination of her treatment, a full psychological evaluation should be completed. This evaluation will provide the therapist with a detailed and objective look into the changes the patient has made. The evaluation will also identify additional treatment issues. Unfortunately, the patient's ability to pay for these services may be limited. During the course of their treatment, many mother-perpetrators have gone through divorces, faced attorney and court costs, paid for therapy, and supported themselves independent from others for the first time. The patient may be able to access funds through child protective agencies, especially if the case remains under the court or agency supervision. If a psychological evaluation can be completed, joint recommendations between the treating therapist and the evaluator can be utilized in any necessary court proceeding. It is through the multidisciplinary team that treatment termination recommendations should be made.

## Coordination Among Professionals

As termination is considered for the mother-perpetrator's individual psychotherapy, the therapist should work with the other mental health professionals involved in the case to establish joint recommendations. Ultimately, a plan for termination of individual therapy is developed and implemented. This plan may recommend that joint or family sessions continue, or that they be adjusted to meet the current needs of the family. Any significant therapeutic changes that might affect contact between mother and child should also be in compliance with the existing court order. If the recommendations are not in the court order, a modified order should be sought by the mother-perpetrator that reflects the current recommendations for the family.

Meadow (1985) suggests that a psychiatrist should play a long-term role with the family once Munchausen by proxy has been identified. The primary focus of this psychiatrist, given that these families are exceedingly difficult and stressful to manage, would be to support the pediatrician who will medically oversee the family. Meadow does not clarify what he means by *long-term treatment,* nor does he identify more clearly the actual treatment role the psychiatrist would take.

## The Father's Role

The role of the child-victim's father and his relationship to the mother-perpetrator should be understood and fully integrated into any decision that professionals make in the case. Because divorce is so prevalent in Munchausen by proxy families, the relationship between the parents is often adversarial and at odds. When the father of the child-victim has been designated the protector, he is often unwilling to give up this role. His perspective must be understood and integrated into the decision process. It is not unthinkable that a father may be so fearful about his child's well-being that he sabotages the reunification between the mother-perpetrator and child-victim.

## Termination of Parental Rights

Usually, if the child-victim is old enough, he or she has been in therapy at the same time as the mother-perpetrator (see Day & Ojeda-Castro, Chapter 12, this volume). An understanding of the cognitive and verbal abilities of the child will assist the professionals and the child's family in discerning the needs of the child. Typically, the majority of trauma occurs to child-victims of Munchausen by proxy syndrome before they have developed verbal abilities. All of the professionals involved in these cases are often most comfortable about the child-victim's well-being if the child is at least able to verbalize responses indicating some understanding of the events and actions that have surrounded him or her.

The conclusion of treatment cases has not always resulted in reunification of the mother-perpetrator and child-victim. In several cases, termination of parental rights has been sought, either by the biological father in civil court and/or as part of a criminal plea bargain agreement. The mother-perpetrators in these cases must then face the final stages of treatment knowing they will not be reunited with their children. In several of these cases, the perpetrators have been able to recognize that they were not able to parent their children. Before they would be able to parent appropriately, they needed to finish their psychological work. This realization helped these mother-perpetrators to accept the termination of their parental rights, as they could see the decision was in their children's best interest. It is a positive prognostic sign when the mother-perpetrator can look beyond her own needs and accept that the needs of her child are more important.

## Unsuccessful Treatment

For a variety of reasons, treatment has not been successful in all of the cases in which Teresa Parnell and I have been involved. We have analyzed our unsuccessful cases and have identified several treatment issues. First, Munchausen by proxy mother-perpetrators with severe personality disorders responded poorly to treatment. The interventions outlined in this book were not successful in engaging these mother-perpetrators in the treatment process. These are patients who, at best, would have little treatment success without the complication of Munchausen by proxy syndrome. Second, child protective workers have become frustrated with the lack of concrete proof of abuse in some cases and have returned child-victims to their mothers because they had no alternative. This has happened particularly in cases involving fabrication rather than induction of illnesses. Some professionals involved in such cases simply do not see the potential danger in returning these children to their mothers. The psychological damage is often abstract, and tends to be minimized. The abusive cycle in these cases is not broken, and there is a strong likelihood that the abusive behavior will reappear.

## Therapist Burnout

Therapists who deal over a long time with abuse cases such as those arising out of Munchausen by proxy syndrome can suffer burnout. Most mental health professionals will see only one case of Munchausen by proxy in their entire careers, and it can be difficult for therapists faced with this disorder to find clinical supervision by someone experienced in the treatment of these families. Most therapists and evaluators learn about these cases through trial and error. It is important that the therapist working with the MBPS mother-perpetrator learn to rely on a cotherapist, to decrease the likelihood of burn-out. Having clinical feedback from another therapist who is familiar with the facts of the case will also provide the therapist with a way to measure his or her success with the patient. The less he or she has to confer with the co-therapist, and the less "crazy" he or she feels, the better the case is going. The therapist must learn to trust his or her instincts in working with the Munchausen by proxy patient, and the experience will prove to be invaluable in the therapist's work with other types of abuse cases.

# 12 Therapy With Family Members

Deborah O. Day
Mercedes D. Ojeda-Castro

> *Most people who believe in the institution of childhood as we know it see it as a kind of walled garden in which children, being small and weak, are protected from the harshness of the world outside until they become strong and clever enough to cope with it. Some children experience childhood in just that way. I do not want to destroy their garden or kick them out of it. If they like it, by all means let them stay in it. But I believe that most young people, and at earlier and earlier ages, begin to experience childhood not as a garden but as a prison.*
>
> *I am not saying that childhood is bad for all children all the time. But Childhood, as a Happy, Safe, Protected, Innocent Childhood, does not exist for many children. For many other children, however good it may be, childhood goes on far too long, and there is no gradual, sensible, painless way to grow out of it or leave it.*
>
> —*J. Holt,* Escape From Childhood: The Needs and Rights of Children, *1975*

Although a few studies have looked at the psychological morbidity and mortality of child-victims of Munchausen by proxy syndrome, no literature exists that addresses psychotherapy with the identified victims. What we know about these children comes from few sources. Even in the many case studies presented in the literature, there are very few references addressing the psychological and developmental state of the child-victims. For the most part, only their medical histories and mortality are addressed.

Woollcott, Aceto, Rutt, Bloom, and Glick (1982) present four case studies of MBPS child-victims. In each of these, they briefly mention interviews conducted with the child-victims. The first patient, a 17-year-old boy, stated when interviewed alone that he wished his mother would not check his temperature so often. However, he also shared in his mother's worries that he was ill. Woollcott et al. describe the second patient as uncomfortable and having little involvement with her peers. She also presented with hysterical features, depression, and sleep disturbance. The third patient, an 8-year-old girl, is described as a friendly, intelligent child. She denied any physical problems and indicated that she wanted to play with other children. In the final case presentation, Woollcott et al. describe a 6-year-old boy. Their only reference to this boy's psychological state is that upon observation, he interacted more appropriately when his mother was not in the room.

McGuire and Feldman (1989) also present a series of case studies. In their discussion, they indicate that the younger child-victims were not allowed to separate from their mothers and develop individual personalities. As a result, they developed withdrawn, hyperactive, and oppositional behaviors. These disturbances were inappropriate for their developmental ages. At the same time, the children learned to "passively tolerate medical procedure." In older children and adolescents, conversion symptoms developed. They were also found to have fabricated their histories and cooperated with their parents' deception of the doctors.

In the literature, there is some discussion of trauma-related symptoms in child-victims. Boros and Brubaker (1992) present the case of CB, a 10-month-old female who was admitted to a hospital because of life-threatening apnea. Only CB's father had witnessed the apneic episodes. While in the hospital, CB had no episodes of apnea and was described as happy and playful. However, when anyone attempted to touch her face, she became hysterical and combative. These behaviors in a preverbal child led the staff to suspect that the child's parents were responsible for her apnea. Other authors have described the psychological as well as the physiological damage done to children by MBPS perpetrating parents (Porter, Heitsch, & Miller, 1994; Sigal, Gelkopf, & Meadow, 1989).

Bools, Neale, and Meadow (1993) studied 54 children who had been victims of Munchausen by proxy syndrome and who received follow-up inclusion in the study 1 to 14 years after fabrication of illness was discovered. Of the 54 children, 30 were in families with their biological mothers and 24 were in out-of-home placements. Bools et al. found that 13 of the children residing with their mothers and 14 of those who were not had a range of disorders, including conduct and emotional disorders and problems relating to school. Overall, 20 children, or 49% of those followed by the researchers, had therapy treatment outcomes that were judged to be unsuccessful. Bools et al. describe a variety of other concerns as well. A substantial number of the children had discovered their mothers' fabrications. School nonattendance among the children was notable, as were such post-traumatic symptoms as fears, avoidance of specific places or situations, and sleep disturbances, including nightmares. One female child presented with hypochondriacal behavior. The presence of such extreme psychological disturbance several years after the abuse is of great concern. This information, along with our own clinical experience, strongly indicates that the child-victims of MBPS are in need of long-term play therapy as a part of the overall treatment plan for the family.

Manthei, Pierce, Rothbaum, Manthei, and Keating (1988) suggest that the youngest child carries the family's burden of pathology. To illustrate their point, they present several Munchausen by proxy cases and recommendations for case management. These recommendations include individual and family therapy.

In all likelihood, the literature regarding child-victims of Munchausen by proxy syndrome is sparse for several reasons, including the young age of most victims, the difficulty in proving cases, the lack of motivation on the part of parents to seek therapy, and the large number of families lost to follow-up after confrontation.

As cases of MBPS are increasingly identified, it is imperative that mental health professionals develop a treatment framework for healing the trauma experienced by these victims, minimizing the developmental damage, and intervening in the intergenerational abuse cycle. Because most victims remain within their families, which include the mother-perpetrators, victim therapy may be a component of establishing safe reintegration into the family. In this chapter, we focus on the common themes and issues that arise in play therapy with Munchausen by proxy syndrome victims. In our practice we have had the opportunity to work with six young child-victims, some in long-term play therapy. The material presented below comes from our collective experiences with these children.

In order to treat victims of Munchausen by proxy effectively, therapists must first have a foundation of knowledge and experience in early childhood development and play therapy (Ammann, 1991; Knoff, 1986; Kratochwill & Morris, 1991; Newman & Newman, 1979; Pfeiffer, 1985; Sattler, 1992; Schaefer & O'Connor, 1983). These children are often developmentally delayed due to their chronic illnesses, repeated hospitalizations, and emotionally deprived environments. This presents specific challenges that must be addressed if play therapy is to be effective.

To begin, each child-victim must receive thorough psychological and developmental evaluations before beginning treatment. In this way, the clinician will have a clear idea of the cognitive, language, and motor skills of the child. The child's skill levels will directly affect his or her ability to play and express him- or herself in the treatment process. In some cases in which delays are severe and the child's environment has been quite deprived, the beginning stages of play therapy may have to focus on providing the child with a safe and enriching environment where he or she can, in effect, learn how to play. In these cases it is also important that the clinician refer the child to an early intervention or preschool program, where a plan can be established to maximize the child's developmental potential.

Additionally, in the majority of Munchausen by proxy syndrome cases, the victims are quite young. Meadow (1982a) and Jones (1987) both have noted that victims are typically under the age of 9, and most are much younger. Rosenberg (1987) reports on

> 67 cases where information about the child's age at the time of diagnosis of MSBP was known, as well as the length of time from onset of symptoms and signs to time of diagnosis. For those 67 cases the mean age at diagnosis was 39.8 months ± 32.1 months; the mean time of onset of symptoms and signs to time of diagnosis was 14.9 months ± 14 months. For all 117 cases the range for age at diagnosis was 1 month to 252 months; the range for time of onset of symptoms and signs to time of diagnosis was days to 240 months. (p. 551)

The typically young age of MBPS child-victims presents specific challenges for clinicians who treat them. These clinicians must have knowledge of the cognitive, emotional, and developmental characteristics that typify young children at various ages (Sattler, 1992). An understanding of developmental concepts such as egocentricity, shyness, dependency, stranger anxiety, separation anxiety, fear of new situations, and distractibility found in preschoolers will form the foundation on which treatment recommendations can be based.

Particular issues appear to be specific to the experiences of Munchausen by proxy syndrome child-victims. These children work in play therapy to resolve issues such as the physical destruction of the self, violation of basic trust, disruptions in attachment, and the incongruous mother image. These children have experienced a fundamental breach in their first and most important relationship: They have experienced inconsistency and victimization by their mothers, the very persons who are supposed to provide them with a foundation of trust and safety. They have been victimized by mothers who have used the mother-child relationship to have their own needs met at the expense of their children's needs.

Despite the significant and potentially devastating effects of this breach, most young child-victims of Munchausen by proxy syndrome do not have difficulty forming bonds or close attachments. Unlike some attachment-disordered children who present for play therapy, they are quite engaging with persons in their environment and can bond with the therapist. They engage in the therapeutic relationship quite readily once initial separation anxiety and stranger anxiety are overcome.

However, therapists must keep in mind that these initial anxieties may be severe in child-victims. They have in many cases experienced repeated painful and intrusive procedures carried out by a variety of medical professionals. As a result, they may have a great deal of initial anxiety when approached by a therapist. This anxiety is exacerbated by the fact that they do not have the strong foundation of a secure attachment to their primary caregivers—their mothers. Thus they struggle with tenuous abilities to trust in the security and safety of their caregivers and in the world around them. In one case in our practice, the child's insecurity and anxiety were so incapacitating that even after repeated attempts to have him separated from his mother, and after the therapist had spent hours attempting to engage him, he continued to be severely anxious and clingy, and cried whenever he was approached by the therapist.

This level of anxiety and insecurity is compounded by the paradoxical nature of the mother-child relationship in Munchausen by proxy syndrome. In the MBPS family system, the mother-child relationship is characterized by an overly enmeshed, supremely attentive mother who, simultaneously, is associated with making the child ill. When mother and child are viewed together, the child may cling to the mother and appear to be overly attached to her. However, the child's clinging and difficulties in separating from the mother are indicative of the degree to which this is a pathological and insecure attachment. It is interesting that when child-victims are separated from their mothers by the courts and placed with other caregivers, they adjust quite well, rarely asking for their mothers after the initial separation. In our experience, they quickly bond with their new caretakers, at a rate not seen in other types of abuse cases.

The child-victim of MBPS copes with the disparity between the overly enmeshed mother and the one who makes the child ill by splitting the idealized mother from the toxic mother. This imagery presents repetitively in the play of child-victims. One child we worked with drew a picture during a session that characterized this paradoxical relationship quite well. He began by drawing a picture of himself, and then superimposed a picture of his mother over it. He went on to draw squiggly lines all over the picture, stating: "That's my mom and me. My mom gets the worms out of me." In the later stages of his treatment, this child focused a great deal on dollhouse play. In this play, there were always two mothers. He described one as "mommy" and the other he called "the mean lady." The mean lady was always feared by the children. In many sessions he talked about the mean lady giving the children "yucky food" that would make the children sick. This is a very interesting dynamic formulation for this child, because his abuse took place when he was preverbal, and he had not been told about what his mother had done to him. It is likely that this play represents the expression of preverbal memories.

Senner and Ott (1989) describe similar drawings done by Susan, a 4½-year-old hospitalized patient suspected to be the victim of Munchausen by proxy. This child's primary nurse recognized the unrealistic parenting expectations placed on this child and identified the mother's inadequate coping skills. The nurse began drawing with Susan and obtained very interesting results. Susan described the first picture of herself: "This is a picture of a crazy girl. She goes around and around in circles. Isn't she crazy? She's standing on her arms. Isn't she crazy? She keeps going around and around in circles. Her legs are touching the ceiling. She can't get her feet on the ground" (p. 353). A second drawing of her family produced equally interesting results. Susan explained, "This is a family doing an experiment. They just keep doing it. I don't know why, but they just keep doing it. The pencil starts here and then, oops, it slips. I don't know why. They just can't help it. It starts here, but then it gets away" (p. 354). During Susan's hospitalization, Senner and Ott report, it was a constant struggle for the team to facilitate normalcy for the child.

In play sessions, the healing process appears to begin as the child-victim engages in regressive play. During this period of the treatment, play frequently consists of regression to early infancy. This includes drinking from baby bottles, crawling on the floor, and talking in baby talk. One young girl with whom we worked spent many sessions hiding under the desk, drinking from a baby bottle and making baby sounds. These sounds developed over sessions into what sounded like painful moaning as she repeatedly whimpered, "Mommy, Mommy." As the girl "grew up" in her sessions, she begin to verbalize increasingly, until the play was elaborated to include a feared monster. She spent a great deal of time hiding under the desk from the monster. This culminated in a session in which she was asked where the monster was and she yelled out, "Mommy!" and began to cry.

It is amazing the extent to which the early pain and emotion of the child-victim is expressed in play. This kind of play allows the child, in effect, to return to the trauma and relive those years in a more satisfactory and healing manner.

We have found that much productive material may be spawned in sessions with MBPS child-victims by having the children bring in their baby books, baby clothes, or pictures of themselves as infants. Even in cases when the abuse took place when the child was preverbal, these kinds of cues appear to aid in the resurfacing of memories that are then acted out in the play. A 4-year-old boy who had been seen in play therapy for 2 years brought in a doll that he had used as his transitional object since infancy. During one session, he was nurturing and caring for the doll, then he suddenly took a pretend sword and cut the doll across its body. He then dropped the sword and began soothing the doll and saying, "Oh, poor baby. It's okay."

Another crucial issue to be addressed in play therapy with child-victims of Munchausen by proxy syndrome is that of distorted self-image. Following months or years as ill children, victims learn to self-identify as sick or fragile; their self-perceptions become distorted. Krener (1994) relates some of these difficulties to the ways in which children learn the expression and experience of emotional and somatic symptoms from their families. Krener notes that if a family's way of expressing tension and distress is through physical symptoms, the child is significantly at risk for developing more unexplained physical symptoms and more psychiatric disorders due to the suggestion, learning, and psychological compliance that take place within the family. Children in such families receive nurturing when they are ill, and they may then continue to rely upon maladaptive methods to get their needs met in interactions with others. This can lead to attempts to maintain their role as sick beyond the actual induction of illness. Often, as these children grow older, they may even participate in the induction or maintenance of their own illness.

One young boy with whom we worked had continued refusing food and making himself throw up well beyond the time that his mother stopped physically inducing any illness in him. As his anxiety increased during his first play therapy session, he was observed to heave and gag until he vomited. All of this boy's life, his investment in being an ill child had been so great that he had refused food and induced vomiting until he required the insertion of a gastric tube for feedings. When he was removed from the care of his mother and received therapy in which he worked on his self-perception and interaction skills, he was finally able to begin eating and become a medically healthy young boy.

In the final stages of play therapy, as the child-victim develops cognitively and emotionally, he or she may be ready to begin reunification with the mother (see Day, Chapter 11, this volume). Before reunification is considered, it is important that the child have the cognitive skills, verbal capacity, and emotional strength to report any induction of illness or to resist any pressure within the mother-child relationship to resume the sick role. For example, one young child-victim with whom we worked began play therapy as his verbal skills began to develop. His mother was progressing in treatment, and unsupervised visitation was suggested. However, the consensus of the multidisciplinary team was that visits should continue to be supervised until the child's verbal skills were more reliable. There is always some risk involved in reuniting the mother-perpetrator and the child-victim—in this case, the decision to wait eased the anxiety of all the professionals involved.

Reunification also depends on the mother's progress in her own psychotherapy and any constraints on contact between mother and child imposed by the court. If contact is deemed to be appropriate, issues related to the child's ability to understand what happened to him or her become important. The child must be able (a) to understand cognitively some aspects of what occurred and (b) to reconcile those events with his or her perception of the mother and what a mother should be. At this point in therapy, joint sessions are extremely helpful for repairing the relationship and helping the mother and child to form healthy attachments to each other, because communication between mother and child in these sessions does not focus or rely on the child being in the ill role.

As a child works on cognitively understanding his or her history as a victim of Munchausen by proxy, he or she expresses awareness of the MBPS behavior on many levels. In many cases this begins in displacement and proceeds through play, until the child is able to discuss directly what occurred. The most distant level of displacement involves acting out the behavior with inanimate objects. One child we worked with played with a toy car that he said repeatedly broke down and had to be towed to a garage. Even when the car was repaired, he insisted that it liked to be towed and wanted to go to the garage. This was a boy who had begun to participate in the fabrication of his illness by self-inducing vomiting.

The next step in the child's addressing the Munchausen by proxy behavior is usually more direct, involving acting out on dolls. This was the case with the boy described previously who used dolls to tell the story of the mean lady who gave the children "yucky food." Next, the child might be able to involve him- or herself in the play directly; for example, the child may want to pretend that he or she is in the hospital and may ask that the therapist act as doctor or mother figure. Finally, the child is expected to be able to talk about his or her understanding of what occurred in the family.

## Psychological and Developmental Evaluations of Child-Victims

We recommend that when a child-victim enters therapy, an initial baseline evaluation be conducted to assess his or her personality and development. Then, when play therapy termination is considered, another evaluation should be completed. In our practice, we have evaluated children ranging in age from infancy through adolescence. We begin with a thorough review of the existing medical, psychological, and developmental records; we also review school records, speech and language evaluation records, and occupational or physical therapy records. MBPS child-victims have typically had multiple consultations and evaluations by the time they enter therapy. The documented information that already exists on a child can help the evaluator to determine the appropriate tests to administer as well as appropriate treatment recommendations.

In our practice, the initial evaluation is designed to assess the cognitive, academic, and personality development of the child. The elements evaluated include social development, fine and gross motor skills, expressive and receptive language skills, and developmental achievement. The intellectual portion of the evaluation includes the use of standardized test instruments appropriate to the child's age. In conducting the personality evaluation, we use multiple objective and projective test instruments. Unfortunately, the tests available for use with very young children are limited, and the reliability of many of these projective instruments decreases with the decreasing age of the child.

In a typical child evaluation, the parents often complete behavioral rating instruments regarding the child. Although we recommend the use of such instruments in Munchausen by proxy cases, it is clear that evaluators should view parental reports in these cases as suspect. The MBPS mother-perpetrator's ratings of her child are likely to be exaggerated. To obtain the most accurate information on the child-victim, the evaluator should ask both the mother and the father to complete the test instruments. If other significant caretakers of the child are available, they should also complete the inventories. If the child is in foster care, the foster parents should complete the instrument to establish the present functioning of the child. The more significant adults provide input, the more valid the description of the child will be.

## Munchausen by Proxy Victims in Later Life

Libow (1994) was the first author to address the psychological outcomes of adults who were victims of Munchausen by proxy as children. Porter et al. (1994) have reported that little follow-up information on Munchausen by proxy survivors is available. Several case reports of adolescents and older child victims have been reported in the literature (Bools et al., 1993; McGuire & Feldman, 1989).

Because of the scant data available, Libow's 1994 symposium contribution warrants a brief review. Libow's study included 10 adult subjects who were eligible for participation because they met the criteria for Munchausen by proxy that Libow had adapted from Rosenberg (1987). These subjects responded to written questionnaires and participated in optional follow-up interviews. Libow analyzed the demographics of the 10 participants, and she includes in the discussion section of her paper details of the limitations of the sample and a description of the findings. She describes the psychological impact of victimization as follows:

> The subjects report having suffered significant emotional and physical problems during their childhoods including problems with growth, eating disorders, nightmares, self-destructive fantasies, high anxiety, and school concentration difficulties—problems likely apparent to adults around them. Yet it appears that in none of these cases did anyone actively intervene to investigate their distress, even when suspicions existed. For most of the subjects, the MBPS abuse stopped only when they left home, or in a few cases, when the child was old enough to actively protest and threaten to tell. Many reported that the MBPS abuse continued with their siblings as the next victim. (pp. 8-9)

This preliminary information provides a captivating glance into the childhood experiences of child-victims. Libow's data serve to reinforce our argument that MBPS child-victims should receive early therapeutic intervention by mental health professionals. Without individual and family treatment, the long-term consequences to child-victims are apparent.

## Siblings

There has been very little published regarding the siblings of identified child-victims. The information that is available is mostly limited to references to siblings' medical histories and/or the circumstances surrounding their deaths (for details, see Parnell, Chapter 3, this volume). When siblings are discussed in the literature, it is in the context of serial Munchausen by proxy cases. No published information is available regarding therapy with the child-victim's siblings, and, unfortunately, we have little to add. However, Teresa Parnell and Deborah Day, the editors of this volume, have been involved in the evaluation and treatment of several sets of siblings in MBPS families with two to four children. These preliminary relationships have yielded some consistent observations.

Each of the child-victims in these families has been either the middle or the youngest child in the family. This child is most closely aligned with the mother, at least superficially, and certainly is the focus of the family. The oldest child is often aligned with the father. This child has taken over tasks within the home to compensate for the mother's absence. The oldest child is often pseudomature, compliant, and overly focused on family issues. He or she may be the keeper of the secrets in the family and may know far more than he or she will reveal during initial evaluation. This child is initially very protective of the mother, but becomes quite angry and blaming toward her. This child has a difficult time resolving the discrepancy between the mother figure and her acknowledged abuse of the child's sibling. This child is also quite traumatized by the loss of the family unit that usually accompanies cases in which there is an admission by the mother-perpetrator. In treatment, the oldest child will need the opportunity to grieve over each of these issues as well as to adjust to a family in which the focus is no longer a sick child.

Parnell and Day have seen several families with a total of three children in which the middle or youngest children have manifested similar personalities and behaviors. This child might be considered the "lost child" in a family, as he or she seems to be ignored while the mother attends to the child-victim and the father is focused on the oldest child. No primary figure attends to or meets the emotional needs of this child, and this may generalize to extended family. This child is sometimes emotionally removed, but acts out in a physical and possibly aggressive manner to obtain the attention he or she craves.

Parnell and Day recommend that the therapist hold joint sessions with the mother-perpetrator and the child-victim's siblings before the mother has sessions with the child-victim. In these sessions with the siblings, the mother-perpetrator should acknowledge her abusive behavior and take responsibility for its impact on the family. These sessions may need to be conducted separately with each sibling, not only because the children's levels of development may differ, but because the oldest child will usually have a far greater need to process these issues with the mother than will other siblings. These sessions may in fact prompt the siblings to disclose various types of abuse they believe the mother has perpetrated toward them. The siblings, especially the oldest child, may challenge directly the mother's supposed therapy progress and whether the child-victim is safe in her care. However, in Parnell and Day's experience, it has been unclear whether the children who react this way are expressing their own opinions or only echoing the concerns of their fathers.

Clearly, the impact on children of the many changes that take place in the family when Munchausen by proxy is diagnosed—the shift from an all-consuming family focus on one child's condition, the discovery of an abusive parent, the eventual parental divorce—cannot be underestimated. It is important that professionals consider the needs of each family member in such cases. All siblings should participate in the family evaluation process, and a treatment plan should be developed and implemented for each child who is old enough to participate. This process will become somewhat less difficult when the research and clinical literature begins to reflect the work of therapists and other professionals with the siblings of child-victims.

## Family Psychotherapy

The literature on the use of family therapy with Munchausen by proxy families consists of a few cursory case reviews. The literature that does exist, however, consistently endorses the use of family therapy, although guidelines or treatment models are missing (Griffith, 1988; Sanders, 1995b). Unfortunately, no one has yet conducted a large, systematic study of the psychosocial factors associated with the parents or families of children diagnosed as Munchausen by proxy syndrome victims (Mercer & Perdue, 1993).

Griffith (1988) outlines the characteristics of family systems in Munchausen by proxy syndrome cases. He begins with two case reports, the psychiatric evaluations and psychological testing utilized in these cases, and a detailed description of the psychological makeup of the family system. Griffith found the following elements in the MBPS family:

- Enmeshment of the parent-child relationships
- Multigenerational themes of exploitative dominance/submission in parent and child relationships, which also continue in a similar manner to victimize the mother in her family of origin
- Intense family group loyalty coupled with little protective concern for the needs of the children as developing individuals; that is, little or no expressed worry over possible physical or psychological trauma to the child that could result from Munchausen by Proxy behavior
- Intergenerational family patterns of illness behavior around chronic medical or somatoform/factitious illness across at least three generations on the maternal side of the family
- A gender reversal of typical sex roles for power and caretaking within the parental couple, such that the wife is more dominant and aggressive and the husband is more caretaking and supportive (p. 434)

Griffith concludes by suggesting that Munchausen by proxy should be seen in the context of the family as a system. This view can yield a more lucid understanding of the behavior and more specific and effective interventions than can an evaluation restricted to individual psychiatric assessments of the involved mother and child. Although they do not describe a psychotherapy case, Rappaport and Hochstadt (1993) also explore the psychosocial history of the caregiver (Munchausen by proxy mother), using an intergenerational model. This approach reiterates Griffith's conclusions.

Sanders (1995b) proposes that the story of factitious or exaggerated illness is coauthored, or that symptoms may be coached through the dynamics of the family. Her study results tentatively support her first hypothesis: "The more active the participation of family members in the presentation of symptoms, the more likely the family is to present a congruent picture of family life" (p. 436). Her second hypothesis is also supported: "The more active the family members are in the presentation of symptoms, the less likely they are to report family changes or stressors" (p. 436). Sanders believes that if the family is approached "with the recognition that the members may have a strongly held story of illness, and that the story is neither right nor wrong, the family may be more open to exploring the possibility of additional or alternative stories" (p. 438). The implication for family therapy "depends on the ability of the family members to be able to move away from an illness story and to be open to an alternative story which will allow the child to move forward in his/her life" (p. 439).

Meadow (1985) envisions a major role for the child psychiatrist in the long-term help of the MBPS family. He recommends early intervention, preferably before and during the stressful confrontation period, and suggests that this early involvement of the psychiatrist will benefit the family therapeutically.

In both the literature and our own practice, the majority of knowledge available regarding treatment of Munchausen by proxy syndrome focuses on individual psychotherapy with the mother-perpetrator. It has been our experience that when the entire family is required to participate in treatment, little cooperation exists. Realistically, we have been able to treat only pieces of the family, primarily the mother-perpetrator and the child-victim.

The lack of long-term family therapy is directly related to MBPS family dynamics. The mother-perpetrators who acknowledge their behavior must begin the intensive uncovering that psychotherapy requires. Due to the significant dysfunction present in these families, other family members are rarely motivated to participate in treatment. Rather, these families begin to break apart as they attempt to keep the family dynamics intact. Family members are often unable to tolerate the changes the mother-perpetrator begins to make in therapy, because these changes threaten the status quo. The mother-perpetrator is likely to come under pressure from family members to leave treatment, and if their attempts fail, marital separation is likely to occur. This dynamic may account for the significant divorce rate in Munchausen by proxy families.

Our individual treatment model focuses on the mother-perpetrator's acknowledgment and acceptance of her abusive behavior. From this acknowledgment, the mother-perpetrator works through a lengthy therapeutic program. Victim empathy is the goal of the therapeutic process. Family therapy also emphasizes acknowledgment and requires a change in the family system. This model is in contrast to Sanders's (1995b) treatment model, in which the therapist and mother-perpetrator work toward changing the story of illness, without placing emphasis on responsibility or victim empathy. Griffith and Slovik (1989) report one case in which long-term family therapy appeared effective in quelling Munchausen by proxy behavior even without the admission of culpability. It is plausible that the family system can be changed in treatment without the abuse being acknowledged. This raises the question of symptom substitution and whether the mother-perpetrator can safely redirect her behavior while remaining in a dysfunctional family system. It is not possible to speculate as to the risk or safety of a child-victim in this situation.

# Part III

## Emerging Issues

# 13 The Criminal Prosecutor's Perspective

Robin Wilkinson
Teresa F. Parnell

> *It is perhaps not surprising that a lawyer or judge would react skeptically to the allegation that a parent is both making her child appear ill and is simultaneously seeking the best possible medical care for the child's condition. In the case we evaluated, the lawyer charged with representing the state on behalf of the child was heard to remark in disbelief, "Now why would a mother do that?"*
> *—David A. Waller, "Obstacles to the Treatment of Munchausen by Proxy Syndrome," 1983*

As an assistant state attorney, the first author of this chapter had been prosecuting child abuse cases for 4 years when the first case of Munchausen by proxy syndrome came to her office. This case intrigued her because she had never prosecuted such a case, nor did she know anyone who had. This case became a trial-and-error learning process, and eventually led to the formulation of this chapter. The first author has now investigated and/or prosecuted eight cases identified as Munchausen by proxy syndrome. She has received calls from other prosecutors who are faced with the same dilemmas she initially faced—Where do they start? How do they investigate such cases? How do they bring these cases before judges and juries? Information on the prosecution of the perpetrators of Munchausen by proxy continues to evolve; we see this evolution as similar to the growth of knowledge in other types of child abuse prosecution.

Only a handful of published articles discuss MBPS cases in the legal arena (Boros & Brubaker, 1992; Emery, 1993; Geberth, 1994; Hanon, 1991; Kahan & Yorker, 1991; Kinscherff & Famularo, 1991; Mitchels, 1983a, 1983b; Sargeant, 1993; Searle, 1993; Sigal, Gelkopf, & Levertov, 1990; Williams, 1986; Yorker & Kahan, 1991). With a few exceptions, such articles have not generally appeared in law reviews, and they do not discuss cases presented for criminal prosecution. Mostly, these articles have contained general overviews of the syndrome, with some discussion of legal issues as they relate to child protective services. There have been a few published cases within the criminal, dependency, and family courts (*In re Colin R.,* 1985; *In the Matter of Jessica Z.,* 1987; *People v. Phillips,* 1981; *People v. Tinning,* 1988; *Place v. Place,* 1987; *State v. Lumbrera,* 1992), as well as some mentions in journal articles of perpetrators having been criminally charged (Bath, Murty, & Gibbin, 1993; Blix & Brack, 1988; Boros & Brubaker, 1992; Feldman, 1994; Grace, Kalinkiewicz, & Drake-Lee, 1984; Hosch, 1987; Lee, 1979; Liston, Levine, & Anderson, 1983; Lorber, Reckless, & Watson, 1980; Samuels, McClaughlin, Jacobson, Poets, & Southall, 1992; Saulsbury, Chobanian, & Wilson, 1984; White, 1985).

This paucity of legal information is one result of the fact that few Munchausen by proxy cases in the literature have received adequate attention from the dependency court, let alone criminal prosecution. The few cases of criminal prosecution mentioned in the literature reflect how difficult it can be for doctors and prosecutors to convince others of the truth of their allegations and to gather sufficient evidence to obtain convictions. The lack of coverage of MBPS in the legal literature arouses concern that awareness of this disorder is minimal within the legal profession, making it difficult for prosecutors to apply knowledge to case prosecution. Attorneys must overcome the tremendous disbelief and discomfort that accompany this unfamiliarity, which, as is noted in other chapters in this volume, is shared by the members of other professions as well.

Munchausen by proxy behavior constitutes a form of child abuse and thus a form of criminal behavior. Law enforcement agencies and prosecutors' offices are responsible for proving or disproving allegations of such criminal activity and for taking action to hold perpetrators legally accountable. Ultimately, this action also serves to protect child-victims, although criminal prosecutors' primary focus is upon alleged perpetrators; the dependency court focuses upon the mechanics of child protection. In Chapter 5 of this volume, Teresa Parnell discusses child protective services intervention via the dependency court; in this chapter we address some issues of coordination between the dependency and criminal courts. The family court may also be involved in Munchausen by proxy syndrome cases via issues of marital separation or dissolution, as may the civil court through malpractice or invasion of privacy actions. In this chapter we focus on criminal prosecution issues.

## Case Law

Very few courts in the United States have addressed or admitted evidence of Munchausen by proxy syndrome. In the first criminal case to address this disorder, a California court allowed an expert witness for the state to testify via a hypothetical question as to whether the mother, accused of murdering an adopted child and willfully endangering the life or health of another child, engaged in Munchausen by proxy syndrome (*People v. Phillips,* 1981). The evidence showed that the mother had deliberately administered a sodium compound in the children's formula. The appeals court upheld the admission of this evidence based on the scientific literature and on the fact that, although motive for murder may not be an essential element for the state to prove, evidence of motive was quite relevant to the state's case in chief.

Two other state courts barred the admission of MBPS evidence in a manslaughter case in which evidence showed the mother had poisoned the child with salt while the child was hospitalized (*Commonwealth v. Robinson,* 1991). In *State v. Lumbrera* (1992), a child homicide trial, a Kansas court struck testimony regarding Munchausen by proxy syndrome because there was no evidence to support the assertion that the defendant suffered from this syndrome. In *Lumbrera,* the mother was charged with suffocating her child, and evidence had been introduced that all of her other five children had died. The causes of death of the other children were not introduced, nor was any other evidence developed to show that the mother had Munchausen by proxy syndrome.

Evidence of MBPS has also been introduced during sentencing, after a plea was entered to a child abuse charge. In *State v. DeJesus* (1993), evidence was presented to show not only that the mother was suffering from Munchausen by proxy syndrome but that the degree of the disorder was so extreme that the woman could not be helped by psychotherapy.

Dependency courts have admitted evidence of Munchausen by proxy syndrome along with expert testimony in proceedings held to determine whether or not parental rights should be terminated. In *In re S.R.* (1991), *In the Matter of Tucker* (1991), *In re Colin R.* (1985), and *Fessler v. State Department of Human Resources* (1989), evidence of MBPS was used to support the requisite findings to terminate parental rights. However, a

Georgia court reversed a finding in support of termination of parental rights with one child when the evidence of the mother's engaging in Munchausen by proxy syndrome with another child was not shown to support that she would necessarily engage in Munchausen by proxy syndrome with this child (*In the Interest of M.A.V.,* 1992). Evidence of Munchausen by proxy syndrome has also been introduced to prove that a child is dependent or in need of services (*In the Interest of B.B.,* 1993).

Evidence regarding Munchausen by proxy syndrome has also been admitted in a divorce proceeding concerning the issue of custody. In *Place v. Place* (1987), the court awarded custody to the father after hearing evidence that the mother of the child subjected the child to repeated and unnecessary invasive medical procedures and that the mother was believed to be a Munchausen by proxy perpetrator.

## The Investigation

Munchausen by proxy syndrome criminal cases are much more complex than most child abuse cases, and the need for investigative involvement is immediate. The prosecutor's involvement in an MBPS case should start when the law enforcement and child protective services investigations begin. The prosecutor needs to be involved in the investigative stage in part because MBPS allegations are often difficult to believe; further, these cases are often chaotic and tend to raise many legal issues. Most law enforcement officers, as well as most child protective service workers, have never investigated an MBPS case. As a result, few prosecutors have experience with Munchausen by proxy perpetrators. Only through a detailed, coordinated effort that involves a high level of communication among disciplines are the dual goals of child protection and perpetrator accountability likely to be achieved.

### The Multidisciplinary Team

A crucial part of the law enforcement investigation and criminal prosecution in a Munchausen by proxy case is the involvement from the beginning of a multidisciplinary team. As soon as an allegation of Munchausen by proxy behavior is made, team staffing should be conducted. The team should include the treating physician, a physician with expertise in MBPS, and anyone else specifically involved in the case, as well as representatives from law enforcement, the hospital administration's legal staff, and child protective services (Hanon, 1991). A social worker or psychologist should also be present to assist the family after confrontation of the mother-perpetrator. The staffing of the multidisciplinary team requires significant coordination and is usually best handled by a child protection team, if one is available (for a detailed discussion of multidisciplinary staffing, see Whelan-Williams and Baker, Chapter 14, this volume).

When the multidisciplinary team first meets, the treating physician should present the findings that aroused suspicion. This may include presentation of alternate hypotheses that were considered and ruled out. Nurses who have observed the mother in the hospital can provide valuable information about the mother's behavior with the child-victim, interaction with staff, and statements made regarding the child's illness. Additionally, nurses often have had contact with other family members and know who has had access to the child and when the access has occurred in relation to the child's symptoms. For the prosecutor, this information provides an overview of the evidence available, how confident the physician is of his or her opinion, and what steps need to be taken to obtain confirmatory evidence.

It is important for the prosecutor to remember that physicians and other medical professionals may be uncomfortable with the process of criminal investigation. Although they will want to protect the child, their participation in building evidence against the child's mother may feel like a betrayal of their usual roles as helping professionals. Additionally, this will require them to take a position against a parent with whom they may have spent considerable time, come to know quite well, and perceive to be an ideal parent. Reactions of shock, disbelief, and disappointment may translate into hostility and criticism toward the individuals conducting the investigation. Additionally, if a consulting physician has been called in to make the diagnosis, the primary physician—who, of course, has a vital role in case investigation and ultimate prosecution—may be particularly resistant.

Once there has been a comprehensive presentation of the case, the prosecutor needs to develop a plan for progressing forward into investigation. The multidisciplinary team members help to ensure that this plan encompasses ethical investigatory techniques and also meets the logistical needs of each discipline. The first issue for all concerned is protection of the child's health. Often, this primary consideration can affect how much evidence can be gathered for possible future prosecution. However, the child's safety has to remain paramount.

Some aspects of the investigation may depend on when in the process of confirming the allegations the staffing of the multidisciplinary team occurs. Although practitioners are supposed to report child abuse at the time they first suspect it has occurred, sometimes physicians do not feel confident enough in their suspicions to consider them anything beyond speculation. Physicians often feel so tenuous about suggesting child abuse that they may take actions to confirm their suspicions before they make any report. In a suspected MBPS case, for example, a physician might attempt to establish a temporal relationship between the mother's presence and the child's symptoms, or might test specimens (i.e., blood, urine, feces) for certain substances.

## Video Surveillance

If a situation exists in which the child is not at extreme risk but more evidence is needed to proceed with prosecution, then law enforcement personnel can work with the hospital and risk management staff to conduct video surveillance to monitor the suspected perpetrator's behavior with the child. To carry out such surveillance, a court order must be obtained, usually through the dependency court; the state's child protection agency can apply for the order as an investigative and protective measure (see Appendix 13.A). In setting up video surveillance, law enforcement personnel need to be aware of their state's laws concerning wiretaps and interception of oral communication. In Florida, pursuant to Florida Statute 934, interception of oral communication is prohibited when a person has reason to believe that his or her communication will not be intercepted; therefore, video surveillance must be conducted with the audio turned off. The charges usually being considered in Munchausen by proxy syndrome cases, except for murder, are not among the exceptions listed in the law concerning interception of oral communication.

During the conduct of video surveillance, a law enforcement officer must be available for 24-hour monitoring; that is, an officer must be present in the video surveillance room every minute. Most MBPS mother-perpetrators rarely leave the hospital, often spending nights with their children. An episode of symptom fabrication or induction, whether smothering, giving the child something to eat, or injecting something into the child's IV line, can happen swiftly and at any time. With fewer people on staff at night, the potential for an occurrence during nighttime hours is, in fact, heightened.

It is interesting to note that in Samuels et al.'s (1992) review of 14 cases of imposed upper-airway obstruction that caused cyanotic episodes, every perpetrator was criminally charged. In all of these cases, covert video surveillance was used. Many hospitals now have specific rooms that are permanently set up with video surveillance capabilities. One concern that has arisen in our work is that we have learned that the mothers on one hospital floor often discuss Munchausen by proxy syndrome and have become aware that a certain hospital room is set up for "catching" these mothers. (For more on video surveillance, see Seibel & Parnell, Chapter 4, this volume.)

## Confronting the Perpetrator

Optimally, confrontation of the MBPS mother-perpetrator occurs when the investigator is prepared with all the necessary information to proceed with full arrest and prosecution of the case. However, realistically, time is of the essence in protecting the child. The potential for harm to the child, as well as the constant presence of the mother, usually results in the need to confront the suspected perpetrator before all the necessary information is in place. However, the multidisciplinary team model provides for swift and efficient action such that sufficient information should be available for authorities to proceed competently (see Whelan-Williams & Baker, Chapter 14, this volume). Together, team members must decide whether there is enough evidence to move forward and confront the alleged perpetrator and, if so, how to handle the confrontation. Obviously, the outcome of the confrontation can have significant impact on any subsequent dependency and criminal cases.

As discussed by Parnell in Chapter 5 of this volume, there is some debate among professionals about who should confront the mother-perpetrator. Most professionals seem to believe that the child's treating physician, who generally has a long-term relationship with the mother, is most likely to obtain a confession. However, it is our experience that many physicians have a hard time believing what is occurring in these cases and therefore feel extremely uncomfortable confronting these mothers. Other professionals believe that law enforcement personnel can be most effective in the initial confrontation (Parnell & Day, 1993). Law enforcement officials also prefer this approach, believing that it increases their ability to gather appropriate information. When a law enforcement officer is to conduct the confrontation, it is often best if the officer is introduced to the suspected mother-perpetrator by a physician she knows well. Although a doctor may not feel comfortable about conducting the confrontation, he or she may be willing to introduce the law enforcement officer to the family and initiate discussion. The law enforcement officer can then invite the mother to discuss the situation. Typically, in such a situation, the mother will agree to talk with the officer. As long as she is not in police custody, she need not be read her Miranda rights.

A noncustodial interview such as that initiated by the method described above represents an effective law enforcement technique; the person has not been arrested and so need not be advised of her right to an attorney. If a law enforcement officer were to approach a suspected mother-perpetrator on his or her own, the question of whether or not she was in custody (and therefore needed to have her rights read to her) might arise. If a suspected mother-perpetrator is arrested or transported to the police station, the officer's ability to complete an effective confrontational interview is limited. Arrest, however, is necessary if the alleged mother-perpetrator is approached, for example, after the law enforcement investigator sees something during video surveillance and she refuses to be interviewed.

We believe it is also a good idea to have a child protective investigator present during the confrontation, because the presence of such an authority will ultimately strengthen the dependency case. This investigator can leave the confrontation and prepare the shelter petition, and will thus be well prepared to report the actual facts of the case in the petition. The investigator will then review the petition with his or her department's attorney, who will determine if there is probable cause to remove the child from the parents' custody.

Confrontation should always occur away from the child's presence and should involve only the alleged mother-perpetrator, in order to protect her privacy and avoid disturbing other patients. Informing other family members, including the suspected perpetrator's spouse, about the situation should occur during a separate interview. Sometimes the physician will want to talk with the other members of the family while the law enforcement officer is conducting the confrontation with the perpetrator. However, the law enforcement officer must make a clear agreement with the physician about such family contact if he or she feels this will adversely influence the investigation. Although the physician may initiate the confrontation and/or family interviews, the law enforcement officer needs to be well versed in the background of the child and the medical evidence. Only when the mother sees that the officer understands what has happened and does not accept the mother's facade is she likely to make a confession.

In conducting the confrontation interview, the law enforcement officer must be extremely careful about making any promises to the mother concerning child protective services. For example, the officer should never suggest that if the mother confesses, her child will be returned to her, or that she will be provided with psychiatric or psychological treatment. Before the confrontation, the multidisciplinary team should hold a discussion to make sure also that the hospital social worker and child protection worker understand that they should not make any statements to the mother such as, "You'll only need treatment" or "You'll get your children back if you talk to us." Such promises can affect whether any further statements made by the mother will be admissible in court. The state could be held to those statements, even though they are not made by law enforcement personnel or the prosecutor (*State v. Chorpenning*, 1974). Of course, such statements also jeopardize the dependency case, because the department would not be acting in good faith.

Depending on the jurisdiction, the prosecutor probably should not be in the room during the confrontation interview, because he or she may then be claimed to be a witness in the case. The prosecutor's main purpose at this point is to oversee the technical aspects of the investigation to ensure proper collection of evidence in case there is a subsequent trial.

It is imperative that the law enforcement officer conducting the confrontation be aware of the tendency of MBPS mother-perpetrators to respond to accusations with staunch denial. These mothers have fooled many professionals for a long time; physicians sometimes even begin to question their own laboratory findings when met with mother-perpetrators' responses to confrontation. It is not unusual, therefore, for a law enforcement officer to experience an internal sense of skepticism when interacting with a suspected mother-perpetrator. This may be especially likely if the mother reacts with calm but persuasive disbelief, along with the presentation of her own "evidence" of the child's illness. Of course, the mother may also react with intense emotion accompanied by threats to harm herself or to remove the child from the hospital. During the multidisciplinary team meeting prior to the confrontation, a discussion of this possibility should lead to a predetermined plan of action for the law enforcement officer.

At the time of the confrontation, the law enforcement investigator needs to document in detail the apparent mental status of the perpetrator, because the McNaughton rule, or insanity defense, is being considered increasingly often in these cases. It may be difficult for a suspected perpetrator to make a successful insanity plea, but nonetheless it is far easier for the investigator to record accurate information concerning the perpetrator's mental status at the time of the confrontation than it is for the prosecutor to try to prove her sanity at a later date. Around the time of the confrontation, the law enforcement officer should also take statements from nurses as to the suspected perpetrator's actions during the previous days, weeks, or months, to prepare for the possibility of an insanity defense. Usually a child abuse statute or some type of attempted murder charge is used to prosecute Munchausen by proxy syndrome cases. These charges involve proving that the alleged perpetrator was aware of the harm she was doing. This is one reason her mental status at the time of the confrontation is so important. Additionally, once the defense has raised the issue of insanity, it becomes the prosecutor's burden to prove that the mother is not insane. Under the McNaughton rule, the standard for many states on insanity asks, Was the person suffering from a mental illness? If so, as a result of that mental illness did she not know right from wrong, or did she understand the consequences of her actions?

The alleged perpetrator should be arrested at the time of the confrontation if probable cause is found. If the perpetrator is released rather than arrested, she will most likely seek an attorney. At that point, if the attorney has any experience in Munchausen by proxy cases, the perpetrator will likely be placed in a psychiatric facility in an attempt to bolster an insanity plea.

## Evidence Collection

While the perpetrator is being confronted with the allegations and the law enforcement officer is seeking a confession, a separate law enforcement officer should be carrying out a seizure order on the child's hospital room (see Appendix 13.B). If there is any probable cause to search the family's home, a search warrant to do so should be obtained simultaneous with the seizure order.

When the alleged mother-perpetrator is taken out of the child's hospital room for the confrontation, she should be asked to leave all of her possessions behind. Evidence of the crime may be in her purse, a diaper bag, or other items she has been keeping with her. The request for a search warrant or seizure order concerning the hospital room and/or residence needs to be quite specific. For instance, it should give a brief history of Munchausen by proxy syndrome, a complete outline of the case, a description of the types of evidence sought, and specifically what law enforcement personnel expect to find. Very few MBPS cases have gone to trial in the United States, and few judges have ever seen search warrant requests that include the details of Munchausen by proxy syndrome. The allegations in these cases can appear ludicrous to persons who are faced with them for the first time. It is imperative that the request for a warrant or other court order inform the judge about this kind of abuse if he or she is going to be able to find probable cause.

The types of evidence sought will, of course, depend on the specific case and the nature of the allegations of symptom induction. The physician can probably help to identify possible nonnatural causes for the types of symptoms presented, and thus guide the search. Examples of possible evidence include syringes, tubing, intravenous materials, prescription and over-the-

The Criminal Prosecutor's Perspective

counter medicines (e.g., ipecac, laxatives, barbiturates), salt, plastic wrap or towels used to suffocate a victim, medical texts or articles, books on Munchausen by proxy syndrome, thermometers, and substances caustic to the skin. Also, evidence may be available from the hospital staff in the form of specimens (blood, urine, emesis, IV fluid, child's formula or milk, stool, and so on) that have already been collected from the child-victim and sometimes from the mother-perpetrator.

Law enforcement officials need to arrange to obtain and preserve this kind of evidence as soon as possible, with strict adherence to chain of custody. In jurisdictions where there are children's hospitals in which these cases arise, law enforcement officials may consider training the medical staff on how to preserve the chain of custody of evidence. A chart should be maintained that shows the complete history of each specimen. This should include a label on each specimen showing the date the specimen was obtained and who obtained it, and the initials of every person who has handled it. If the child-victim has been on an apnea monitor, the machine may be equipped with an internal recorder that will need to be downloaded.

The items noted above are only a few examples of the kinds of evidence that may be collected. The potential sources of symptom induction are almost endless. Again, the prosecutor will need to depend on the physician, the multidisciplinary team, and the research literature, as well as his or her own creativity, in considering all the possible sources of external evidence to support the suspected Munchausen by proxy syndrome diagnosis.

## Family Interviews

While the confrontation and collection of evidence are occurring, the hospital social worker or child protection worker should be contacting other family members. A decision must be made as to whether the child is going to be taken into the custody of child protective services, returned to the mother, or placed in the custody of another family member (see Parnell, Chapter 5, this volume). This issue, although it should be discussed by the multidisciplinary team, may not be decided until the outcome of the confrontation is clear. Investigators should be aware that many family members are going to react to the allegations with disbelief and are not going to be supportive of prosecution.

Many Munchausen by proxy perpetrators do eventually divorce, but only after their nonoffending spouses have been involved in treatment, realized the extent of the pain their children went through, and then understood that their wives directly caused the pain. All of the couples involved in the cases we have dealt with are now divorced. There are many reasons for dissolution of the family that may have impacts on the criminal case—for example, allegations of a domineering or abusive nonoffending spouse and a break-down in the marital relationship. Initially, the entire family presents as a functioning unit. There is no disclosure of abuse or discord. Some mother-perpetrators will deny that they have been abused by their spouses in order to make sure their children remain in the spouses' care. Others exaggerate spouse abuse to deflect blame. The more the prosecutor knows about the nonoffending spouse and other possible family issues, the more prepared he or she will be in prosecution for what the defense will probably argue.

Once the suspected perpetrator is arrested, the prosecutor should seek a guardian ad litem for the child if one has not already been appointed by the court (see Hadley, Chapter 16, this volume). Because the nonoffending spouse is at least initially unlikely to be supportive of prosecution, there needs to be an adult involved in the case whose primary concerns are the child's welfare and the child's needs.

## Charges

Aggravated child abuse can be prosecuted under four theories, only two of which apply to Munchausen by proxy: (a) aggravated battery on a child under the age of 18, and (b) willful torture, which is defined as causing unnecessary pain and suffering. Most MBPS cases are argued under both theories. Cases in which symptoms have been exaggerated rather than induced usually are limited to the argument of willful torture, owing to the unnecessary and painful medical procedures the child has undergone as a result of the mother-perpetrator's actions. Physical abuse cases are easier to prove, be-cause the causal effects of the perpetrator's actions and the injuries to the child are more apparent.

If the child-victim dies, the accused perpetrator can be charged with first- or second-degree murder. Many states have a felony murder rule that allows a charge of first-degree murder to be brought when a child dies from the perpetration of felony child abuse. Attempted second-degree murder is charged along with aggravated child abuse in cases where the child has survived but his or her health was in great danger due to the mother-perpetrator's actions. The purpose of a negotiated plea is to protect the child-victim. Maintaining either charge as part of the plea can ensure the future protection of the child.

## Bond

Due to the manipulation involved in MBPS mother-perpetrators' behavior, prosecutors also need to consider carefully the conditions of bond. In most of these cases, bond will be set low enough for the family to make bail. Only in first-degree murder cases does bond reach a significant amount; it is even more likely in such cases that there will be no bond. In Florida, conditions of bond in child abuse cases include no contact between the suspected mother-perpetrator and the child-victim. The prosecutor should ensure that such conditions are relayed to the dependency court, so that contact continues to be restricted. Additionally, the prosecutor should ask for conditions that restrict communication between the alleged mother-perpetrator and the child-victim. If the court is looking at the possibility of allowing communication, this needs to be regulated first by court order and coordinated by a therapist knowledgeable about Munchausen by proxy syndrome cases. Additionally, whoever has custody of the child needs to monitor any written or telephone communication between mother and child.

Most Munchausen by proxy child-victims, due to their long-term hospital stays, have developed very close relationships with the offending parents. It is imperative that the prosecutor collaborate with the dependency attorney to discuss restrictions on perpetrator-victim contact. We are aware of situations in which there was no exchange of information between the dependency and criminal courts, and the mother-perpetrators ended up with fewer restrictions in one court due to lack of information and/or the mothers' misrepresentation of information.

## Preparation for Prosecution

As soon as a prosecutor becomes involved in an MBPS case, he or she should try to obtain copies of as many articles as possible on this disorder. Good sources for such material include university libraries and the medical experts involved in the case. Although Munchausen by proxy syndrome is discussed increasingly in prosecution seminars, that information is likely to be superficial and is often not fully digested by prosecutors who have not experienced such cases. Lack of familiarity with or knowledge of Munchausen by proxy syndrome on the part of law enforcement officers or prosecutor will delay and possibly ruin the investigative process. Skepticism and lack of understanding of the dynamics of such cases can lead a prosecutor to pursue the needed information only reluctantly and halfheartedly. A careful review of the literature, however, may reveal a case that is eerily similar to the one being prosecuted.

It is imperative that the prosecutor have a comprehensive understanding of Munchausen by proxy syndrome, because one of his or her first goals will be to educate others, such as the judge, who have never seen a case of this type. It may be especially helpful for the prosecutor to provide others with copies of the literature on particular cases similar to the case on trial. This can add to the credibility of what are often bizarre allegations. As a prosecutor, the first author of this chapter makes it a point to provide the most relevant articles and a copy of the *DSM-IV* (American Psychiatric Association, 1994) section on Munchausen by proxy to the judge and to the defense attorney prior to any hearing or sentencing. We also recommend that the prosecutor use experts to educate the judge during bond hearings and sentencing.

## Medical Records

Next, the prosecutor needs to obtain the complete medical file of the child-victim as soon as possible. Most investigations will occur while the child is in the hospital, but other medical records, inpatient and outpatient, should be obtained as well. The prosecutor needs to subpoena records from any other hospitals in the area, even if there has been no mention from the family that the child has been admitted there. Many MBPS perpetrators will move from hospital to hospital as medical personnel become suspicious. The prosecutor also needs to work with child protective services to determine whether the family has moved from another state. If so, the prosecutor will need to contact the child protection agency in each state where the family has lived to determine if there have been previous abuse reports and to canvass for medical records in those areas. This step is very important to the case prosecution, because prior records and samples can establish a pattern of behavior. For example, in one case, a physician who had formerly seen the child-victim in another state was contacted, and it was discovered that he had preserved a specimen from the child because he had a suspicion of Munchausen by proxy. After he was contacted, he retrieved the specimen and had it tested; syrup of ipecac was found to be present in the specimen.

Law enforcement personnel must obtain as much information as possible about the allegations, the suspect, and the victim through the medical records. For effective prosecution, the prosecutor must ensure that the diagnostic procedure conducted by the physician expert and the investigative procedure conducted by the law enforcement officer is completed thoroughly. The investigation should include a review of all medical records, including hospital admissions and the symptoms observed, diagnoses made, and treatments provided during all hospital stays. The records review should take note of any changes in the victim's condition during or after contact with the parent, the diagnostic impressions of anyone who treated the child, any difficulty treating professionals may have had in finding anything conclusive, any evidence of the child's not responding to treatment, and any discrepancies between the records and parent reports. We should note that it is not unusual for different physicians who have treated a child to disagree as to the diagnosis of Munchausen by proxy syndrome. It is important for the prosecutor to know and understand any dissenting professionals' opinions and how the professionals reached those opinions.

Nurses' notes on their contacts with critically ill children can be especially helpful for investigators, as they usually reflect visits by the parents and other family members and observations of the parents' interactions with the child. These notes can help the prosecutor to understand the family dynamics, and they are also useful for proving who has had access to the child. (For more information on appropriate procedures for reviewing medical records, see Seibel & Parnell, Chapter 4, this volume.)

The law enforcement investigation should also include interviews with the alleged perpetrator's immediate and extended family, parents of other children hospitalized at the same time, neighbors of the suspected MBPS family, day-care workers and teachers who have had contact with the child-victim, and any third parties who have supposedly viewed the child's symptoms. A check should also be conducted for any births and deaths of siblings of the child-victim that have not been reported to medical personnel. In one notable case in which the first author was involved as prosecutor, the suspected mother-perpetrator's first child had died. She came to the attention of authorities when Munchausen by proxy was suspected in her second child. There had been no previous confrontation of the mother regarding her first child, even though there had been suspicions of Munchausen by proxy. Law enforcement officers and prosecutors should be aware that the mother-perpetrators can be some of the smoothest liars they will ever encounter. As has been mentioned previously in this volume, some mother-perpetrators fabricate about many aspects of their lives, not just their children's illness.

## Experts

As soon as the defense discloses the name of a therapist, psychologist, or psychiatrist who is evaluating or treating the perpetrator, the prosecutor should subpoena those records with notice to defense counsel or the defendant. The prosecutor may need to obtain a court order to overcome the confidential nature of the doctor-patient relationship; his or her argument in such circumstances will usually be that an exception to confidentiality exists in cases of child abuse (if allowed by statute)—this is another excellent opportunity for the prosecutor to educate the judge. The prosecutor should then depose the defense's professional expert in order to discover what additional social and medical history has been made available to him or her.

The prosecutor must keep in mind that mental health professionals are not immune to the disbelief experienced by many others regarding Munchausen by proxy cases. Additionally, MBPS mother-perpetrators often appear quite normal during interviews and psychological testing, and are able to provide very plausible explanations for the "misunderstandings" that have led to their arrest. As a result, mental health professionals who are inexperienced in MBPS cases can be drawn into advocating for these mothers.

An additional concern for the prosecutor is that the mental health expert who will be needed to testify for the state may or may not be educated about Munchausen by proxy syndrome. If a psychological defense, such as insanity, is going to be used, the kind of expert who normally would testify, a professional in the area of forensic psychiatry or psychology, usually will have had no exposure to MBPS cases. By the same token, a professional who has worked on Munchausen by proxy cases may have no experience in performing forensic examinations. Therefore, the prosecutor may need to educate his or her selected expert, either in the area of the insanity defense or in Munchausen by proxy syndrome. (For more on the usefulness of mental health experts for a variety of purposes in the prosecution and sentencing of Munchausen by proxy mother-perpetrators, see Day, Chapter 6, and Parnell, Chapter 7, this volume.)

Because Munchausen by proxy syndrome is largely a medical diagnosis, a cornerstone of the prosecution's case will be the medical experts. These may include the physicians who actually treated the child, a consulting physician who made the diagnosis of Munchausen by proxy, and an outside expert who has reviewed the child's entire medical record to confirm the diagnosis and address any lingering concerns with alternate diagnoses. Outside experts often have extensive experience in reviewing medical records and normally have also worked in other areas of child physical abuse or sexual abuse. The medical experts can be very helpful in educating the prosecutor about complex medical procedures and diagnoses. We discuss the use of various experts during trial later in this chapter.

## Coordination With the Dependency Court

There are only a few states in which dependency actions are prosecuted by the same agency that prosecutes criminal cases. Florida's agency in charge of child protective services, the Department of Children and Families Services, does the actual prosecution in dependency cases, rather than the criminal prosecutor's office. Coordination of legal action by the two agencies should start from the beginning of the investigation. Ideally, a legal representative from child protective services and a child protective services worker should be present at the first staffing of the case, before the confrontation. At that point, discussion will occur about whether to file a dependency action, whether to take the child into protective custody, and how to set up the testimony of the expert witness from the medical staff to show that the child is at risk. Because the immediate issue is always to protect the child, the initial focus is on collecting sufficient evidence to obtain a child protective custody order and to file a petition for dependency. The gathering of sufficient evidence to justify the initiation of criminal proceedings is important, but it may not be possible in all cases. Initiation of dependency proceedings to separate the child from the suspected perpetrator also prevents recurrence of the injury and helps to establish connection between the perpetrator's presence and the symptoms, which will further strengthen the criminal case. It is important to note that in the dependency case, the state's burden of proof is less stringent than in a criminal action. In Florida, the state need only prove by a preponderance of the evidence that the child has been abused, abandoned, or neglected. In some cases there may not be enough evidence to obtain a criminal conviction, but there is enough to protect the child through dependency, and possibly termination of parental rights. Of course, dependency is temporary; without termination of parental rights, the child will be returned to the parent eventually unless the family court or criminal court orders some form of long-term protection.

In the dependency case, more information is generally forthcoming from the family, including the nonoffending spouse, than in the criminal prosecution. The criminal prosecutor seeks to put the offending parent in jail, or at least to have her labeled as a child abuser and placed on probation. In dependency court, parents are seeking to maintain their parental rights, and they are therefore more likely to reveal information. Exchange of information between the dependency and criminal courts should begin immediately, because cases often move more rapidly in the dependency court. The defense attorney is going to start discovery in the dependency action. Depending on the defense attorney, the prosecutor may or may not be notified of depositions. A good relationship between the prosecutor and the lawyer who is working the dependency case will ensure that the prosecutor is notified when key depositions are being conducted. Once the depositions are done in the dependency action, they may never be set in the criminal court. Information provided by experts and copies of medical records may also be exchanged.

## Jury Selection

In child physical abuse cases, prosecutors traditionally try to exclude conservative jurors as well as any who believe in the adage "Spare the rod and spoil the child." In child sexual abuse cases, prosecutors want the jury to include educated parents and other individuals who have contact with children. In jury selection on a Munchausen by proxy case, the prosecutor should look for educated individuals with conservative views who are not prone to accept a mental illness or insanity defense. Jurors who live responsible lives and who believe people are responsible for their own actions meet these criteria. The prosecutor might also want to consider avoiding mental health professionals, but accepting physicians, nurses, and other medical professionals as jurors. It is important that the jurors be well educated, because they will need to understand complicated medical testimony.

The prosecutor might attempt to educate potential jurors briefly on Munchausen by proxy in voir dire, so that he or she may observe any attitudes they reveal and thus identify which individuals may be most sympathetic to the state's case. Once the prosecutor speaks to the jury, he or she will have at least an impression of their beliefs about child abuse in general. Because Munchausen by proxy syndrome is so rare and few cases have been tried in front of juries, no useful profile of the prosecution-friendly juror has been developed.

## Prosecution

The goal of prosecution in the MBPS case is to prove that the poor physical condition of the child was intentionally caused by another individual.

Specifically, the prosecution needs to establish clearly that the mother intentionally caused the symptoms/illness in the child, or that her behaviors, in an intentional attempt to simulate illness, led to injury or death of the child. The prosecutor must prove each element required by the statute of criminal law for which the perpetrator is being tried. Cases with which we are familiar have involved charges of aggravated child abuse, attempted second-degree murder, and first-degree murder (see Table 13.1).

For effective prosecution of such charges, the prosecutor need not prove that the mother-perpetrator exhibits a pattern of behavior called Munchausen by proxy syndrome, especially if the direct evidence of abuse is strong (e.g., a videotape). In fact, the prosecutor may choose not to introduce this relatively new, difficult, and sometimes puzzling concept at all. Some courts have failed to allow admission of evidence concerning MBPS or to qualify experts in the disorder. Additionally, the use of the word *syndrome* may focus the judge and jury on mental illness rather than on intentional injury to the child. Even if the court does allow testimony concerning Munchausen by proxy, it is sometimes difficult to establish that the case in question fits exactly the elements present in other cases of the syndrome.

However, introduction of the concept of Munchausen by proxy syndrome may be helpful or even necessary in some cases. The prosecutor must consider the strength of the direct evidence of abuse, how bizarre the actual allegations are, and the skill of the expert witnesses. Given the difficulty most persons have in comprehending such behavior, it may be helpful for the judge and jury to know that the behavior has a recognized name, that there have been other confirmed cases around the world, and that there have been known cases similar to the one currently being prosecuted. The motivation of the perpetrator is also explained for the judge and jury when the concept of Munchausen by proxy syndrome is presented in court.

Whether or not the prosecutor chooses to discuss Munchausen by proxy explicitly, successful prosecution will depend on his or her ability to educate the judge and jury about something unthinkable. As a prosecutor becomes acclimated to the bizarre nature of MBPS cases, he or she may tend to lose sight of the apparent discrepancy between the seemingly ideal mother the defendant appears to be and the monster mother the prosecutor must ask the judge and jury to believe exists. The prosecutor must remain focused on proving the criminally abusive behavior in order to obtain a conviction and thus ensure the accountability that will protect the child-victim and perhaps initiate rehabilitation of the perpetrator.

In the vast majority of MBPS cases, there is no direct evidence (i.e., witnessed behavior); therefore, these cases usually rest on circumstantial

**TABLE 13.1   Details of Selected MBPS Case Prosecutions**

| Allegations | Charges | Convicted of | Sentence |
|---|---|---|---|
| Fecal injection | attempted second-degree murder; aggravated child abuse | pled to attempted second-degree murder | community control, probation with visitation restrictions; treatment |
| Urine and fecal injection into IV | attempted second-degree murder; aggravated child abuse | pled to aggravated child abuse; adjudication withheld | probation, community control, supervised visitation; treatment |
| Administration of ipecac | attempted second-degree murder; aggravated child abuse | pled to attempted second-degree murder; adjudication withheld | time served, 15 years probation; agreed to forfeit parental rights, visitation only with father's consent; treatment |
| Administration of ipecac[a,b] | first-degree murder | pled to second-degree murder | 17 years in state prison |
| Administration of ipecac | attempted second-degree murder; aggravated child abuse | pretrial diversion; record expunged after 9 months | pretrial diversion; 1 year of treatment |
| Administration of laxative | aggravated child abuse | aggravated child abuse; adjudication withheld | probation; treatment |
| Presentation of own blood as child's | aggravated child abuse | pretrial diversion, but failed to meet conditions, so case is pending | pretrial diversion; treatment (stopped attending) |

NOTES: a. Same perpetrator as in preceding case.
      b. Insanity defense.

evidence. Thus the prosecutor needs to present evidence to eliminate other possible causes of the child's condition. First, the medical experts must testify as to their belief that an exhaustive diagnostic process was conducted in which no medical or other cause was found to account for the child's condition. Although the prosecution's experts may describe the child as being completely normal once the Munchausen by proxy abuse was detected and ended, it is imperative that they be well versed in the specific medical issues once considered as possible diagnoses. As we have noted, Munchausen by proxy mothers usually garner considerable support, and there may be some disagreement among physicians involved with the case regarding the diagnoses indicated earlier. Waller (1983) describes one case of repeated factitious infections in which the mother was able to call upon five physicians to testify to her integrity as a parent. Schreier and Libow (1994) describe an MBPS case in which nine physicians testified, several on behalf of the defense; in addition, five nurses testified to the mother's caring, loving parenting.

Most Munchausen by proxy cases require considerable medical testimony, and expert witnesses may need assistance in preparing testimony that is clear, concise, and presented in lay terminology as much as possible. Use of visual aids—such as slides, transparencies, charts, graphs, dolls, scale models, computers, and calendars—may be especially indicated for the presentation of information on medical procedures, methods of treatment, and the child's condition. Again, the goal is to make the presentation of technical information as understandable and interesting to the judge and jury as possible.

Most states' child abuse statutes require proof of injury for conviction. For this reason, it is more difficult to prove a case in which symptoms have been exaggerated than one in which symptoms have been induced. In an exaggeration case, the prosecutor must show that the mother-perpetrator's exaggeration of symptoms caused the child to suffer from unnecessary medical procedures. The prosecutor must further demonstrate that the physician's choices of medical procedures were based on the mother's reporting of symptoms. In accomplishing this, it is particularly important that the prosecutor not lose sight of the child-victim among the impersonal-sounding, technical medical testimony. The prosecutor must elicit testimony that keeps in the forefront of the minds of the judge and jury the image of an innocent, healthy child undergoing unnecessary physical suffering. If the nonoffending parent is cooperating with the prosecution, he can testify to the pain and suffering he observed in his child. Next, the prosecutor must try to demonstrate that the alleged mother-perpetrator was responsible for that unnecessary suffering.

The prosecutor needs to establish a temporal relationship between the presence of the mother-perpetrator and the child-victim's symptoms. He or she may accomplish this in part by presenting the testimony of others (family members, medical staff, teachers, day-care workers) who saw no symptoms outside the presence of the mother. Nurses' notes and observations can also be particularly helpful. Evidence of a temporal relationship is strengthened by proof that the mother was the only person with access to the child *every* time symptoms occurred. Of course, it is extremely difficult to obtain such proof, especially because most Munchausen by proxy abuse occurs in the hospital, where multiple individuals have access to the child simultaneously. Additionally, if the mother has caused physical damage to the child with her methods of symptom induction, the child may now have bona fide symptoms that do occur in the presence of others, although they are secondary to the mother's actions. At the very least, the prosecutor needs to demonstrate that the mother had the opportunity to engage in deceptive behavior with the child, keeping in mind that the perpetrator's abusive actions could be achieved in very brief periods of time.

The most powerful evidence of a temporal relationship between the mother's presence and the child's symptoms comes from the child's physical condition following the intervention of child protective services and thus separation from the mother. A hallmark of the Munchausen by proxy case is the dramatic and remarkable change that takes place in the child's condition following this separation. The judge and jury need to see evidence of the child's current condition, with complete lack of previous symptomatology. A medical expert can clearly demonstrate that the only changes in the child's "treatment" regime have been *removal* of the mother from the child and an *absence* of medical treatment. Before and after photographs of the child may be helpful, as well as large charts documenting the symptoms before and after separation. Pediatric developmental charts can clearly show the weight changes the child has experienced (weight change is particularly dramatic in poisoning cases), and jury members are likely to be familiar with such charts from visits to their own children's doctors. Testimony from a nurse regarding the child's condition in the hospital and the resulting limitations on normal childhood behavior may be particularly useful when juxtaposed with testimony from the child's current caregiver about the child's now healthy condition.

The prosecutor may also need to prove that the alleged mother-perpetrator has the medical knowledge that would enable her to cause the child's injuries. Many MBPS mothers have had some kind of health care-related training, and they often comment on that training, or even employment in a health care field, to others while in the hospital setting. The prosecutor needs to present to the judge and jury any information of this type that has been discovered in the investigation.

Unfortunately, prosecutors must realize that they will never be able to prove some Munchausen by proxy syndrome cases. When many different people have had access to a child-victim, it is sometimes impossible to prove beyond a reasonable doubt that the mother is the one who has been harming the child.

## Experts

Expert witnesses are used by the prosecution for three main purposes in an MBPS case: to educate the judge and jury about Munchausen by proxy syndrome, to review the medical history of the child-victim, and to bring together these two elements to prove the mother's intentional abusive actions. One expert may testify for all three purposes, or different experts may testify concerning different points.

Generally, there will be available to testify multiple physicians who have been involved in the child's care and are familiar with his or her medical history. One or more of these physicians may be able to render opinions regarding the Munchausen by proxy diagnosis. However, we are familiar with cases in which physicians have been accused of promulgating this diagnosis because of their own failure to identify a child's medical conditions. Therefore, it may be preferable for the prosecutor to use an outside medical expert with expertise in medical records review and Munchausen by proxy. It is imperative that this expert conduct a careful review of all medical information regarding the child before testifying (see Seibel & Parnell, Chapter 4, this volume). He or she can then bring together the medical evidence with other information to support the diagnosis of Munchausen by proxy syndrome. The outside expert may also be responsible for educating the judge and jury on the syndrome.

The prosecutor must consider carefully the manner in which all of this testimony is to be presented, including how many experts to use and in what sequence. In determining strategy, the prosecutor should weigh the complexity of the case and the resources available. One possible formula is as follows:

1. A psychologist, psychiatrist, or pediatrician can testify first as an independent expert whose sole purpose is to educate the judge and jury

about MBPS. This expert need not have interviewed the patient or reviewed records for the current case.

2. Medical professionals (primary and specialist physicians, nurses, nutritionists, and so on) involved with the child's care can then testify. These individuals will be able to inform the judge and jury of the child's chronological medical history up until the Munchausen by proxy diagnosis, including all diagnoses considered, treatments rendered, the child's condition, and so on. This testimony may include the process leading to suspicion of abuse.

3. A psychologist, psychiatrist, or pediatrician who is an expert in Munchausen by proxy and who has reviewed all pertinent data about the case can testify next. Preferably, this individual will have personally interviewed or evaluated the mother-perpetrator as part of his or her review. This expert will bring together all of the information presented to make a definitive diagnosis. If the case is extremely medically complex or unclear, a physician may be needed to fill this role. Otherwise, a psychologist can be very helpful in explaining to the judge and jury all aspects of the perpetrator's life and psychological functioning.

## Sentencing

In our opinion, adjudication of Munchausen by proxy mother-perpetrators is vital to ensure child-victims' continued safety and to track this offender population appropriately. Although a child-victim's safety is often taken care of in the dependency court, criminal sanctions may bolster the provisions of the dependency court. Often the criminal courts can monitor a perpetrator more stringently and for a longer period of time. Even if the dependency court terminates parental rights, there is nothing to stop a mother from relocating, giving birth to another child, and beginning her pattern of abuse all over. Community control or probation can at the very least provide some monitoring of the movements of convicted perpetrators. As is noted throughout this volume, the staunch denial of the MBPS mother-perpetrator and her often exemplary behavior outside of the Munchausen by proxy make it exceedingly difficult to prove a case without a confession. Therefore, the courts in many jurisdictions may be anxious to resolve such cases with plea bargains that ensure the safety of the child-victims, some level of case monitoring, and treatment for the perpetrators.

As for the penalties resulting from prosecution in these cases, a lot depends on the specific statute involved, along with the specific court in which the prosecutor happens to practice. In cases in which the child-victim has died, or in which two children have been abused, the perpetrator will normally receive some incarceration. On the other hand, for mother-perpetrators who find themselves before the court for the first time in their lives, or in cases in which the allegations are not considered life threatening, courts normally lean toward probation or community control with mandatory mental health treatment.

The major concern for a prosecutor is whether the mother-perpetrator will reoffend; therefore, the prosecutor needs to ask for long-term probation. As noted in other chapters of this volume, psychological treatment of the MBPS mother-perpetrator takes many years. Lengthy probation or probation after incarceration will ensure continued psychotherapy and decrease the risk of a mother's reoffending. Even if the mother is in therapy and making progress and the child is well protected by being in the custody of the nonoffending spouse or another family member, the court must consider and the prosecutor must ask for restrictions on contact between mother and child. To date, there is simply not enough information available in the research literature on long-term outcomes of Munchausen by proxy cases for anyone to assess adequately the long-term risk of harm to the child.

When a mother-perpetrator is placed on probation, the prosecutor can ask the judge to consider some particular terms and restrictions. For example, each of the mother-perpetrator's children should have a medical examination once a year by a physician chosen by the nonoffending spouse or by child protective services, if that agency is still involved. The defendant may also be required to turn over to the court the records of any medical visits made by her children. The best arrangement is for the court to require continued medical care by a physician familiar with the case and the allegations. If contact between mother and child is allowed, the prosecutor should recommend that the court require supervised visitation, to protect the child. Again, the prosecutor must look at the family dynamics and how the family is doing at that time to decide whether the nonoffending spouse should be allowed to be the supervisor of visitation. (One concern is that the Munchausen by proxy abuse occurred when the nonoffending spouse was in a close relationship with the perpetrator; therefore, he may not be the best person to supervise visitation.)

Although the dependency court will address many of these issues, the prosecutor must not assume that these restrictions will be sufficient. The prosecutor can obtain guidance on these issues from the mental health experts involved in the case (see also Parnell, Chapter 5, this volume). Mental health experts can also advise the prosecutor as to which perpetrators may be most amenable to treatment. Additionally, the prosecutor should make a distinction between perpetrators who place themselves in therapy from the very beginning of the investigation, are cooperative with child protective services, and/or go along with the plan of child protective services concerning visitation and supervision and those who maintain staunch denial of the allegations.

## Some Closing Thoughts From the First Author

When I first began prosecuting cases involving Munchausen by proxy, I pushed for prosecution because of the horror of seeing a child go through unnecessary medical procedures and not having a normal childhood, normal relationships, or normal friendships. In spite of my asking for prison sentences for offenders, most of the judges leaned more toward community control or probation. Looking back on these cases, I am able to see that the perpetrators have made great progress in therapy thus far. In addition to not reoffending, only one woman has violated any aspect of her probation or community control. More important, most of the perpetrators have totally changed; their self-esteem has improved, their demeanor and appearance have changed, and their entire presentation as persons has altered. Most of them have divorced, but they have moved forward to create new and productive lives.

Now when I view these cases, I believe that some of these women are truly mentally ill, and although this may not rise to the level of an insanity defense, I believe that their mental illness needs to be considered in any determination of appropriate criminal resolution. In prosecuting these cases for the past 4 years, I have not seen reoffenders. That is always going to be a concern, as will the question of how long perpetrators will stay in treatment. However, I have seen good progress in my several years of following multiple cases in which the women have not received prison but have received appropriate therapy directed at their Munchausen by proxy behavior.

# APPLICATION AND AFFIDAVIT FOR VIDEO SURVEILLANCE ORDER AND SEIZURE ORDER

IN THE NINTH JUDICIAL CIRCUIT,
IN AND FOR ORANGE COUNTY, FLORIDA     OPD Case # _____
STATE OF FLORIDA
COUNTY OF ORANGE

BEFORE ME, Judge _____ in and for Orange County, Florida, personally came **Investigator** _____, a member of the Orlando Police Department, who being first duly sworn, deposes and says that Affiant has reason to believe that certain laws have been and are being violated in and on certain premises and the curtilage thereof in Orange County, Florida.

These premises are described as follows:

_____ Hospital, [street address], Orlando, Orange County, Florida, a ___-story building, Room No. ___ located on the ___ floor or such other room as the child may be located in. The room number is located on the wall outside of the door. The room has a bathroom. Located in the room is a hospital crib, a chair which makes out into a single bed and various storage cabinets.

This being the premises occupied by the child, _____, [race/gender], DOB: _____, patient/victim, the mother _____, [race/gender], DOB: _____, and under the control of _____ Hospital and that there is now being kept or administered on said premises and curtilage certain substances, to wit: Fecal matter and any containers or paraphernalia which might be used to contain or administer such fecal matter such as syringes or other device(s) which are being kept and used in violation of the laws of the State of Florida. Fecal matter is a substance obtained after a person defecates and is most likely located in a toilet. This substance is believed to be administered intravenously by syringe, usually directly into the victim's intravenous central line. Said administration of fecal matter into the blood-stream is in violation of the State of Florida to wit:

Florida State Statute 827.03 (Aggravated Child Abuse)

The facts tending to establish the grounds for this application and the probable cause of Affiant believing that such facts exist are as follows:

Page 1 of 4     Initials ____

_____

NOTE: Special thanks to Lee Freeman O'Brien, Police Legal Advisor for the Orlando Police Department, for her contributions to this sample document.

OPD Case # _____

Your Affiant, _____, has been a member of the Orlando Police Department, Orlando, Florida, since _____. Your Affiant studied basic police procedures at the _____ Police Academy, Orange County, Florida, where your Affiant studied the laws of Florida pertaining to child abuse, lewd acts, sexual battery and other Florida Statutes. Your Affiant attended a 40-hour Crimes Against Persons School at _____. Your Affiant has completed a 24-hour course in investigation of abused, battered and neglected children at _____. Your Affiant is currently assigned to the Youth Section, within the Special Investigations Division, Orlando Police Department.

On [month/day/year], [rank] [A], with the Orlando Police Department, received a telephone call from [B], M.D., referencing a possible child abuse case. On [month/day/year], your Affiant and [A] obtained the following information from Dr. [B], a Pediatrician and recognized expert in the field of diagnosis and treatment of child abuse. Dr. [B] advised that he was notified by the child's attending physician, Dr. [C], about his concerns for the child's health. Dr. [C] stated that this child has a long history of undiagnosed gastrointestinal problems and other medical problems and has had extensive evaluations by many specialists and that the child's illness remains undiagnosed. According to Dr. [C], suspicious incidents involving this child have caused him to be concerned that the child may be a victim of Munchausen by Proxy Syndrome. Dr. [C] stated that in the past, the child has had intravenous lines which had been sutured in place and which unexplainably have come out, and most recently the child has developed an illness caused by organisms called fecal flora, the presence of which was ascertained as a result of three blood cultures taken from the child which were reviewed by several medical personnel to confirm their accuracy. The presence of these unexplained occurrences and the presence of the fecal flora are, according to Dr. [B], associated with Munchausen by Proxy Syndrome.

Munchausen by Proxy Syndrome is a form of child abuse in which a disorder or illness of the child is fabricated by the parent. The responsible parent, typically the mother, constantly seeks medical treatment for acute illnesses which are often present but false or induced by the responsible parent through various means, including the introduction of foreign substances or poisons.

Dr. [B] and other physicians who are attending or have attended to this child believe that this child's symptoms are consistent with Munchausen by Proxy Syndrome.

Your Affiant requests a Video Surveillance Order and Seizure Order to videotape persons within Room No. _____, or such other room as the child may be located in, at _____ Hospital located on the _____ floor of [street address], Orlando,

OPD Case # _____

Orange County, Florida, for any actions that would indicate how fecal matter is being obtained, collected and placed within an object used to inject said fecal matter into the victim's bloodstream. Due to the secretive nature of the actions of perpetrators in such cases, there is little evidence which is available to link the perpetrator to the administration of toxins to victims. Due to the exigent nature of the offense it is your Affiant's belief that videotaping of the activities in the child's hospital room is necessary to clearly establish the identity of the perpetrator.

Additional information received indicates that [child] was hospitalized on [month/day/year] and one week prior to [month/day/year] and then again on [month/day/year]. Blood cultures were taken which resulted in the positive test for fecal matter. Since [month/day/year] the child has been in the room, and the only time he could have been infected with fecal matter is when he has been left unattended.

According to Dr. [B], the only way the blood cultures can test positive for fecal flora is through venous injection, and this child has a central intravenous line for feeding and medical purposes.

The mother exhibits classic signs that may be associated with the syndrome, such as

—living in the hospital room 24 hours a day,
—developing close friendships with hospital staff, and
—given access to hospital computer in order to read medical test results.

Furthermore, Dr. [B] states that 99% of the perpetrators of this syndrome are the natural mothers of the child.

The mother will be informed by hospital staff that the child may be reassessed, which according to the experts may cause the mother to react compulsively by possibly injecting the child.

Traditional investigative methods such as interviewing, undercover surveillance, informants and witnesses are ineffective and are often inadequate for the detection of such evidence, or are so time-consuming as to create an unnecessary delay and potential further injury and/or death to the victim. Your Affiant has diligently interviewed experienced medical personnel who are knowledgeable about the child's medical history and believes that there are no other reasonable means to further isolate the cause of the child's medical condition.

WHEREFORE, Affiant makes this affidavit and prays the issuance of a Video Surveillance Order and Seizure Order in due form of law for the entry of the above-described premises, for the installation of a video surveillance camera to be

OPD Case # _____

placed in the above-described premises for said evidence heretofore described, and for the video monitoring and recording thereof for a period not to exceed [number of hours or days, not to exceed 30 days] from installation, and for the subsequent seizure and safekeeping of any electronic recording of same, subject to the Order of a Court having jurisdiction thereof, by the duly constituted officers of the law. The investigating/executing officers and others will make every effort to minimize surveillance of nonpertinent activity, but only to the extent that the child is not placed at risk of threatened harm. Affiant further prays for authority to search the above-described premises and any persons thereon reasonably believed to be connected with the said illegal activity described in this order and if the same or any part thereof be present to seize said items.

_____
AFFIANT

SWORN TO and SUBSCRIBED before me this _____ day of _____, 19_____.

_____
JUDGE

# Appendix 13.B

# VIDEO SURVEILLANCE ORDER
# AND SEIZURE ORDER

IN THE NINTH JUDICIAL CIRCUIT,
IN AND FOR ORANGE COUNTY, FLORIDA      OPD Case # _____
STATE OF FLORIDA
COUNTY OF ORANGE

TO: _____, CHIEF OF THE ORLANDO POLICE DEPARTMENT AND/OR ANY OF HIS POLICE OFFICERS OR AGENTS THEREOF,

WHEREAS, complaint on oath and in writing, supported by affidavit, having been made this day before the undersigned,

WHEREAS, said facts made known to me have caused me to certify and find that there is probable cause to believe that certain laws have been and are being violated in and on certain premises and the curtilage thereof in Orange County, Florida. These premises are described as follows:

_____ Hospital, [street address], Orlando, Orange County, Florida, a ___-story building, Room No. ___, located on the ___ floor or such other room as the child may be located in. The room number is located on the wall outside of the door. The room has a bathroom. Located in the room is a hospital crib, a chair which makes out into a single bed and various storage cabinets.

This being the premises occupied by the child, _____, [race/gender], DOB: _____, patient/victim, the mother _____, [race/gender], DOB: _____, and under the control of _____ Hospital and that there is now being kept or administered on said premises and curtilage certain substances, to wit: Fecal matter and any containers or paraphernalia which might be used to contain or administer such fecal matter such as syringes or other device(s) which are being kept and used in violation of the laws of the State of Florida. Fecal matter is a substance obtained after a person defecates and is most likely located in a toilet. This substance is believed to be administered intravenously by syringe usually directly into the victim's intravenous central line. Said administration of fecal matter into the blood stream is in violation of the State of Florida to wit:

Florida State Statute 827.03 (Aggravated Child Abuse)

AND WHEREAS, the facts establishing the grounds for this application being set forth in the affidavit of **Investigator** _____, a member of the Orlando Police Department, incorporated by reference herein.

NOW, THEREFORE, you and either of you, with such lawful assistance as may be necessary, are hereby commanded, in the daytime, nighttime or on Sunday as the exigencies of the situation may require, to enter and search the aforesaid premises together with such adjacent areas as is necessary, for the purpose of installing video surveillance equipment, and for recording such activity for evidence as listed above, and for preservation of same. The duration of such video surveillance is not to exceed [number of hours or days, not to exceed 30 days] from installation and activation; and video surveillance shall be limited to such periods of time when the child victim and/or suspect perpetrator listed above is in the room under surveillance; the surveilling officers and/or other personnel shall make every effort to minimize surveillance of nonpertinent activity, but only to the extent that the child is not placed at risk of threatened harm. If the evidence named herein or any part thereof be found pursuant to this order, you are hereby authorized to seize and secure same, giving proper receipt therefor and delivering a completed copy of this order to the person in charge of the premises, or in the absence of any such person, leaving a completed copy where the property is found, and making a return of your doings under this order within ten (10) days of the date hereof, and you are further directed to bring said property so found and also the bodies of the person or persons in possession thereof before the Court having jurisdiction of this offense to be disposed of according to law.

WITNESS my hand and seal this _____ day of _____, 19____.


_____
JUDGE

OPD Case # _____

# INVENTORY AND RECEIPT

Needle box

Garbage bag

Miscellaneous items from bed pan on top of small dresser

Roll of tape/rusty nail with tape

DATED this _____ day of _____, 19____.

_____
OFFICER

OPD Case # _____

# RETURN

STATE OF FLORIDA
COUNTY OF ORANGE

Received this Seizure Order on the _____ day of _____, 19___, and executed the same in Orange County, Florida, on the _____ day of _____, 19___, by searching the premises described therein and by taking into my custody the property described in the above Inventory and Receipt and by having read and delivered a copy of this Seizure Order and Inventory and Receipt to _____.

_____
OFFICER

I, _____, the officer by whom the Order was executed, do swear that the above Inventory and Receipt contains a true and detailed account of all of the property taken by me on said Order.

_____
OFFICER

SWORN TO and SUBSCRIBED before me this _____ day of _____, 19_____.

_____
DEPUTY COURT CLERK

# 14 A Multidisciplinary Hospital Response Protocol

Sue Whelan-Williams
Toni D. Baker

> *Be prepared to put in a lot of time. Major expenditures of time go to the family, social services, the courts, the police, coordinating medical and nursing staff, and sorting out staff conflicts. Disbelief and anger at the diagnosis are often present among medical and nursing staff.*
> *—Donna Rosenberg, "Web of Deceit: A Literature Review of Munchausen Syndrome by Proxy," 1987*

Many articles have been written regarding the difficulty of identifying and confirming individual cases of Munchausen by proxy syndrome (Kahan & Yorker, 1991; Meadow, 1982a; Rosenberg, 1987). Kaufman, Coury, Pickrell, and McCleery (1989) note:

Despite a ten-year history of cases in the literature, Munchausen by Proxy Syndrome remains difficult to detect. Obstacles include staff perception of mothers as ideal parents, perpetrators' denial of allegations, the legal and psychiatric systems' skepticism that a parent would victimize her own child, and the ease with which perpetrators change physicians at the first hint of suspicion. (pp. 141-142)

A few articles in recent years have suggested that a multidisciplinary approach is most effective in overcoming these obstacles (Baldwin, 1994; Hanon, 1991; Meadow, 1985; Mercer & Perdue, 1993; Mitchell, Brummitt, DeForest, & Fisher, 1993). In fact, representatives from various professions are usually drawn into MBPS cases, but often in rather disjointed response to the various crises that erupt when such cases are suspected and probable perpetrators are confronted. The deception and manipulation manufactured by the Munchausen by proxy mother-perpetrator generate strong emotions in all the professionals who become involved. The differing perspectives of professionals on the mother's alleged behavior, which are fueled by these emotions, generally undermine what otherwise could be a good working relationship among professionals. However, very few authors have even mentioned the need for multidisciplinary coordination, let alone outlined any defined policy and procedure that can provide a process by which suspected Munchausen by proxy syndrome cases can be handled.

An effective multidisciplinary approach to identifying, confirming, and confronting MBPS cases requires a planned, objective, coordinated response that can be put into effect immediately upon suspicion of a case. By following such a designated protocol, professionals can prevent many of the problems that can otherwise arise in the diagnosis of Munchausen by proxy syndrome. In this chapter, we present a model protocol for addressing MBPS cases that we helped to develop at Arnold Palmer Hospital for Children and Women in Orlando, Florida. From June 1990 to February 1993, eight cases of Munchausen by proxy syndrome were identified, reported, investigated, and confirmed at this hospital. Six of the children were inpatients; two were diagnosed on an outpatient basis. A ninth case was identified and confirmed in February 1994. In eight of these nine cases, the suspected perpetrators confessed. Although no empirical data exist that clearly indicate why the confession rate was so high, we believe that the manner in which the protocol guides the intervention process played a major role. Below, we outline the steps in the protocol used at Arnold Palmer Hospital for Children and Women and why we believe each step is an important part of an investigation into suspicions of Munchausen by proxy syndrome. We believe that the framework we describe can be useful for the creation of similar protocols in other settings as well.

An article by Masterson and Wilson (1987) provides a baseline reference for the protocol described below. These authors outline an in-hospital multidisciplinary "evaluation process" that provides for specific pathways of intervention in cases of factitious illness in children. They suggest that "the diagnostic process is greatly facilitated with a multidisciplinary team and inpatient hospitalization of the child" (p. 22). During this hospitalization, the team (social worker, psychologist or psychiatrist, and medical staff) conducts an evaluation of the child in the hospital and in the absence of the parents. Masterson and Wilson recommend that a team meeting format be used during the evaluation and when findings are presented to the parents, in order to prevent staff splitting and distortion by the parents. Their protocol does not include agencies external to the hospital until *after* the diagnosis is made and the alleged perpetrator has been confronted. Some of the cases Masterson and Wilson discuss did not involve reporting to outside agencies at all, suggesting that treatment follow-through was their focus.

We believe that the hospital's multidisciplinary team must expand on this idea of case flow by integrating into the protocol agencies external to the hospital, including those that hospital personnel must contact at the point of *suspicion* of child abuse. These agencies include child protective services, which receives and investigates suspected child abuse cases under the mandatory reporting law, and law enforcement. Decisions regarding the investigation and confrontation process must be made in concert by the attending physician and representatives of the hospital administration, law enforcement, and child protective services. Whether or not the perpetrator agrees to participate in psychotherapy is an issue for child protective services and possibly the courts. Additionally, the involvement of agencies external to the hospital strengthens the efficacy of the protocol in the community when outpatient cases are suspected.

The primary issues to be addressed in the development of a protocol are basically the same regardless of the number or types of professionals involved in the investigation of child abuse in the community. A multidisciplinary "child protection team" is the ideal structure already in place in many areas to bring together the various professionals vital to the investigation of a Munchausen by proxy syndrome case (i.e., law enforcement, child protective services, physicians, psychologists, and social workers). A child protection team is a hands-on group of professionals, skilled at decision making, who can provide evaluation and consultation in difficult abuse cases (Whitworth, 1989). The professionals who serve on such a team often have worked closely together for some time and routinely practice a multidisciplinary approach to the investigation of child abuse. We recommend that a child protection team be involved in the development of any protocol designed to address MBPS cases, although we should note that even the members of such a team are often not prepared for the confusion and complexity of these abuse cases, or the intense coordination among professionals that they require.

## The Protocol

The first step in the protocol used at Arnold Palmer Hospital for Children and Women occurs when an attending or consulting physician first questions the medical findings on a particular child (see Figure 14.1, Step 1). The physician must have someone objective and experienced to turn to when suspicions of Munchausen by proxy syndrome emerge; in this protocol, the child protection team medical director is the contact person for any physician with such suspicions (Step 2). (If a hospital does not have a special team of professionals available to investigate abuse cases, a member of the medical staff should be designated as the liaison for all Munchausen by proxy syndrome case contacts.) Our experience has shown that MBPS cases are difficult to diagnose, especially in children with actual chronic medical conditions. The child protection team medical director (or other designated contact physician) must develop expertise in rare chronic medical conditions as well as Munchausen by proxy cases. Additionally, he or she must establish a trusting relationship with other physicians and with the external agencies concerned with issues of child abuse. He or she may also be called upon to be a credible expert witness in court.

After the attending physician consults with the child protection team medical director, a determination is made as to whether the medical findings indicate the need for further investigation (Step 3). Obviously, this consultation and the resulting decision must occur immediately upon the attending physician's first formulation of suspicion, as most states' child abuse statutes mandate prompt reporting. Such immediate action would not be possible in a busy medical center without a predetermined protocol in place and the commitment of all the professionals involved. Once the medical staff suspects that a true case of Munchausen by proxy syndrome exists, a number of people must be notified, including child protective services, law enforcement, and the hospital administration (Step 4). These individuals/agencies may in turn notify others (e.g., the prosecuting attorney's office). It is vital that the protocol identify specifically all internal and external participants who must be notified, and that a procedure be established so that notification is virtually simultaneous. One individual, such as the child protection team case coordinator, should be responsible for the actions required in Step 4; unless these are completed in a timely manner, the emergency staffing (Step 5) will not be possible.

The emergency staffing should be held immediately after Step 4 is complete, so that representatives of the various disciplines can develop a unified action plan for the investigation. The emergency staffing ensures

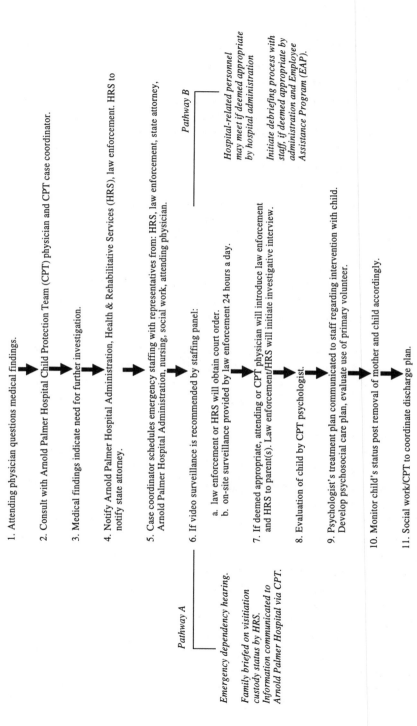

1. Attending physician questions medical findings.

2. Consult with Arnold Palmer Hospital Child Protection Team (CPT) physician and CPT case coordinator.

3. Medical findings indicate need for further investigation.

4. Notify Arnold Palmer Hospital Administration, Health & Rehabilitative Services (HRS), law enforcement. HRS to notify state attorney.

5. Case coordinator schedules emergency staffing with representatives from: HRS, law enforcement, state attorney, Arnold Palmer Hospital Administration, nursing, social work, attending physician.

6. If video surveillance is recommended by staffing panel:
   a. law enforcement or HRS will obtain court order.
   b. on-site surveillance provided by law enforcement 24 hours a day.

7. If deemed appropriate, attending or CPT physician will introduce law enforcement and HRS to parent(s). Law enforcement/HRS will initiate investigative interview.

8. Evaluation of child by CPT psychologist.

9. Psychologist's treatment plan communicated to staff regarding intervention with child. Develop psychosocial care plan, evaluate use of primary volunteer.

10. Monitor child's status post removal of mother and child accordingly.

11. Social work/CPT to coordinate discharge plan.

*Pathway A*

*Emergency dependency hearing.*

*Family briefed on visitiation custody status by HRS.*
*Information communicated to Arnold Palmer Hospital via CPT.*

*Pathway B*

*Hospital-related personnel may meet if deemed appropriate by hospital administration*

*Initiate debriefing process with staff, if deemed appropriate by administration and Employee Assistance Program (EAP).*

**Figure 14.1.** Arnold Palmer Hospital for Children and Women/Community Munchausen Syndrome by Proxy Protocol
SOURCE: Orlando Regional Healthcare System. Used with permission.

direct and speedy communication among all parties involved in the case, and can include many people. At Arnold Palmer Hospital for Children and Women, most agencies that take part in the investigation are structured with three layers of personnel, all of which may become involved: the line staff member who actually conducts the investigation, his or her immediate supervisor, and agency administrators (who can ensure immediate approval if policy exceptions are necessary). The hospital also provides its own cadre of participants (as would most hospitals), including the administrator on call, the attending physician, the child protection team medical director, a representative of risk management, a psychologist, nurse manager, primary nurse from the unit where the child was admitted, and any psychosocial staff members who have been directly involved with the family.

Even though emergency case conferences can often become very cumbersome, we believe that all of the professionals identified in the protocol are crucial to successful case coordination and intervention. Certainly, hospital staff members often have key information that proves helpful during the investigative phase. However, the team must also be aware that due to the strong, conflicting emotions aroused by these cases, some staff members who attend the conference may report back to the mother about the investigation that has begun. As with any successful case conference, especially one with so many participants, it is essential that the primary objectives of the conference are clear to all participants and that a strong facilitator be appointed to guide the process. The facilitator should not be someone who is involved in the actual investigation of the case. The use of an outside facilitator is necessary anytime a case conference involves five or more people, to ensure that all parties provide input and that consensus is reached on the intervention plan, the goal of which is to make a determination whether or not the case in question is a case of abuse.

The first five steps of the MBPS protocol used at Arnold Palmer Hospital for Children and Women are designed to address several communication problems that might obstruct the case investigation process if they are not resolved at the outset. It is critical for any hospital to establish a systematic method for interdisciplinary and interagency communication that can be utilized throughout the course of investigation of suspected cases of Munchausen by proxy syndrome. All external agencies have their own policies and procedures that regulate their intervention processes, and these must be taken into consideration when an MBPS protocol is written. Problems of coordination can be minimized if each agency is encouraged to provide input to the proposed protocol prior to its implementation. Also, agencies that have been involved in the development of the protocol are likely to provide the types of support necessary in the investigation of these potentially lethal cases.

There will be times when, due to the complexity of Munchausen by proxy cases, the traditional methods of reporting and investigating suspected child abuse and neglect might need to be modified. For example, in the state of Florida, the agency in charge of child protective services (the Department of Health and Rehabilitative Services) is mandated to speak with the parents within 24 hours of a report of suspected child abuse or neglect. This requirement can interfere with the investigation of MBPS cases, which sometimes involve a need to conduct video surveillance to confirm the allegations (a process that in turn often requires a court order). If each agency involved is committed to the protocol, special arrangements can often be made to work around the usual procedures.

Before the MBPS protocol was in place at Arnold Palmer Hospital for Children and Women, many disruptive arguments arose at case conferences regarding video surveillance and perpetrator confrontation (Steps 6 and 7). Although all the agencies concerned with child abuse cases assert that their primary interest is the protection of the children, the various agencies' agendas for meeting that ultimate goal may be different. Law enforcement officials have a mandate to try to prove that a crime has been committed, and they are concerned with gathering appropriate evidence for the prosecutor. Physicians are primarily responsible for the child's physical well-being. Hospital administrators may feel a responsibility to protect both the rights of the patient and the rights of the parents.

The use of video surveillance in suspected cases of Munchausen by proxy is complex and replete with contradictions as to the legal right to monitor a room without consent (Epstein, Markowitz, Gallo, Holmes, & Gryboski, 1987; Fiatal, 1989; Kahan & Yorker, 1991). The consensus is that the decision to use video surveillance should be made on a case-by-case basis. Further, the need for a court order seems to depend, in part, on who initiates the process (law enforcement or the hospital). In our hospital, we prefer that law enforcement or child protective services pursue an order from the court to carry out video surveillance when a case of Munchausen by proxy syndrome is suspected (for some details on such court orders, see Wilkinson & Parnell, Chapter 13, this volume). The existence of a court order eliminates any argument that videotaped evidence was procured through illegal means. Further, the need to pursue a court order can function as an additional control, minimizing the arbitrary use of video surveillance without strong physician belief that Munchausen by proxy syndrome exists. We recommend that any hospital team developing an MBPS protocol consult with the hospital's risk management department and legal counsel regarding video surveillance.

The negotiation of our protocol actually began after the first case in our hospital in which videotaping was initiated by law enforcement. The case involved a 5-year-old child who was hospitalized for fevers, etiology unknown. The child's fever typically subsided within 24 hours of hospitalization. Additionally, during the course of the hospitalization, the child was moved from a private room to a nursery for observation. The child's mother did not like having to leave the private room, and after a few days in the nursery insisted on being moved back to the private room. It was noted by the nurse that the child did not spike a fever the entire time in the nursery. Extensive tests, including a complete immune evaluation, were conducted, resulting in no diagnosis. The child would spike a fever again each time the physician considered discharge. The physician isolated nonhuman pathogens in the child's bloodstream and suspected that some type of bacteria were being injected through the child's central intravenous line.

It was decided by all agencies involved that law enforcement would install video equipment in the child's room and monitor activity in the room to see if the mother was injecting anything into the child's intravenous line. When she was indeed observed doing so, she was confronted by law enforcement, arrested, and taken to the police station. It was only after she was shown the videotape that she confessed, stating that she used a hypodermic needle and contaminated the needle by rubbing it on the toilet seat or by using dirty water from the toilet. On at least six occasions while the child was hospitalized at Arnold Palmer, the mother put contaminated water into her child's intravenous line. Prior to this admission, the child had been evaluated at several other hospitals over a 3-year period.

Once the multidisciplinary group confirms a diagnosis of Munchausen by proxy syndrome, the issue of confrontation needs to be addressed (Step 7). We recommend that the initial part of the confrontation be conducted by the primary or consulting physician who has confirmed the suspicion of Munchausen by proxy syndrome. This physician should introduce the medical evidence of MBPS to the alleged perpetrator. This confrontation should occur in the presence of a law enforcement officer, a child protective services investigator, and a mental health professional. Because Munchausen by proxy syndrome presents in the medical arena, the suspected mother-perpetrator needs to understand the medical evidence that validates the allegations. After this initial confrontation, the case should be turned over to law enforcement. In our setting, we have yet to agree completely on this format (for other perspectives, see Seibel & Parnell, Chapter 4, and Parnell,

Chapter 5, this volume). We have decided after much discussion to evaluate each case individually to determine who is the best person to confront the alleged perpetrator. Law enforcement is the only agency guaranteed participation during any and all confrontations.

In his article on management of Munchausen by proxy syndrome, Meadow (1985) notes, "I am sure the person who conducts [the confrontational] interview should be the pediatrician who has known the family and the child the longest and who has uncovered the deception" (p. 391). However, we have found that in the majority of cases in which we have been involved, the primary pediatricians have not wanted to confront the suspected parents. Many were angry that they had been deceived by the parents. In one particular case, the primary pediatrician had been treating the patient's true medical complications for several years and wanted to continue caring for the child after the case was identified. He felt that his being involved with the confrontation would alienate the family, and he might lose touch with the patient.

After confrontation, an issue that needs immediate attention is the psychological well-being of the child. In each of the cases identified in our hospital, once the alleged perpetrator admitted to the crime, she was removed from the hospital by law enforcement. When this occurs, because of the relationship between the mother and the child-victim, the child protection team psychologist is asked to evaluate the child within 24 hours and make recommendations to the psychosocial team regarding ongoing support for the child and family (Step 8).[1] These recommendations are then incorporated into the medical record for action by the child life specialist and social worker (Step 9). Other family members' needs are dealt with by child protective services at this point (Pathway A).

The status of the child-victim continues to be monitored in the hospital for an indefinite period (Step 10). Even if the child is not suffering from a bona fide medical illness, there are often residual medical effects of the mother-perpetrator's actions that must be fully resolved. Additionally, child placement issues will be considered within the court system and may take time to arrange, especially if the child has ongoing medical problems. During this time the nursing staff must be prepared to monitor closely the child's physical and emotional progress now that the suspected source of illness (i.e., the mother) is removed. In some cases the mother is allowed continued access to the child, which is supervised by the nurses. Therefore, it is important that all staff have a realistic understanding of the potential lethality of these cases and the potential for continued perpetration even when contact is supervised.

The final step in the protocol (Step 11) is the coordination of a discharge plan that addresses all the needs of the child. Once again, each discipline/ agency that is part of the team may have different expectations regarding the discharge plan. The role of the hospital does not always end when the child is discharged. Several of the children in cases at Arnold Palmer Hospital also suffered from genuine chronic medical conditions and were routinely seen in various outpatient clinics. It is necessary for the social worker to remain in close contact with the child protection team case coordinator and the child protective services worker to ensure that wherever the child is placed, doctors familiar with the case will continue to have medical access to the child.

Following the confrontation of the suspected perpetrator in every MBPS case with which we have been involved, one of the most difficult issues has been staff reaction to the identification of the case (Pathway B). Several of the cases were identified on the same pediatric floor of the hospital. Once a case was identified, psychosocial/employee assistance program staff were made available to help other staff members process the multitude of conflicting emotions related to caring for a patient and his or her parent with this syndrome. As in most cases of chronic pediatric illness, staff members develop close relationships with the children and their families in Munchausen by proxy cases. Indeed, the closeness that develops in MBPS cases can be especially intense. These mothers are usually viewed by staff quite positively; they are often supportive when staff members are frustrated by the child's lack of improvement, they initiate personal interaction with staff members, and they often have medical knowledge that leads them to be more conversational with staff than other parents. These close ties can backfire once Munchausen by proxy syndrome has been confirmed. Staff members feel betrayed, angry, and hurt. On occasion, they may overidentify with the family and refuse to believe that the caretaker is actually the instrument of the child's pain and suffering. The staff reactions we have seen have been consistent with the descriptions found in the literature.

Although many articles have included comments about professionals' reactions to Munchausen by proxy syndrome, this issue has represented not much more than a passing concern in the research literature. This is unfortunate for several reasons: Medical professionals are vital in the detection of Munchausen by proxy syndrome, the feelings of betrayal by the family that professionals experience after MBPS is detected are very strong, and these feelings have long-term implications for staff interactions with child patients' families. Blix and Brack (1988) conducted one study of the effects of a case on nurses in a large midwestern children's hospital. Twenty pediatric nurses completed an open-ended questionnaire regarding how they felt about the case, how it affected their subsequent interaction with their patients' parents, and how they coped with knowledge of the case personally and professionally. Overall, the responses suggested that the nurses felt professionally unprepared to deal with the case. Many reacted with feelings of shock, disbelief, and nausea, as well as anger toward the parents, the diagnosing physician, and themselves. The mother's alleged behavior was in direct opposition to their prior view of her as supportive, loving, and concerned. Thus the nurses had difficulty accepting the veracity of the allegations, and some felt that it changed their relationship with parents in general, making them less trusting and more vigilant.

In a brief discussion of staff issues, Chan, Salcedo, Atkins, and Ruley (1986) mention staff concerns with "child abuse by proxy," in other words, the conflicts staff experience over their role in subjecting a child to dangerous and painful treatments for no medical reason. Chan et al. comment on the need for hospitals to help staff members to understand the dynamics of these cases, as well as to prepare them for the typical responses accused parents will make when confronted. Chan et al. suggest that all involved medical staff be informed as soon as MBPS is suspected, but we believe that disclosing suspicions to so many staff members at this early stage may conflict with the need to obtain confirmatory evidence (see Day, Chapter 6, this volume). Certainly, once the suspected mother-perpetrator has been confronted, the medical staff should be given all of the pertinent information on the case. This delay in sharing information with all staff may create additional feelings of betrayal among staff members—betrayal by the hospital—and sympathy for the family. Nonetheless, it may be necessary for professionals to keep their suspicions closely guarded for a time in order that they may gather the evidence necessary to protect the child.

A number of problems can arise when the hospital does not provide a forum in which staff can deal with the issues raised by the detection of an MBPS case. For instance, the emotional trauma experienced by staff on such a case may strain coworker relationships. Also, without adequate understanding of Munchausen by proxy family dynamics, information about the diagnosis, and resolution of the often intense personal emotions these cases can stimulate, staff members may not be willing or able to protect adequately a child-victim whose contact with the perpetrating parent is now restricted. Further, unresolved issues about the case may lead staff to be reluctant to acknowledge signs of Munchausen by proxy syndrome in future cases, or to be overzealous in suspecting Munchausen by proxy syndrome. Most important, these issues may interfere with staff members' abilities to provide the best possible care to all future pediatric patients and their families. The hospital can help to ensure the emotional well-being of staff and good quality of future care by attending to the needs of staff exposed to cases of Munchausen by proxy syndrome, and by developing and implementing a critical stress debriefing plan.

## Note

1. *Editors' note:* We are aware of cases, both personally and in the literature, in which in-hospital evaluations of children via psychiatric or psychological consultations were used in isolation to assist in identification of cases of Munchausen by proxy syndrome. However, we caution strongly against such a practice without multidisciplinary team support. Such consultations, although a standard part of hospital practice and certainly useful in other types of cases, are far too limited in scope for MBPS cases and are likely to produce "normal" findings.

# 15 The School System Perspective

Karen O. Palladino

*All employees or agents of the district school board have an affirmative duty to report all actual or suspected cases of child abuse or neglect, have immunity from liability if they report such cases in good faith, and have a duty to comply with child protective investigations and all other provisions of law relating to child abuse and neglect.*
*—Florida Statute 232.50 (1)*

I first became aware of the type of child abuse called Munchausen by proxy syndrome a few years ago when a very difficult parent was identified as being in violation of Florida's compulsory school attendance law. The child's school originally reported to the Hospital Homebound Office that it was having difficulty with a parent who was not sending her child to school due to the child's purported medical problems and was instead attempting to procure homebound instruction. The mother asserted that the child was too ill to attend school and presented notes from various doctors to support her claim. However, the notes reflected no specific condition that appeared serious enough to warrant homebound instruction. When the school social worker was dispatched for a home visit, neither the parent nor the child was found at home during the school day. The mother did not return any telephone calls. When a school district representative made a telephone inquiry to one of the child's physicians to inquire how the medical problem prevented the child from attending school, the physician indicated that the child probably could go to school. However, the mother had expressed to the physician a desire to have the student on homebound services. When the school contacted the mother and told her that homebound services had been refused for her daughter, she flew into a rage. She threatened a lawsuit, insulted and threatened school board staff, and accused school personnel of trying to kill her daughter. One week later, the mother presented a statement from yet another physician requesting homebound instruction for the child because of a new medical problem.

Along with the new request, the school office began to receive from the mother a barrage of extensive medical records on the child, records accumulated over many years. Unbelievably, none of the medical diagnoses involved any serious illness that would typically require homebound instruction. The child's medical records indicated diagnoses that included obesity (this student's weight exceeded 150 pounds when she was a fourth grader), asthma, bronchial ailments, kidney and urinary tract infections/problems, mysterious nonspecific heart ailments, suspected seizures, and possible migraine headaches. The mother then began sending the school the medical records of her other children and copies of years of prescription printouts from pharmacies in the area. After weeks of harassment, threats, and more physicians' statements, the child was placed on homebound instruction, with the stipulation that the school district would arrange for an independent medical evaluation at the district's expense to determine if the student was truly in need of homebound services. At this point, the district staff felt that the mother had simply worn them down; they took this course of action as the path of least resistance, to buy some time for further investigation. In the meantime, at least the child would be receiving an education.

Shortly after the child was placed on homebound instruction, the mother began calling school officials with numerous complaints about the quality of the teacher provided, her unhappiness with the schedule set up for the instruction, and how the entire situation was upsetting her family routine. She began each of her calls with a detailed account of all the personal family problems she was experiencing. She reported that she had recently been in an accident, and that because of this she was now involved in litigation. She also reported that she was involved in a litigious action out of state, and in still another legal dispute over an injury her child had incurred at a former school. The story became so incredible that it was becoming awkward and embarrassing for staff to confront the mother on each and every issue that arose.

Finally, the school district received the independent physician's report on the contracted examination of the child. It was an eye-opener. This doctor could not find any serious medical condition in the child other than obesity. He did not find any indication that she needed an inhaler for her asthmatic condition or any reason she should be missing school. He reported that he believed the child's mother to be suffering from Munchausen by proxy syndrome.

As director of administrative support services for the school district, I began to research this strange syndrome. Unfortunately, the literature available on the subject was rather sparse, especially articles that could assist school personnel in identifying the characteristics of this type of abuse. What I was able to find, however, suddenly made sense of many isolated, seemingly unrelated, bits of information in this case. After I discussed the doctor's findings and the information I had uncovered in my research with district-level personnel, the school district contacted the local child abuse hot line and made a report. The hot-line staff were hardly receptive; this was apparently not the type of report they typically received, and they were reluctant to give it much credence. An investigation was conducted, and school personnel were invited to attend several staffings with school and school district personnel; representatives of the Department of Health and Rehabilitative Services, Children's Medical Services, and the Children's Home Society of Florida; and the Family Services Planning Team.[1] Several months later, the child was removed from the home and placed in foster care.

Once separated from her mother, the child flourished. She was removed from homebound services, attended school regularly, did not use her asthma inhaler at all, and even received an award at the County Science Fair. She progressed from having 76 absences from school the previous school year to only 3 in the year following her placement in foster care. The mother was allowed supervised visitation and was ordered to undergo a psychological evaluation. The child's obesity was addressed, but her mother did try to bring the girl's "favorite foods" to her when she visited. The child was also required to submit to weekly urine tests, to be sure nothing was being introduced into her system to sabotage her progress.

Unfortunately, the child was eventually returned to the mother's home, only to be removed again. Months after the second separation, she was again returned to the custody of her mother. In that school year, as a matter of follow-up, the child's new school was contacted (the mother had taken her out of the previous school) by officials checking on her attendance. It was found that she was again displaying a pattern of excessive absences. When the school was questioned as to why there had been no follow-up concerning these absences, the response was that the child had always brought a doctor's note. The local child protective services office was then informed that the child was in the same situation as before. Staff there reported that the case had been closed after a few months of satisfactory performance on the part of the mother. The child had been returned to the mother by a judge over the objection of child protective services, and the judge would not consider removing the child again. There was nothing to be done, unless another abuse report was filed. The student's history was then explained to the personnel at her new school, and another abuse report was made. This time, the person who took the hot-line call was familiar with Munchausen by proxy syndrome, and very little explanation was needed. Two days later, the mother went to the school and demanded to know if anyone had been to the school looking at her child's records; she also wanted to know who had made the abuse report. The mother told the school guidance counselor that the personnel at her child's former school were all liars, and that the three psychiatrists who had evaluated her were all liars also. These events all took place very recently, and I have no further information on the status of this case.

What I find to be most frustrating about working on Munchausen by proxy syndrome cases is they are so time-consuming. In addition, Munchausen by proxy syndrome is so recently recognized that there have been very few articles published in school-related journals to assist school professionals in recognizing and dealing with child-victims of this disorder (see Kahan & Yorker, 1990; Mercer & Perdue, 1993). Most articles on the subject have appeared in medical or other noneducation journals (e.g., the *American Journal of Orthopsychiatry* and *Archives of Disease in Childhood*) and have not discussed issues relevant to school-based detection and management. This is unfortunate, because school professionals are among the most likely persons to be able to suspect and recognize MBPS abuse, especially in older children, owing to the fact that schools have the expectation of daily contact with almost all children ages 5 through 18.

The older the child, the more important the role of the school professional becomes, because an older child-victim may begin to share in the mother-perpetrator's pathology, siding with her or covering for her. It is critical that school personnel be alert to the symptoms described in the preceding chapters of this book. Although no one single indicator or combination of indicators is absolute reason to suspect a parent of Munchausen by proxy abuse, educators and others in school settings should be aware of the signs that can indicate a strong underlying problem within the family unit that may need investigation. The earlier the abuse is detected, the earlier treatment can begin.

To assume this important role in child protection, school staff must be educated to recognize the nonmedical aspects of Munchausen by proxy syndrome. School districts should arrange for administrators, social workers, school psychologists, and other selected staff to attend seminars on this topic, or should bring in consultants to provide training. I describe below some indicators of possible MBPS abuse to which school personnel should be alert; these should be considered in conjunction with guidelines described elsewhere in this book (see especially Parnell, Chapter 3). This list is based upon information that should be readily accessible to school personnel. It is important to remember, however, that school personnel are not responsible for making the diagnosis of Munchausen by proxy syndrome—that is a medical diagnosis. This list of indicators is intended simply to aid school personnel in determining whether particular cases warrant abuse reports and/or referral for medical review.

## Indicators for the School Professional

1. *School attendance problems.* Chronic absenteeism, whether explained or unexplained, should be investigated. Physician statements from a variety of sources, including or other than the family physician, may be suspect. Particular note should be made if a parent claims that the child has a severe or life-threatening illness, but takes the child only to walk-in clinics rather than specialists. On the other hand, some parents may present doctors' notes from many specialists, each possibly with a different diagnosis. Each new doctor may not be aware that the child is being treated or medicated by other doctors. Only the person at the school who is receiving all the doctors' notes might be able to piece this together. School personnel should also remember that physicians' notes or letters are not sufficient documentation of illness, as the parent may present only those that she wants someone to see. Additionally, physicians' findings may be based on fabricated information or a lack of awareness that other medical professionals are involved with the child's care.
2. *Requests for hospitalized/homebound services.* Parent requests for hospitalized/homebound services for a child who has one or more different mild medical problems, no one of which would seemingly require homebound services, should be questioned. The Individuals with Disabilities Education Act requires that all students must be provided an education in the least restrictive environment, and this means that even extremely medically fragile children are still attending school. When a parent claims that her child cannot come to school

at all because the child has headaches, allergies, or stomachaches, this may indicate that the case should be referred to the school's child study team for review, to determine if a psychological evaluation is needed.

3. *Parent accusations that the school is making the child ill.* A parent may claim that the school has environmental elements that aggravate the child's respiratory problems, asthma, or allergic reactions. Alternatively, a parent may assert that teachers are subjecting her child to "mental or emotional abuse." The MBPS mother may feel that no one should ever question her child's honesty or integrity, and may consider it unacceptable for teachers to discipline or challenge the child.

4. *Parent presentation of extensive medical history file to explain child's illness.* If a parent presents extensive medical records on the child, the school nurse or physician, if available, should review them with an eye to such invasive procedures as spinal taps, exploratory surgery, blood studies, and allergy tests—evidence that there has been a continued search for "the" diagnosis. Also, the person reviewing the records should check on the prescription medications the child has received or is currently receiving, and the dosages. If the person conducting the records review is not a nurse or physician, he or she will need to consult with a school or county health services professional in order to understand this information and to judge whether or not the child's treatments and medications have been appropriate.

5. *Child reported to be too ill to come to school due to respiratory ailments.* School personnel should investigate to see if the parent has tried to eliminate elements in the home that would aggravate such a condition (e.g., pets, carpets, deodorizers, smoking).

6. *Child reported to be too ill to come to school, but is involved in other activities.* School personnel should be concerned if they know that a child who has been absent due to illness has been seen out with his or her parents during the school day or on weekends; for instance, a child's friends may report having seen him or her at the movies, restaurants, or shopping malls.

7. *Child appears to be suffering from impaired psychosocial development* due to dysfunction on the part of a parent, which further affects the medical issues. Social skills limitations or the handling of stress with illness behavior are common dysfunctions in the MBPS victim. Additionally, by conducting a social history interview with the child, school personnel may uncover information that indicates misrepre-

sentations or falsehoods on the part of the parent that would substantiate medical fabrication.

8. *Unreasonable requests from a parent.* School personnel should be wary of a parent who demands that unreasonable accommodations be made for her child, or who disagrees with a reasonable treatment plan proposed by the school but cannot offer substantive reasons for doing so. The Munchausen by proxy mother will often go over the heads of the school personnel who are trying to work with her to seek backup for her position from a higher authority.

9. *A symbiotic parent-child relationship.* School personnel should be able to recognize an unusually enmeshed parent-child relationship. The MBPS mother often seems to have a psychological need to have her child with her at all times.

10. *Hysterical personality in a parent.* The Munchausen by proxy parent often appears to be overwhelmed by disasters in her life and seems compelled to tell others about the "horrible" things that are happening to her. She may describe at great length the details of her life, which can sound like a soap opera. An MBPS mother may be described as being overly passionate. Everything she does, whether it is related to her child or not, reflects urgency. She must see someone *right now,* she cannot wait; if something does not happen immediately, some great disaster will befall her. She does not wait for others to respond to what she has said before she resumes talking, often speaking at a decibel level far above normal conversation. When she is in the school office, she is the focus of attention.

11. *It appears that the parent wants to punish the school system.* School personnel should take note of any parent who appears to have some kind of grudge against the school or the school system because of a past hurt or grievance, real or imagined.

12. *Parent becomes hostile and threatens legal action.* The Munchausen by proxy mother may be likely to threaten legal action against the school if she is questioned about her motives. School personnel should realize that this is probably a fear response; the mother has learned through experience that such threats can often get the school to back off.

13. *The parent takes no real action to solve what she says are her child's problems.* School personnel may observe that a parent appears to pay lip service to her concerns about her child, but actually does nothing that will really address those concerns.

14. *The parent declares that "other" professionals are in agreement with her regarding the child's condition, but fails to produce proof to substantiate her claims.*

Finally, it is important for educators and others in the school setting to remember that Munchausen by proxy syndrome should not necessarily be ruled out simply because a child has a genuine previously diagnosed disorder. The presence of any of the indicators listed above should alert school personnel to take a careful look at that child's case.

## Plan of Action

Following are some specific suggestions for actions that school personnel should take if they suspect that a child is a victim of Munchausen by proxy abuse (i.e., if several of the above-listed indicators are present):

1. Review the problems with the child study team at the child's school. Even if the consensus of the group is that there is no abuse, any school employee who truly suspects abuse is obligated by law to make an abuse report.
2. *Make an abuse hot-line call,* and then follow up with the local child protective services office required to conduct an investigation.
3. Attend all meetings with child protective services and other agencies that are involved in providing needed services to children. Remember that the allegations in Munchausen by proxy cases are so hard for some professionals to believe that the possibility of abuse of this kind may be dismissed unless someone is present who has carefully considered the situation and has compiled a variety of pertinent information.
4. Cooperate with all investigations, providing information if requested.
5. Appear in court to provide testimony or records if requested.
6. Stand your ground if you think you are right. You are the child's advocate, or you would not have gotten this far.
7. Follow up on the case, even if a child who was removed from a parent's home is later returned to her. These cases require long-term follow-up.
8. Keep confidentiality. If you know who made the abuse report, protect that person's anonymity; never reveal this person's identity to the parent. If you fail to keep this confidence, you may prevent the person from making any other report in the future, and thereby jeopardize the

health and safety of a child. Most states have laws that prevent such disclosure.

School personnel who become involved in suspected cases of Munchausen by proxy syndrome quickly learn that they are incredibly exhausting, time-consuming, and emotionally draining. These are very difficult cases, in large part because of the personal attacks, abuse, threats, criticism, and devaluing aimed by the MBPS parent at anyone who gets in her way. Further, the time investment takes away from all of the other work that school personnel must accomplish. For these reasons, many cases are never reported; they are just too hard.

With continued education and dissemination of information on the subject, Munchausen by proxy syndrome may become more easily recognized and may be diagnosed earlier. The schools play a critical role in the discovery of MBPS abuse in children ages 5 through 18, because school personnel have more contact with children than do the representatives of any other agency or institution. Educators and others in the school setting must accept the importance of their role, and not be afraid, if it becomes necessary, to question a parent's intent or to challenge societal views regarding family privacy. School personnel have a responsibility to do the right thing for the benefit of the child.

## Note

1. The Department of Health and Rehabilitative Services investigates all abuse/ neglect allegations in Florida. The Family Services Planning Team assists families at high risk for removal of a child due to psychological or behavioral problems by taking a team approach to treatment planning, case management, and funding for recommended interventions. Although funded by the Department of Health and Rehabilitative Services, the Family Services Planning Team is operated through contract with a private agency. In the county where this case occurred, Children's Home Society had the contract at the time. Children's Medical Services, also funded by the Department of Health and Rehabilitative Services, provides medical services to children with chronic medical conditions.

# 16 The Guardian ad Litem

Ralph V. Hadley III

Under Florida law, if the Department of Health and Rehabilitative Services has filed a complaint with the juvenile court alleging that a child is "dependent" by reason of neglect or abuse, the court has the power to appoint a guardian ad litem for the child. This person is uniquely positioned in abuse and neglect cases to protect the best interest of the child. The guardian ad litem has a huge advantage over all the other participants in the case in that he or she has no particular ax to grind; his or her only concern is the protection of the child-victim client. Because the guardian ad litem is appointed for this limited purpose and enters the case without prejudgment as to its merits, the role is unique.

In cases involving alleged abuse arising out of Munchausen by proxy syndrome, it is critical that the guardian ad litem first understand the nature and complexity of this disorder. As discussed in depth in the preceding chapters of this book, Munchausen by proxy encompasses many parent behaviors surrounding the child's physical condition. However, parent behavior typically fits into two categories: The parent either proactively causes symptoms (such as the administration of syrup of ipecac) or falsely reports nonexistent or exaggerated symptoms (see Parnell, Chapter 2, this volume). In either instance, the goal of the parent is to cause medical attention to be focused on the child, normally involving repeated examinations and tests. Even in cases in which the afflicted parent has only falsely reported symptoms, the guardian ad litem should understand that the child has been placed at risk of psychological injury as well as physical pain caused by often invasive and therefore risky examination procedures (see Day and Ojeda-Castro, Chapter 12, this volume). Further, the guardian ad litem must be tuned in to the fact that the offending parent almost always appears to be a concerned, caring, and loving parent and, almost without exception, is indignant and displays shock at the allegations brought against her. As will be set forth below, understanding the nature and complexity of Munchausen by proxy syndrome will enable the guardian ad litem to play a pivotal role in the case. It is my opinion that a guardian ad litem should be appointed in every case involving allegations of Munchausen by proxy syndrome.

When a guardian ad litem is appointed to his or her first Munchausen by proxy case, he or she should immediately access the available publications on the topic.[1] There have been numerous articles published in various medical journals about this affliction, and most professionals who have access to these articles are happy to share them with a guardian ad litem. Otherwise, the guardian can obtain them from any major library through a database search. In addition, the guardian ad litem should discuss MBPS with professionals who have experience in diagnosing and/or treating the syndrome, in order to be apprised of the latest developments in this field. One thing my experience has shown me is that the knowledge about and understanding of this difficult mental disorder is expanding at an exponential rate. Because Munchausen by proxy syndrome is a fairly recently discovered phenomenon, there is much that is still not understood about this illness; this makes the guardian ad litem's understanding of current developments in the research even more critical.

Often, the guardian ad litem in an MBPS case must work under a significant handicap: The client is too young or is otherwise mentally disadvantaged and cannot communicate effectively with the guardian. Unlike other abuse and neglect cases, Munchausen by proxy syndrome cases almost always involve children who cannot communicate with their guardians. Another factor found in most Munchausen by proxy cases is disbelief on the part of the nonoffending spouse and other family members.

The guardian ad litem should conduct a thorough investigation of the case, similar to that conducted by the other professionals involved (as described in Chapters 3, 4, and 5 of this volume). The potential ramifications of Munchausen by proxy behavior are too serious for the guardian to depend only on information gathered by others. Additionally, because of the nonadversarial nature of the guardian ad litem's role, he or she can conduct an investigation on a substantially different level from the one conducted by other authorities. In many instances, the attorneys representing the alleged perpetrator will allow the guardian ad litem to interview their client informally, without the necessity of taking a deposition or using other formal discovery proceedings. Likewise, the other family members will normally make themselves available to the guardian ad litem to be interviewed, so that the guardian may understand the case and the people involved. Because such interviews can be conducted in a nonthreatening manner, without the formality that accompanies court proceedings, they are often very valuable in helping the guardian ad litem to understand the dynamics of the family and the issues that led up to the allegations being investigated.

In addition to conducting interviews with all family members and/or other interested parties on an informal basis, the guardian ad litem should seek to obtain medical authorizations from the alleged offending parent that will permit treating physicians to release records and to be interviewed by the guardian ad litem. The court order appointing the guardian ad litem contains a provision specifically directing all medical practitioners who have treated the child to release the records to the guardian ad litem and to cooperate with him or her.

The guardian ad litem also has the inherent authority to file a motion with the court to require that the alleged offending parent submit to a complete psychological and psychiatric evaluation. If the guardian ad litem has been effective in obtaining a medical release from the alleged offending parent, he or she should use that release to obtain the medical records, and then should supply those records to the evaluating psychologist and psychiatrist prior to the evaluation. It can also be very effective if the guardian ad litem schedules a preevaluation conference with the psychiatrist and psychologist to apprise them of any facts gleaned during the interview process or the guardian's investigation. Often these facts can be very helpful to the evaluating mental health practitioners in getting to the heart of the matter during the relatively brief evaluation process. The psychological and psychiatric evaluations are extremely helpful tools for the guardian ad litem: He or she can use them to gain an understanding of what has led to the abuse allegations, to assess the potential for perpetrator rehabilitation, and to determine whether reunification of the alleged perpetrator with the child-victim is appropriate and, if so, under what circumstances.

When conducting interviews of treating physicians, the guardian ad litem should pay particular attention to the child's primary treating pediatrician. This aspect of the guardian ad litem's investigation takes on added significance if there has been a tendency on the part of the parent to change pediatricians repeatedly. As has been noted elsewhere in this volume, the tendency of a parent to change the child's doctors frequently can be one of the indications of a Munchausen by proxy problem.

Although the guardian ad litem should cooperate at all times with counsel for the Department of Health and Rehabilitative Services and, where appropriate, with the prosecutor, this cooperation must by necessity be limited, owing to the underlying mandate of the guardian ad litem to protect the interest of the child. The interest of the child can often be protected to maximum degree through open communication among all parties and the guardian ad litem. However, the guardian ad litem should be prepared to protect and preserve confidences when this serves the interest of his or her client. Although such a statement seems axiomatic, the guardian ad litem should be aware that some prosecutors, in their zeal to obtain a conviction, are willing to overlook or ignore the best interest of the child. In addition, the guardian ad litem must be prepared to enlighten and educate the judge assigned to the case if he or she is unfamiliar with this particular syndrome. Because I have been assigned to several of these cases, I have developed a significant library of articles and various publications describing this particular mental illness, and I routinely photocopy these articles and send them to the presiding judge to make sure the court is fully apprised of current developments.

Because most dependency actions (in Florida as well as in many other states) operate with the long-term goal of reuniting the child with the parent, the guardian ad litem in a Munchausen by proxy syndrome case must always be sensitive to that fact. Therefore, one of the threshold issues the guardian ad litem must address in an MBPS case concerns whether or not reunification is an appropriate long-range goal. The family interviews and mental health evaluations of the alleged perpetrator are most critical to the guardian in reaching this determination; as indicated above, it is best if the needed interviews can be carried out in informal settings, as unrecorded discussions. This is not to imply that depositions and other formal discovery methods should not be employed with any parties who are otherwise unwilling or unable to cooperate. For instance, in one case in which I acted as guardian ad litem, the mother was accused of administering syrup of ipecac to her baby in order to induce illness. All efforts on my part to address the case informally and to act as a mediator were resisted. However, as I developed the case more fully, I discovered that the mother involved had previously lost a baby under circumstances chillingly similar to those found in the case I was handling. The authorities subsequently exhumed the body of this baby and discovered significant traces of syrup of ipecac. The mother was indicted and pled guilty to the murder of that child. It is important that the guardian ad litem be willing to explore alternatives in obtaining access to needed information in a Munchausen by proxy case. The guardian ad litem's client cannot afford for the guardian to be timid in seeking out the truth about the fundamental underlying issues.

Owing to the guardian ad litem's unique role, he or she is often in a position to act somewhat in the role of mediator. As advocate of the child's position, the guardian ad litem can seek the middle ground between state agencies and the embattled parent. For the same reason, the guardian's recommendations tend to carry great weight with the court. The role of mediator can be especially important during the adjudicatory or trial phase of the case, when the state is required to present evidence to the court that the child is neglected or abused as defined by the statute and therefore "dependent" on the protection of the court. It is this stage of the proceedings that historically is the most acrimonious, and in which the state and the accused parent find themselves at opposite ends of the spectrum.

In a Munchausen by proxy case, the nature of the allegations implies that the offending parent suffers from a mental illness. As this kind of case does in fact deal with allegations of mental illness, the guardian ad litem can often use the knowledge and insight he or she has gained in conducting the investigation to craft a compromise settlement during the adjudicatory phase of the proceedings. Historically, in such a compromise settlement the parent acknowledges that there is a problem and agrees to a plan to seek mental health treatment for the problem. The threshold issue that must be addressed in the attempt to reach a compromise settlement is the offending parent's willingness to acknowledge the existence of a mental health problem.[2] In the absence of such an acknowledgment, no plan devised by a guardian ad litem, even with the best psychological and psychiatric guidance, will be effective. Even under the best of circumstances, therapy solutions are often unclear and difficult to craft. The guardian ad litem should not hesitate to discuss a proposed treatment plan with the evaluating professionals (both psychiatrist and psychologist can be helpful).

The case plan designed by a guardian ad litem in a Munchausen by proxy case should be put into effect only with a concurrence of the evaluating mental health professionals. Offending parents in these cases are historically among the most clever of child abusers, and their long-term prognoses are among the least viable. Because the Munchausen by proxy perpetrator is so cunning, the guardian ad litem must be extremely sensitive to the fact that some parents may be accused of being Munchausen by proxy abusers when in fact they are only caring parents. In the absence of clear and convincing proof, the above-outlined investigative methodology can be extremely helpful to the guardian ad litem in making his or her own determination as to the validity of the allegations. It should be noted that clear and convincing proof is less often available in cases involving fabrication or exaggeration than in cases in which symptoms have been induced. (As mentioned earlier, however, the guardian ad litem should be aware that cases of the former type still represent significant potential for harm to the child.)

The same tools will assist the guardian ad litem in that rare case in which the best interest of the child mandates an attempt to terminate the parental rights of the offending parent. Because the attempt to sever a mother's rights in relation to her child is such an extreme measure, it should be undertaken only in those cases where there does not appear to be any other method available to ensure the safety of the child. In the one Munchausen by proxy case in which I moved for severance, it was clear that the offending parent suffered from a sufficiently severe mental illness that none of the recommended therapies or treatments would ever ensure the safety of my client. Another factor, of course, is the parent's willingness to take the steps necessary to solve the problem. It is not unusual in an MBPS case to have a "you can lead a horse to water" type of situation. In those instances in which a parent refuses to undergo therapy and treatment, or, in the alternative, where no treatment is going to be effective to ensure the safety of the child, the guardian ad litem must consider requesting termination of the perpetrator's parental rights. The guardian ad litem is uniquely positioned in this instance to move forward with a request for termination, even if state agencies have made no such request.

Because of the inherent nature of a Munchausen by proxy case, it is clearly incumbent upon the guardian ad litem to take a much more proactive role than would normally be expected in a guardianship case. Munchausen by proxy cases are far more complex and difficult than are typical abuse or neglect cases. MBPS cases are harder to prove and more difficult for most people to understand, and the severity of Munchausen by proxy syndrome runs the gamut from mild to extreme. The judgment calls that the guardian ad litem must make are often some of the most difficult he or she will ever face as a lawyer; they can seldom be made with the confidence and the certainty that each of us would like to have when dealing with a client's very life. The guardian ad litem must keep in mind that in all but the most extreme cases, the law mandates that the child eventually be returned to the offending parent, and it is the guardian's responsibility to see to it that this return takes place under the best possible circumstances.

## Notes

1. In conducting a database search for material on Munchausen by proxy syndrome, one needs to be sure to use the phrase *by proxy,* as in one or all of the following terms: *Munchausen by proxy syndrome, Munchausen syndrome by proxy, Munchausen by proxy,* and *factitious disorder by proxy.* Otherwise, one will obtain references for Munchausen syndrome and factitious disorder, disorders in which the person fabricates and/or induces symptoms of illness in him- or herself rather than in the child. These issues are discussed by Parnell in Chapter 2 of this book.

2. *Editors' note:* As Parnell discusses in Chapter 5 of this book, we feel strongly that the acknowledgment must specifically identify the Munchausen by proxy abuse behaviors, if not the diagnostic label. Otherwise, the mother-perpetrator may agree that she has a mental health problem and seek treatment, but without ever agreeing to address the main concerns for the child-victim's welfare.

# References

Abe, K., Shinozima, K., Okuno, A., Abe, T., & Ochi, H. (1984). Munchausen's syndrome in children: Bizarre childhood and laboratory features. *Acta Paediatrica Japan, 26,* 539-543.

Ainsworth, M. D. S. (1985). Patterns of infant-mother attachment: Antecedents and effects on development. *Bulletin of the New York Academy of Sciences, 61,* 771-791.

Alexander, R., Smith, W., & Stevenson, R. (1990). Serial Munchausen syndrome by proxy. *Pediatrics, 86,* 581-585.

American Psychiatric Association. (1980). *Diagnostic and statistical manual of mental disorders* (3rd ed.). Washington, DC: Author.

American Psychiatric Association. (1987). *Diagnostic and statistical manual of mental disorders* (3rd ed., rev.). Washington, DC: Author.

American Psychiatric Association. (1994). *Diagnostic and statistical manual of mental disorders* (4th ed.). Washington, DC: Author.

Ammann, R. (1991). *Healing and transformation in sandplay: Creative processes become visible.* La Salle, IL: Open Court.

Asher, R. (1951). Munchausen's syndrome. *Lancet, 1,* 339-341.

Atoynatan, T. H., O'Reilly, E., & Loin, L. (1988). Munchausen syndrome by proxy. *Child Psychiatry and Human Development, 19,* 3-13.

Baldwin, M. A. (1994). Munchausen by proxy: Neurological manifestations. *Journal of Neuroscience Nursing, 26*(1), 18-23.

Barker, J. C. (1962). The syndrome of hospital addiction: A report on the investigation of seven cases. *Journal of Mental Science, 108,* 167-182.

Bath, A. P., Murty, G. E., & Gibbin, K. P. (1993). Munchausen syndrome by proxy: Otolaryngologists beware! *Journal of Laryngology and Otology, 107*(2), 151-152.

Benedek, E., & Schetky, D. (1985). Allegations of sexual abuse in child custody and visitation disputes. In D. Schetky & E. Benedek (Eds.), *Emerging issues in child psychiatry and the law.* New York: Brunner/Mazel.

Berkner, P., Kastner, T., & Skolnick, L. (1988). Chronic ipecac poisoning in infancy: A case report. *Pediatrics, 82,* 384-386.

Black, D. (1981). The extended Munchausen syndrome: A family case. *British Journal of Psychiatry, 138,* 466-469.

Blix, S., & Brack, G. (1988). The effects of a suspected case of Munchausen's syndrome by proxy on a pediatric nursing staff. *General Hospital Psychiatry, 10*, 402-409.

Bools, C. N., Neale, B. A., & Meadow, S. R. (1992). Co-morbidity associated with fabricated illness (Munchausen syndrome by proxy). *Archives of Disease in Childhood, 67*, 77-79.

Bools, C. N., Neale, B. A., & Meadow, S. R. (1993). Follow-up of victims of fabricated illness (Munchausen syndrome by proxy). *Archives of Disease in Childhood, 69*, 625-630.

Bools, C. N., Neale, B. A., & Meadow, S. R. (1994). Munchausen syndrome by proxy: A study of psychopathology. *Child Abuse & Neglect, 18*, 773-788.

Boros, S. J., & Brubaker, L. C. (1992). Munchausen syndrome by proxy case accounts. *FBI Law Enforcement Bulletin, 61*(6), 16-20.

Bourchier, D. (1983). Bleeding ears: Case report of Munchausen syndrome by proxy. *Australian Paediatric Journal, 19*, 256-257.

Bowlby, J. (1988). *A secure base: Parent-child attachment and healthy human development.* New York: Basic Books.

Briere, J. N. (1989). *Therapy for adults molested as children: Beyond survival.* New York: Springer.

Briere, J. N. (1992). *Child abuse trauma: Theory and treatment of the lasting effects.* Newbury Park, CA: Sage.

Bussey, K., Lee, K., & Grimbeek, E. J. (1993). Lies and secrets: Implications for children's reporting of sexual abuse. In B. Goodman & B. Bottoms (Eds.), *Child victims, child witnesses: Understanding and improving testimony* (pp. 147-168). New York: Guilford.

Butler, M. (1985). Guidelines for feminist therapy. In L. B. Rosewater & L. E. A. Walker (Eds.), *Handbook of feminist therapy: Women's issues in psychotherapy* (pp. 32-38). New York: Springer.

Byard, R. W., & Burnell, R. H. (1994). Covert video surveillance in Munchausen syndrome by proxy: Ethical compromise or essential technique? *The Medical Journal of Australia, 160*, 352-356.

Carrell, S. (1984, March). Texas nurse found guilty of killing child. *American Medical News*, pp. 1-27.

Chan, D. A., Salcedo, J. R., Atkins, D. M., & Ruley, E. J. (1986). Munchausen syndrome by proxy: A review and case study. *Journal of Pediatric Psychology, 11*(1), 71-80.

Clarke, E., & Melnick, S. C. (1958). The Munchausen syndrome or the problem of hospital hoboes. *American Journal of Medicine, 25*, 6-12.

Commonwealth v. Robinson, 565 N.E.2d 1229 (Mass. Ct. App. 1991).

Courtois, C. (1988). *Healing the incest wound: Adult survivors in therapy.* New York: W. W. Norton.

Courtois, C. (1991, Fall). Theory, sequencing and strategy in treating adult survivors. *New Directions for Mental Health Services, 51*, 47-59.

Croft, R. D., & Jervis, M. (1989). Munchausen's syndrome in a 4-year-old. *Archives of Disease in Childhood, 63*, 740-741.

Crouse, K. A. (1992). Munchausen syndrome by proxy: Recognizing the victim. *Pediatric Nursing, 18*, 249-252.

Darbyshire, P. (1986, February). Licensed to kill? *Nursing Times, 12,* 22-25.

Davies, N. (1993). *Murder on Ward Four.* London: Chatto & Windus.

Day, D. O. (1994, August). Long-term therapy with the Munchausen mother. In T. F. Parnell (Chair), *Munchausen by proxy syndrome: Advances in diagnosis, treatment, and legal management.* Symposium conducted at the 102nd Annual Meeting of the American Psychological Association, Los Angeles.

Dine, M. S., & McGovern, M. E. (1982). Intentional poisoning of children—an overlooked category of child abuse: Report of seven cases and review of literature. *Pediatrics, 70,* 32-35.

Egginton, J. (1990). *From cradle to grave: The short lives and strange deaths of Marybeth Tinnings's nine children.* New York: Jove.

Eisendrath, S. J. (1989). Factitious physical disorders: Treatment without confrontation. *Psychosomatics, 30,* 383-387.

Ekstein, R., & Caruth, E. (1972). *Keeping secrets in tactics and techniques in psychoanalytic therapy.* New York: Science House.

Elkind, P. (1989). *The death shift: The true story of nurse Genene Jones and the Texas baby murders.* New York: Viking Penguin.

Emery, J. (1993). Child abuse, sudden infant death syndrome, and unexpected infant death. *American Journal of Diseases of Children, 147,* 1097-1100.

Emery, J. E., Gilbert, E., & Zugibe, F. (1988). Three crib deaths, a babyminder and probable infanticide. *Medicine, Science and Law, 28,* 205-211.

Eminson, D. M., & Postlethwaite, R. J. (1992). Factitious illness: Recognition and management. *Archives of Disease in Childhood, 67,* 1510-1516.

Epstein, M. A., Markowitz, R. L., Gallo, D. M., Holmes, J. W., & Gryboski, J. D. (1987). Munchausen syndrome by proxy: Considerations in diagnosis and confirmation by video surveillance. *Pediatrics, 80,* 220-224.

Erickson, W. D., Luxenburg, M. G., Walbek, N. H., & Seely, R. K. (1987). Frequency of MMPI two point code types among sex offenders. *Journal of Consulting and Clinical Psychology, 55,* 566-570.

Feldman, M. (1994). Denial in Munchausen syndrome by proxy: The consulting psychiatrist's dilemma. *International Journal of Medicine, 24*(2), 121-128.

Feldman, M. D., Ford, C. V., & Reinhold, T. (1994). *Patient or pretender: Inside the strange world of factitious disorders.* New York: John Wiley.

Fessler v. State Department of Human Resources, 567 So.3d 301 (Ala. Civ. App. 1989).

Fiatal, R. A. (1989). Lights, camera, action: Video surveillance and the Fourth Amendment (Part 1). *FBI Law Enforcement Bulletin, 58*(1), 23-30.

Finkelhor, D. (1984). *Child sexual abuse: New theory and research.* New York: Free Press.

Fisher, G. C., Mitchell, I., & Murdoch, D. (1993). Munchausen's syndrome by proxy: The question of psychiatric illness in a child. *British Journal of Psychiatry, 162,* 701-703.

Folks, D., & Freeman, A. (1985). Munchausen's syndrome and other factitious illness. *Psychiatric Clinics of North America, 8,* 263-278.

Ford, C. V., King, B. H., & Hollender, M. H. (1988). Lies and liars: Psychiatric aspects of prevarication. *American Journal of Psychiatry, 14,* 554-562.

Foreman, D. M., & Farsides, C. (1993). Ethical use of covert videoing techniques in detecting Munchausen syndrome by proxy. *British Medical Journal, 307,* 611-613.

Frederick, V., Luedtke, G. S., Barrett, F. F., Hixson, S. D., & Burch, K. (1990). Munchausen syndrome by proxy: Recurrent central catheter sepsis. *Pediatric Infectious Disease Journal, 9,* 440-442.

Friedrich, W. N. (1988). Child abuse and sexual abuse. In R. L. Greene (Ed.), *The MMPI: Use with specific populations* (pp. 246-258). Philadelphia: Grune & Stratton.

Frost, J. D., Jr., Glaze, D. G., & Rosen, C. L. (1988). Munchausen's syndrome by proxy and video surveillance [Letter]. *American Journal of Diseases of Children, 142,* 917-918.

Geberth, V. J. (1994). Munchausen syndrome by proxy (MSBP): An investigative perspective. *Law and Order, 42*(8), 95-97.

Geelhoed, G. C., & Pemberton, P. J. (1985). SIDS, seizures or 'sophageal reflux? *The Medical Journal of Australia, 143,* 357-358.

Gilbert, L. A. (1980). Feminist therapy. In A. M. Brodsky & R. Hare-Mustin (Eds.), *Women and therapy: Assessment, research, and practice.* New York: Guilford.

Gilbert, R. W., Pierse, P. M., & Mitchell, D. P. (1987). Cryptic otalgia: A case of Munchausen syndrome in a pediatric patient. *Journal of Otolaryngology, 16,* 231-233.

Godding, V., & Kruth, M. (1991). Compliance with treatment in asthma and Munchausen syndrome by proxy. *Archives of Disease in Childhood, 66,* 956-960.

Goodwin J. (1982). *Sexual abuse: Incest victims and their families.* Boston: John Wright-PSG.

Goodwin, J., Sahd, D., & Rada, R. (1978). Incest hoax: False accusations, false denials. *Bulletin of the American Academy of Psychiatry and Law, 6,* 269-276.

Goss, P. M., & McDougall, P. N. (1992). Munchausen syndrome by proxy: A cause of preterm delivery. *The Medical Journal of Australia, 157,* 814-817.

Grace, A., Kalinkiewicz, M., & Drake-Lee, A. B. (1984). Covert manifestations of child abuse. *British Medical Journal, 289,* 1041-1042.

Green, A. H., & Schetky, D. H. (1988). True and false allegations of child sexual abuse. In D. H. Schetky & A. H. Green (Eds.), *Child sexual abuse: A handbook for health care and legal professionals* (pp. 104-124). New York: Brunner/ Mazel.

Green, M., & Solnit, A. J. (1964). Reactions to the threatened loss of a child: A vulnerable child syndrome. *Pediatrics, 34,* 58-66.

Griffith, J. L. (1988). The family systems of Munchausen syndrome by proxy. *Family Process, 27,* 423-437.

Griffith, J. L., & Slovik, L. S. (1989). Munchausen syndrome by proxy and sleep disorders medicine. *Sleep, 12,* 178-183.

Guandolo, V. L. (1985). Munchausen syndrome by proxy: An outpatient challenge. *Pediatrics, 75,* 526-530.

Guyer, M., & Ash, P. (1986). *Child abuse allegations in the context of adversial divorce.* Paper presented at the annual meeting of the American Academy of Psychiatry and the Law, Los Angeles.

Hall, G. C. N., Maiuro, R. D., Vitaliano, P. P., & Proctor, W. D. (1986). The utility of the MMPI with men who have sexually assaulted children. *Journal of Consulting and Clinical Psychology, 54,* 493-496.

Halsey, N. A., Tucker, T. W., Redding, J., Frentz, J. M., Sproles, T., & Daum, R. S. (1983). Recurrent nosocomial polymicrobial sepsis secondary to child abuse. *Lancet, 2,* 558-560.

Hanon, K. (1991). Child abuse: Munchausen syndrome by proxy. *FBI Law Enforcement Bulletin, 60*(12), 8-11.

Hathaway, S. R., & McKinley, T. C. (1983). *Minnesota Multiphasic Personality Inventory: Manual.* New York: Psychological Corporation.

Herman-Giddens, M. E., & Berson, N. L. (1989). Harmful genital care practices in children: A type of child abuse. *Journal of the American Medical Association, 261,* 577-579.

Hersen, M., Kazdin, A., & Bellack, A. (Eds.). (1983). *The clinical psychology handbook.* New York: Pergamon.

Hochhauser, K. G., & Richardson, R. A. (1994). Munchausen syndrome by proxy: An exploratory study of pediatric nurses' knowledge and involvement. *Journal of Pediatric Nursing, 9,* 313-320.

Hodge, D., Schwartz, W., Sargent, J., Bodurtha, J., & Starr, S. (1982). The bacteriologically battered baby: Another case of Munchausen by proxy. *Annals of Emergency Medicine, 11,* 205-207.

Holt, J. (1975). *Escape from childhood: The needs and rights of children.* New York: Ballantine.

Hosch, I. A. (1987). Munchausen syndrome by proxy. *MCN: American Journal of Maternal Child Nursing, 12,* 48-52.

Hvizdala, E. V., & Gellady, A. M. (1978). Intentional poisoning of two siblings by prescription drugs: An unusual form of child abuse. *Clinical Pediatrics, 17,* 480-482.

Hyler, S. E., & Sussman, N. (1981). Chronic fictitious disorder with physical symptoms (the Munchausen syndrome). *Psychiatric Clinics of North America, 4,* 365-376.

Hyman, P. E., DiLorenzo, C., Beck, D., Hamilton, A. B., & Zelter, L. K. (1994). Munchausen's syndrome-by-proxy (MBP) and chronic intestinal pseudo-obstruction (CIP): Overlapping phenotypes [Abstract]. *Journal of Pediatric Gastroenterology and Nutrition, 19,* 332.

Ifere, O. A., Yakubu, A. M., Aikhionbare, H. A., Quaitey, G. E., & Taqi, A. M. (1993). Munchausen syndrome by proxy: An experience from Nigeria. *Annual of Tropical Paediatrics, 13,* 281-284.

In re Colin R., 493 A.2d 1083 (Md. Ct. App. 1985).

In re S.R., 599 A.2d 364 (Vt. 1991).

In the Interest of B.B., 500 N.W.2d 9 (No. 155, 91-1610) (Iowa 1993).

In the Interest of M.A.V., 425 S.E.2d 377 (Ga. Ct. App. 1992).

In the Matter of Jessica Z., 135 Misc.2d 520, 515 N.Y.S.2d 370 (No. 7309, N-86) (N.Y. Fam. Ct., Jan. 27, 1987).

In the Matter of Tucker, 578 N.E.2d 774 (Ind. 1991).

Jani, S., White, M., Rosenberg, L. A., & Maisami, M. (1992). Munchausen syndrome by proxy. *International Journal of Psychiatry in Medicine, 22,* 343-349.

Janofsky, J. S. (1986). Munchausen syndrome in a mother and daughter: An unusual presentation of folie à deux. *The Journal of Nervous and Mental Disease, 174,* 368-370.

Jones, D. P. H. (1987). The untreatable family. *Child Abuse & Neglect, 11,* 409-420.

Jones, D. P. H., & McGraw, J. M. (1987). Reliable and factitious accounts of sexual abuse to children. *Journal of Interpersonal Violence, 2,* 27-45.

Jones, J. G., Butler, H. L., Hamilton, B., Perdue, J. D., Stern, H. P., & Woody, R. C. (1986). Munchausen syndrome by proxy. *Child Abuse & Neglect, 10,* 33-40.

Jones, V. F., Badgett, T. J., Minella, J. L., & Schuschke, L. A. (1993). The role of the male caretaker in Munchausen syndrome by proxy. *Clinical Pediatrics, 32,* 245-247.

Jureidini, J. (1993). Obstetric factitious disorder and Munchausen syndrome by proxy. *The Journal of Nervous and Mental Disease, 181,* 135-137.

Kahan, B. B., & Yorker, B. C. (1990). Munchausen syndrome by proxy. *Journal of School Health, 60*(3), 108-110.

Kahan, B. B., & Yorker, B. C. (1991). Munchausen syndrome by proxy: Clinical review and legal issues. *Behavioral Sciences and the Law, 9*(1), 73-83.

Kalichman, S. C. (1993). *Mandated reporting of suspected child abuse: Ethics, law, and policy.* Washington, DC: American Psychological Association.

Karpel, M., & Strauss, E. (1983). *Family evaluation.* New York: Gardner.

Katz, R. L., Mazer, C., & Litt, I. F. (1985). Anorexia nervosa by proxy. *The Journal of Pediatrics, 107,* 247-248.

Kaufman, K. L., Coury, D., Pickrel, E., & McCleery, J. (1989). Munchausen syndrome by proxy: A survey of professionals' knowledge. *Child Abuse & Neglect, 13,* 141-147.

Kellerman, J. (1993). *Devil's waltz.* New York: Bantam.

Kempe, C. H. (1975). Uncommon manifestations of the battered child syndrome. *American Journal of Diseases of Children, 129,* 1265.

Kempe, C. H., Silverman, F. N., Steele, B. F., Droegemueller, W., & Silver, H. K. (1962). The battered-child syndrome. *Journal of the American Medical Association, 181,* 17-24.

Kernberg, O. F. (Ed.). (1989). Narcissistic personality disorder. *Psychiatric Clinics of North America, 12,* 553-570.

Kernberg, O. F., Selzer, M. A., Koenigsberg, H. W., Carr, A. C., & Appelbaum, A. H. (1989). *Psychodynamic psychotherapy of borderline patients.* New York: Basic Books.

Kim, D. S. (1986). How physicians respond to child maltreatment cases. *Health and Social Work, 11,* 95-106.

Kinscherff, R., & Famularo, R. (1991). Extreme Munchausen syndrome by proxy: The case for termination of parental rights. *Juvenile and Family Court Journal, 40,* 41-53.

Knoff, H. M. (Ed.). (1986). *The assessment of child and adolescent personality.* New York: Guilford.

Kohl, S., Pickering, L. K., & Dupree, E. (1978). Child abuse presenting as immunodeficiency disease. *The Journal of Pediatrics, 93,* 466-468.

Kohut, H., & Wolf, E. (1978). The disorders of the self and their treatment: An outline. *International Journal of Psychoanalysis, 59,* 413-425.

Kovacs, C., & Toth, E. (1993). Factitious diabetes mellitus and spontaneous hypoglycemia. *Diabetes Care, 16,* 1294-1295.

Kratochwill, T., & Morris, R. (Eds.). (1991). *The practice of child therapy* (2nd ed.). New York: Pergamon.

Krener, P. (1994). Factitious disorders and the psychosomatic continuum in children. *Current Opinions in Pediatrics, 6,* 418-422.

Lacey, S. R., Cooper, C., Runyan, D. K., & Azizkhan, R. G. (1993). Munchausen syndrome by proxy: Patterns of presentation to pediatric surgeons. *Journal of Pediatric Surgery, 28,* 827-832.

Lansky, S. B., & Erickson, H. M., Jr. (1974). Prevention of child murder. *Journal of American Academy of Child Psychiatry, 13,* 691.

Lee, D. A. (1979). Munchausen syndrome by proxy in twins. *Archives of Disease in Childhood, 54,* 646-647.

Leeder, E. (1990). Supermom or child abuser? Treatment of the Munchausen mother. *Women and Therapy, 9*(4), 69-88.

Leonard, K. F., & Farrell, P. A. (1992). Münchausen's syndrome by proxy: A little-known type of abuse. *Postgraduate Medicine, 91*(5), 197-204.

Lerman, H. G. (1986, August). *Women in context: Contributions of feminist therapy.* Workshop presented at the 94th Annual Meeting of the American Psychological Association, Washington, DC.

Lerner, H. G. (1983). Female dependency in context: Some theoretical and technical considerations. *American Journal of Orthopsychiatry, 53,* 697-705.

Lerner, H. G. (1993). *The dance of deception.* New York: HarperCollins.

Levin, S. M., & Stava, L. (1987). Personality characteristics of sex offenders: A review. *Archives of Sexual Behavior, 16,* 57-59.

Libow, J. A. (1994, August). Munchausen by proxy victims in later life. In T. F. Parnell (Chair), *Munchausen by proxy syndrome: Advances in diagnosis, treatment, and legal management.* Symposium conducted at the 102nd Annual Meeting of the American Psychological Association, Los Angeles.

Libow, J. A., & Schreier, H. A. (1986). Three forms of factitious illness in children: When is it Munchausen syndrome by proxy? *American Journal of Orthopsychiatry, 56,* 602-611.

Light, M. J., & Sheridan, M. S. (1990). Munchausen syndrome by proxy and apnea (MBPA): A survey of apnea programs. *Clinical Pediatrics, 29,* 162-168.

Lim, L. C. C., Yap, H. K., & Lim, J. W. (1991). Munchausen syndrome by proxy. *Journal of Singapore Paediatric Society, 33*(1-2), 59-62.

Liston, T. E., Levine, P. L., & Anderson, C. (1983). Polymicrobial bacteremia due to Polle syndrome: The child abuse variant of Munchausen by proxy. *Pediatrics, 72,* 211-213.

Loftus, E. (1993). The reality of repressed memory. *American Psychologist, 48,* 518-537.

Lorber, J., Reckless, J. P. D., & Watson, J. B. G. (1980). Non-accidental poisoning, the elusive diagnosis. *Archives of Disease in Childhood, 55,* 643-646.

Love, P., with Robinson, J. (1990). *The emotional incest syndrome: What to do when a parent's love rules your life.* New York: Bantam.

Lyall, E. G., Stirling, H. F., Crofton, P. M., & Kelnar, C. J. (1992). Albuminuric growth failure. A case of Munchausen syndrome by proxy. *Acta Paediatrica, 81,* 373-376.

Main, D. J., Douglas, J. E., & Tamanika, H. N. (1986). Munchausen's syndrome by proxy. *The Medical Journal of Australia, 145,* 300-301.

Makar, A. F., & Squier, P. J. (1990). Munchausen syndrome by proxy: Father as a perpetrator. *Pediatrics, 85,* 370-373.

Manthei, D. J., Pierce, R. L., Rothbaum, R. J., Manthei, U., & Keating, J. P. (1988). Munchausen syndrome by proxy: Covert child abuse. *Journal of Family Violence, 3,* 131-140.

Masterson, J. (1981). *Narcissistic and borderline disorders.* New York: Brunner/ Mazel.

Masterson, J. F., & Wilson, J. (1987). Factitious illness in children: The social worker's role in identification and management. *Social Work in Health Care, 12*(4), 21-30.

Mayo, J. P., & Haggerty, J. J. (1984). Long-term psychotherapy of Munchausen syndrome. *American Journal of Psychotherapy, 38,* 571-578.

McCoid, A. H. (1965). The battered child and other assaults upon the family: Part one. *Minnesota Law Review, 50,* 1-58.

McCreary, C. P. (1975). Personality differences among child molesters. *The Journal of Personality Assessment, 39,* 591-593.

McGuire, T. L., & Feldman, K. W. (1989). Psychological morbidity of children subjected to Munchausen syndrome by proxy. *Pediatrics, 83,* 289-292.

Meadow, R. (1977). Munchausen syndrome by proxy: The hinterland of child abuse. *Lancet, 2,* 343-345.

Meadow, R. (1982a). Munchausen syndrome by proxy. *Archives of Disease in Childhood, 57,* 92-98.

Meadow, R. (1982b). Munchausen syndrome by proxy and pseudo-epilepsy. *Archives of Disease in Childhood, 57,* 811-812.

Meadow, R. (1984). Fictitious epilepsy. *Lancet, 2,* 25-28.

Meadow, R. (1985). Management of Munchausen syndrome by proxy. *Archives of Disease in Childhood, 60,* 385-393.

Meadow, R. (1990a). [Letter to the editor]. *Child Abuse & Neglect, 14,* 289-290.

Meadow, R. (1990b). Suffocation, recurrent apnea, and sudden infant death. *The Journal of Pediatrics, 117,* 351-357.

Meadow, R. (1993a). False allegations of abuse and Munchausen syndrome by proxy. *Archives of Disease in Childhood, 68,* 444-447.

Meadow, R. (1993b). Non-accidental salt poisoning. *Archives of Disease in Childhood, 68,* 448-452.

Meadow, R. (1994). Who's to blame—mothers, Munchausen or medicine? *Journal of the Royal College of Physicians of London, 28,* 332-337.

Meadow, R., & Lennert, T. (1984). Munchausen by proxy or Polle syndrome: Which term is correct? *Pediatrics, 74,* 554-556.

Meichenbaum, D. (1992). Evolution of cognitive behavior therapy. Origins, tenets and clinical examples. In J. Zeig (Ed.), *The evolution of psychotherapy* (Vol. 2, pp. 114-122). New York: Brunner/Mazel.

Mercer, S., & Perdue, J. (1993). Munchausen syndrome by proxy: Social work's role. *Journal of the National Association of Social Workers, 38*(1), 74-81.

Mills, R. W., & Burke, S. (1990). Gastrointestinal bleeding in a 15-month-old male: A presentation of Munchausen's syndrome by proxy. *Clinical Pediatrics, 29,* 474-477.

Milner, J. S., & Chilamkurti, C. (1991). Physical abuse perpetrator characteristics: A review of the literature. *Journal of Interpersonal Violence, 6,* 345-366.

Mitchell, I., Brummitt, J., DeForest, J., & Fisher, G. (1993). Apnea and factitious illness (Munchausen syndrome) by proxy. *Pediatrics, 92,* 810-814.

Mitchels, B. (1983a). Munchausen syndrome by proxy: Protecting the child. *Journal of the Forensic Science Society, 23,* 105-111.

Mitchels, B. (1983b). Munchausen syndrome by proxy: Protection or correction? *New Law Journal, 164*(5), 133, 165-168.

Money, J., & Werlwas, J. (1976). Folie a deux in the parents of psychosocial dwarfs: Two cases. *Bulletin of the American Academy of Psychiatry and the Law, 4,* 351-362.

Morris, B. (1985). Child abuse manifested as factitious apnea. *Southern Medical Journal, 78,* 1013-1014.

Mortimer, J. G. (1980). Acute water intoxication as another unusual manifestation of child abuse. *Archives of Disease in Childhood, 55,* 401-403.

Murphy, W. D., & Peters, J. M. (1992). Profiling child sexual abusers: Psychological considerations. *Criminal Justice and Behavior, 19,* 24-37.

Murphy, W. D., Rau, T. J., & Worley, P. J. (1994). Offender treatment: The perils and pitfalls of profiling child sex abusers. *APSAC Advisor, 7*(1), 3-4, 28-29.

My sister-in-law was starving her baby. (1991, October). *Good Housekeeping,* pp. 26-29.

Myers, J. E. B. (Ed.). (1994). *The backlash: Child protection under fire.* Thousand Oaks, CA: Sage.

Newman, B., & Newman, P. (1979). *Development through life: A psychosocial approach.* Homewood, IL: Dorsey.

Nicol, A. R., & Eccles, M. (1985). Psychotherapy for Munchausen syndrome by proxy. *Archives of Disease in Childhood, 60,* 344-348.

Oppenoorth, W. H. (1992). Treatment of Munchausen syndrome by proxy with clinical psychiatric family therapy and hypnotherapy: A case description. *Tijdschrift voor psychotherapie, 18*(1), 12-21.

Orenstein, D. M., & Wasserman, A. L. (1986). Munchausen syndrome by proxy simulating cystic fibrosis. *Pediatrics, 78,* 621-624.

Outwater, K. M., Lipnick, R. N., Luban, N. L., Ravenscroft, K., & Ruley, E. J. (1981). Factitious hematuria: Diagnosis by minor blood group typing. *The Journal of Pediatrics, 98,* 95-97.

Palmer, A. J., & Yoshimura, G. J. (1984). Munchausen syndrome by proxy. *Journal of the American Academy of Child Psychiatry, 23*(4), 503-508.

Parnell, T. F., & Day, D. O. (1993, August). *Munchausen syndrome by proxy: Evaluation and treatment.* Workshop presented at the 101st Annual Meeting of the American Psychological Association, Toronto.

People v. Phillips, 122 Cal. App.3d 69, 175 Cal. Rptr. 703 (No. CR 19871) (Cal. Ct. App. July 28, 1981).

People v. Tinning, 536 N.Y.S.2d. (1988).

Peters, J. (1976). Children who are victims of sexual assault and the psychology of offenders. *American Journal of Psychotherapy, 30,* 398-421.

Pfeiffer, S. I. (Ed.). (1985). *Clinical child psychology: An introduction to theory, research and practice.* New York: Grune & Stratton.

Pickford, E., Buchanan, N., & McLaughlan, S. (1988). Munchausen syndrome by proxy: A family anthology. *The Medical Journal of Australia, 148,* 646-650.

Place v. Place, 525 A.2d 704 (N.H. 1987).

Plassman, R. (1994). Munchausen syndromes and factitious diseases. *Psychotherapy and Psychosomatics, 62*(1-2), 7-26.

Pope, H. G., Jonas, J. M., & Jones, B. (1982). Factitious psychosis: Phenomenology, family history, and long-term outcome of nine patients. *American Journal of Psychiatry, 139,* 1480-1483.

Porter, G. E., Heitsch, G. M., & Miller, M. M. (1993). Munchausen syndrome by proxy [Letter to the editor]. *Medical Journal of Australia, 158,* 720.

Porter, G. E., Heitsch, G. M., & Miller, M. D. (1994). Munchausen syndrome by proxy: Unusual manifestations and disturbing sequelae. *Child Abuse & Neglect, 18,* 789-794.

Proesmans, W., Sina, J., Debucquoy, P., Renoirte, M., & Eeckels, R. (1981). Recurrent acute renal failure due to non-accidental poisoning with glafenin in a child. *Clinical Nephrology, 16,* 207-210.

Quinsey, V. L., Arnold, L. S., & Pruesse, M. G. (1980). MMPI profiles on men referred for a pretrial psychiatric assessment as a function of offense type. *Journal of Clinical Psychology, 36,* 410-417.

Rand, D. C. (1989). Munchausen syndrome by proxy as a possible factor when abuse is falsely alleged. *Issues in Child Abuse Accusations, 1*(4), 32-34.

Rand, D. C. (1990). Munchausen syndrome by proxy: Integration of classic and contemporary types. *Issues in Child Abuse Accusations, 2*(2), 83-89.

Rand, D. C. (1993). Munchausen syndrome by proxy: A complex type of emotional abuse responsible for some false allegations of child abuse. In H. Wakefield & R. Underwager (Eds.), *Solomon's dilemma: False allegations in divorce and custody.* Springfield, IL: Charles C Thomas.

Rappaport, S., & Hochstadt, N. J. (1993). Munchausen syndrome by proxy (MSPB): An intergenerational perspective. *Journal of Mental Health Counseling, 15,* 278-289.

Raspe, R. E. (1785). *Singular travels, campaigns, and adventures of Baron Munchausen.* London: Cresset.

Ravenscroft, K., Jr., & Hochheiser, J. (1980, October). *Factitious hematuria in a six-year-old girl: A case example of Munchausen syndrome by proxy.* Paper presented at the annual meeting of the American Academy of Child Psychiatry, Chicago.

Reich, P., Lazarus, M., Kelly, M. J., & Rogers, M. P. (1977). Factitious feculent urine in an adolescent boy. *Journal of the American Medical Association, 238,* 420-421.

Richardson, G. F. (1987). Munchausen syndrome by proxy. *American Family Physician, 36*(1), 119-123.

Richtsmeier, A. J., & Walters, D. B. (1984). Somatic symptoms as a family myth. *American Journal of Diseases of Children, 138,* 855-857.

Robins, P. M., & Sesan, R. (1991). Munchausen syndrome by proxy: Another women's disorder? *Professional Psychology: Research and Practice, 22,* 285-290.

Rogers, D., Tripp, J., Bentovim, A., Robinson, A., Berry D., & Goulding R. (1976). Non-accidental poisoning: An extended syndrome of child abuse. *British Medical Journal, 1,* 793-796.

Rosen, C. L., Frost, J. D., Jr., Bricker, T., Tarnow, J. D., Gillette, P. C., & Dunlavy, S. (1983). Two siblings with recurrent cardiorespiratory arrest: Munchausen syndrome by proxy or child abuse? *Pediatrics, 71,* 715-720.

Rosenberg, D. (1987). Web of deceit: A literature review of Munchausen syndrome by proxy. *Child Abuse & Neglect, 11,* 547-563.

Rosenberg, D. (1994). Munchausen syndrome by proxy. In R. M. Reece (Ed.), *Child abuse—Medical diagnosis and management* (pp. 266-278). Philadelphia: Lea & Febiger.

Roth, D. (1990). How "mild" is mild Munchausen syndrome by proxy? *Israel Journal of Psychiatry and Related Sciences, 27*(3), 160-167.

Rubin, L. G., Angelides, A., Davidson, M., & Lanzkowsky, P. (1986). Recurrent sepsis and gastrointestinal ulceration due to child abuse. *Archives of Disease in Childhood, 61,* 903-905.

Sale, I., & Kalucy, R. (1980). An observation of the genesis of Munchausen syndrome: A case report. *Australia and New Zealand Journal of Psychiatry, 14,* 61-64.

Samuels, M. P., McClaughlin, W., Jacobson, R. R., Poets, C. F., & Southall, D. P. (1992). Fourteen cases of imposed upper airway obstruction. *Archives of Disease in Childhood, 67,* 162-170.

Samuels, M. P., & Southall, D. P. (1992). Munchausen syndrome by proxy. *British Journal of Hospital Medicine, 47,* 759-762.

Sanders, M. J. (1995a, August). A narrative approach to therapy with the Munchausen by proxy syndrome family. In T. F. Parnell (Chair), *Evaluation and treatment of the Munchausen by proxy family system.* Symposium conducted at the 103rd Annual Meeting of the American Psychological Association, New York.

Sanders, M. J. (1995b). Symptom coaching: Factitious disorder by proxy with older children. *Clinical Psychology Review, 15,* 423-442.

Sargeant, G. (1993, June). Mother's medical obsessions endanger child, judge rules. *Trial,* pp. 96-97.

Sattler, J. M. (1992). *Assessment of children* (3rd ed.). New York: Author.

Saulsbury, F. T., Chobanian, M. C., & Wilson, W. G. (1984). Child abuse: Parental hydrocarbon administration. *Pediatrics, 73,* 719-721.

Schaefer, C. E., & O'Connor, K. J. (Eds.). (1983). *Handbook of play therapy.* New York: John Wiley.

Schreier, H. A. (1992). The perversion of mothering: Munchausen syndrome by proxy. *Bulletin of the Menninger Clinic, 56,* 421-437.

Schreier, H. A., & Libow, J. A. (1993a). *Hurting for love: Munchausen by proxy syndrome.* New York: Guilford.

Schreier, H. A., & Libow, J. A. (1993b). Munchausen syndrome by proxy: Diagnosis and prevalence. *American Journal of Orthopsychiatry, 63,* 318-321.

Schreier, H. A., & Libow, J. A. (1994). Munchausen by proxy syndrome: A modern pediatric challenge. *The Journal of Pediatrics, 125*(pt. 2 suppl.), S110-S115.

Scott, R. L., & Stone, D. A. (1986). MMPI profile considerations in incest families. *Journal of Consulting and Clinical Psychology, 54,* 364-368.

Searle, M. (1993). Munchausen syndrome by proxy: A guide for California attorneys. *Western State University Law Review, 20,* 393-426.

Senner, A., & Ott, M. J. (1989). Munchausen syndrome by proxy. *Issues of Comprehensive Pediatric Nursing, 12,* 345-357.

Sgroi, S. (1989). *Vulnerable populations* (Vol. 2). Lexington, MA: Lexington.

Sheridan, M. (1989). Munchausen syndrome by proxy. *Health and Social Work, 14*(1), 53-58.

Sheridan, M. S. (1994). Parents' reporting of symptoms in their children: Physicians' perceptions. *Hawaii Medical Journal, 53,* 216-217, 221-222.

Siegel, P. T. (1990, August). *How to interview a mother suspected of Munchausen syndrome by proxy.* Paper presented at the 98th Annual Meeting of the American Psychological Association, Boston.

Sigal, M. D., Altmark, D., & Carmel, I. (1986). Munchausen syndrome by adult proxy: A perpetrator abusing two adults. *The Journal of Nervous and Mental Disease, 174,* 696-698.

Sigal, M. D., Altmark, D., & Gelkopf, M. (1991). Munchausen syndrome by adult proxy revisited. *Israel Journal of Psychiatry and Related Sciences, 28*(1), 33-36.

Sigal, M. D., Gelkopf, M., & Levertov, G. (1990). Medical and legal aspects of the Munchausen by proxy perpetrator. *Medicine and Law, 9,* 739-749.

Sigal, M. D., Gelkopf, M., & Meadow, S. R. (1989). Munchausen by proxy syndrome: The triad of abuse, self-abuse and deception. *Comprehensive Psychiatry, 30,* 527-533.

Single, T., & Henry, R. L. (1991). An unusual case of Munchausen syndrome by proxy. *Australia and New Zealand Journal of Psychiatry, 25,* 422-425.

Smith, K., & Killam, P. (1994). Munchausen syndrome by proxy. *MCN: American Journal of Maternal Child Nursing, 19,* 214-221.

Smith, N. J., & Ardern, M. H. (1989). More in sickness than in health: A case study of Munchausen syndrome by proxy in the elderly. *Journal of Family Therapy, 11,* 321-334.

Sneed, R. C., & Bell, R. F. (1976). The dauphin of Munchausen: Factitious passage of renal stones in a child. *Pediatrics, 58,* 127-130.

Southall, D. P., & Samuels, M. P. (1993). Ethical use of covert videoing for potentially life threatening child abuse: A response to Drs Foreman and Farsides. *British Medical Journal, 307,* 613-614.

Southall, D. P., Stebbens, V. A., Rees, S. V., Lang, M. H., Warner, J. O., & Shinebourne, E. A. (1987). Apnoeic episodes induced by smothering: Two cases identified by covert video surveillance. *British Medical Journal, 274,* 1637-1641.

Stancin, T. (1990, August). *Educating medical personnel about Munchausen syndrome by proxy.* Paper presented at the 98th Annual Meeting of the American Psychological Association, Boston.

Stankler, L. (1977). Factitious skin lesions in a mother and two sons. *British Medical Journal, 97,* 217-219.

State v. Chorpenning, 291 So.2d 54 (Fla. 2nd DCA 1974).

State v. De Jesus, 93 WL 171866 (No. CR92-73269) (Conn. Super. 1993).

State v. Lumbrera, 845 P.2d 609 (Kans. 1992).

Stevenson, R., & Alexander, R. (1990). Munchausen syndrome by proxy presenting as a developmental disability. *Journal of Developmental and Behavioral Pediatrics, 11,* 262-264.

Stone, F. (1989). Munchausen-by-proxy syndrome: An unusual form of child abuse. *Social work: The Journal of Contemporary Social Work, 70,* 243-246.

Sullivan, C. A., Francis, G. L., Bain, M. W., & Hartz, J. (1991). Munchausen syndrome by proxy: 1990. A portent for problems? *Clinical Pediatrics, 30,* 112-116.

Sussman, N. (1989). *Comprehensive textbook of psychiatry* (5th ed., Vol. 2). Baltimore: Williams & Wilkins.

Sutphen, J. L., & Saulsbury, F. T. (1988). Intentional ipecac poisoning: Munchausen syndrome by proxy. *Pediatrics, 82*(pt. 2), 453-456.

Taylor, S., & Hyler, S. E. (1993). Update on factitious disorders. *International Journal of Psychiatry in Medicine, 23,* 81-94.

Tec, L. (1975). Precursors of Munchausen's syndrome in childhood [Letter to the editor]. *American Journal of Psychiatry, 132,* 757.

Turk, L. J., Hanrahan, K. M., & Weber, E. R. (1990). Munchausen syndrome by proxy: A nursing overview. *Issues in Comprehensive Pediatric Nursing, 13,* 279-288.

Turner, S., Calhoun, K., & Adams, H. (Eds.). (1981). *Handbook of clinical behavior therapy.* New York: John Wiley.

U.S. Department of Health and Human Services. (1988). *Study findings: Study of national incidence and prevalence of child abuse and neglect, 1988.* Bethesda, MD: Westat.

Verity, C. M., Winckworth, C., Burman, D., Stevens, D., & White, R. J. (1979). Polle syndrome: Children of Munchausen. *British Medical Journal, 2,* 422-423.

Waller, D. A. (1983). Obstacles to the treatment of Munchausen by proxy syndrome. *Journal of the American Academy of Child Psychiatry, 22,* 80-85.

Waring, W. W. (1992). The persistent parent. *American Journal of Diseases of Children, 146,* 753-756.

Warner, J. O., & Hathaway, M. J. (1984). Allergic form of Meadow's syndrome (Munchausen by proxy). *Archives of Disease in Childhood, 59,* 151-156.

Wartik, N. (1994, February). Fatal attention. *Redbook,* pp. 62-69.

White, S. T. (1985). Surreptitious warfarin ingestion. *Child Abuse & Neglect, 9,* 349-352.

Whitworth, J. M. (1989). The Florida child protection team system. *APSAC Advisor, 2*(3), 4.

Williams, C. (1986). Munchausen syndrome by proxy: A bizarre form of child abuse. *Family Law, 16,* 32-34.

Williams, C., & Bevan, V. T. (1988). The secret observation of children in hospital. *Lancet, 1,* 780-781.

Wolfe, D. A. (1987). *Child abuse: Implications for child development and psychopathology.* Newbury Park, CA: Sage.

Woollcott, P., Aceto, T., Rutt, C., Bloom, M., & Glick, R. (1982). Doctor shopping with the child as proxy patient: A variant of child abuse. *Journal of Pediatrics, 101,* 297-391.

Yorker, B. C., & Kahan, B. B. (1991). The Munchausen syndrome by proxy variant of child abuse in the family courts. *Journal, Juvenile and Family Court, 42*(3), 51-58.

Yudkin, S. (1961). Six children with coughs: The second diagnosis. *Lancet, 2,* 561-563.

Zitelli, B. J., Seltman, M. F., & Shannon, R. M. (1987). Munchausen's syndrome by proxy and its professional participants. *American Journal of Diseases of Children, 141,* 1099-1102.

Zitelli, B. J., Seltman, M. F., & Shannon, R. M. (1988). Munchausen's syndrome by proxy and video surveillance. *American Journal of Diseases of Children, 142,* 918.

Zohar, Y., Avidan, G., Shvili, Y., & Laurian, N. (1987). Otolaryngologic cases of Munchausen's syndrome. *Laryngoscope, 97,* 201-203.

# Index

295

# About the Authors

**Toni D. Baker** obtained her bachelor of science degree in 1982 with a major in social work and a minor in psychology. She obtained her master of social work degree from Florida State University in 1990. She is currently employed as a Project Coordinator for Arnold Palmer Hospital for Children and Women in Orlando, Florida, where she has previously held positions as Operations Manager for the Psychosocial Grant Programs and as Department Manager for the Child Protection Team. She is also currently an Administrator for Behavioral Health for the Orlando Regional Healthcare System. She has approximately 9 years' experience in the field of child abuse and neglect in several different roles, from investigator to operations manager. In addition, she has a number of years of direct clinical experience with families in which there was suspected child abuse and/or neglect. Through her supervisory role with the Child Protection Team and Arnold Palmer Hospital for Children and Women, she has had the opportunity to develop, with other key hospital personnel, an in-hospital protocol for identifying suspected Munchausen by proxy syndrome cases. She copresented on Munchausen by proxy syndrome at the Fourth European Conference on Child Abuse and Neglect.

**Deborah O. Day** received her doctorate in clinical psychology from Florida Institute of Technology in 1985. She is a licensed psychologist, licensed mental health counselor, certified family mediator, and certified family mediator trainer. She is currently in private practice with Psychological Affiliates, Inc., of Winter Park, Florida. Her specialties include individual psychotherapy and psychological evaluations, and her forensic expertise includes divorce/custody, child abuse issues, battered women, sexual harassment, and trauma. She has testified as an expert in several nationally recognized cases, and has appeared on numerous local television shows; she is also a frequent speaker at national professional meetings. She is the

Consultant/Clinical Supervisor for the Child Protection Team in Florida's Orange, Osceola, and Seminole Counties, and currently serves as Chair of the Psychology Department at Columbia/Winter Park Memorial Hospital. Dr. Day serves on the Judical Nominating Commission for the Florida Supreme Court. She is a member of the Association of Family and Conciliation Courts, for which she serves on the custody subcommittee. She is Cochair of the Mental Health Professionals in Litigation Committee of the Family Section of the Florida Bar, and Chair of the Advisory Board for the Sexual Abuse Treatment Program. She is a member of the American Psychological Association, the Florida Psychological Association, the Southeastern Psychological Association, the Florida Association of Professional Family Mediators, and the National Association of Counsel for Children.

**Ralph V. Hadley III** is an attorney in private practice in Winter Park, Florida. He graduated from the University of Florida with a bachelor's degree in 1965 and a juris doctor in law in 1968. He has been admitted to the bar (Florida and California) for more than 27 years. Although his practice is concentrated in the commercial and banking field, he has undertaken the representation of abused and neglected children on a pro bono basis for the past 15 years. During that time, he has represented more than 50 children who were alleged by the Florida Department of Health and Rehabilitative Services to be abused or neglected; 5 of these cases have involved Munchausen by proxy syndrome. In recognition of his pro bono representation of children, he received the Legal Aid Society Award of Merit from the Orange County Legal Aid Society in 1987 and the "Judge J. C. 'Jake' Stone" Legal Aid Society Distinguished Service Award in 1989; he was also the recipient of the Florida Bar President's Pro Bono Service Award in 1992.

**Mercedes D. Ojeda-Castro** received her B.A. in psychology with honors from Emory University in 1984 and her M.A. in developmental psychology in 1986 from Columbia University. She received a second M.A. in clinical psychology from the University of Michigan in 1988 and a Ph.D. in clinical psychology from the University of Michigan in 1995. She is a Psychological Resident at Psychological Affiliates, Inc., in Winter Park, Florida, a private practice setting serving children, adolescents, and adults with specialization in child abuse, spouse abuse, custody/divorce, and Munchausen by proxy syndrome. She also specializes in early childhood and play therapy. She is a member of the Board of Directors for United Cerebral Palsy of Central Florida and of the Advisory Board for the J. D. Holloway Early Intervention Clinic. She was also appointed by Governor Lawton Chiles to the Health and

Human Services Board of District 7. She is a member of the American Psychological Association, the Florida Psychological Association, the Association for Play Therapy, and the Florida Association for Play Therapy.

**Karen O. Palladino** is Director of Administrative Support Services for the Brevard County School District, Melbourne, Florida. She received a bachelor of arts from the University of Central Florida in elementary education, and an M.Ed. in special education and Ed.D. in elementary education from Mississippi State University. Her experience includes classroom teaching, school-based administration, and instruction of graduate students at several universities over the past 23 years. She holds certification in the state of Florida as a school psychologist, teacher for exceptional students and early childhood, and school administrator. In her current position, one of her responsibilities is coordination of the Hospital/Homebound Program for the school district. It is in this capacity that she first became aware of Munchausen by proxy syndrome and, with other professionals, identified students who had suffered MBPS abuse. She has provided educators, guidance counselors, and school psychologists with information that may help them to recognize troubled families. In November 1995 she was a copresenter, with Dr. Teresa Parnell, on the topic of Munchausen by proxy syndrome from the school system perspective at the 22nd Annual Conference of the Florida Association of School Psychologists. She has made numerous presentations to school district staff on the detection of MBPS abuse and now includes this topic in her work with graduate students as an adjunct faculty member of Nova Southeastern University.

**Teresa F. Parnell** received her bachelor of arts degree in 1984 from Flagler College and her master of science degree in clinical psychology in 1988 from the University of Central Florida. She received her doctoral degree in clinical psychology in 1990 from the Florida Institute of Technology. She is a licensed psychologist and certified county/family mediator for Psychological Affiliates, Inc., in Winter Park, Florida, a private practice setting serving children, adolescents, and adults with specialization in child sexual abuse, custody/divorce, domestic violence, trauma, and forensic issues. She is also an adjunct faculty member at Nova Southeastern University, where she teaches courses in a master's program, and is one of a team of psychologist consultants to the Orange/Osceola/Seminole County Multi-Disciplinary HRS/CPT Case Management Staffing. She has testified as an expert witness in criminal, dependency, and family courts. She is a past member, past president, and past vice president of the Board of Directors for Safehouse of

Seminole, a domestic violence shelter. Along with a colleague, she developed an educational program titled "Divided Loyalties: Promoting Shared Parenting Through Education," which is court approved for mandatory attendance by divorcing parents in Orange/Osceola/Seminole Counties. She has been involved in several applied research projects that have resulted in presentations at national and regional conventions as well as publications in professional journals. She is a member of the American Psychological Association, the Association of Family and Conciliation Courts, the Southeastern Psychological Association, the Florida Psychological Association, and the American Professional Society on the Abuse of Children.

**Matthew A. Seibel** received his B.S. in molecular, cellular biology from the University of Colorado in 1977. He received his medical degree in 1981 from Howard University College of Medicine in Washington, D.C. He served as Senior Pediatric Resident at the University of Florida, Gainesville, from 1983 to 1984. He is board certified in pediatrics and is a practicing pediatrician with the Orlando Health Care Group. He is on staff at Arnold Palmer Hospital for Children and Women, where his practice involves pediatric resident education. His consultation at Arnold Palmer Hospital has resulted in the diagnosis of numerous cases of Munchausen by proxy syndrome. Since 1988, he has been the Medical Director of the tri-county Child Protection Team. He performs medical evaluations and provides consultations for suspected child abuse victims. As an expert in child abuse, he frequently provides forensic testimony in dependency and criminal court proceedings. He has presented a number of papers at national conferences and has been recognized nationally and internationally for his medical expertise in the diagnosis of Munchausen by proxy syndrome. He is a Fellow of the American Academy of Pediatrics.

**Sue Whelan-Williams** is the Site Administrator for South Seminole Hospital, which is affiliated with the Orlando Regional Healthcare System (ORHS). She has been with ORHS since 1980, when she joined that organization's Child Protection Team as Junior Case Coordinator. In addition to functioning for years as a coordinator of interdisciplinary services on the diagnostic end of the child abuse continuum, she cofounded a support group for sexually abused adolescent girls. Her interest in Munchausen by proxy syndrome was captured when she became the first coordinator on the Orlando team to be involved in an MBPS case. In 1985, she became the first clinical supervisor of the Child Protection Team, and later that year she was promoted to Manager of the program, a position she has held since. In 1989, she also became the Administrator for Psychosocial Services at the Arnold Palmer Hospital for Children and Women, where, owing to her background in child abuse, she became the point hospital administrator for all Munchausen by proxy syndrome cases. She and Toni Baker developed a Munchausen by proxy syndrome protocol in collaboration with the Child Protection Team medical director and key community advocates. She has presented nationally and internationally on the subject of child abuse and the value of a collaborative approach to diagnosis/intervention. She is particularly interested in the dynamics of interdisciplinary practice in health care and the outcome of benefits of such synergy.

**Robin Wilkinson** is the Division Chief of the Sex Crimes/Child Abuse Division of the State Attorney's Office in Orlando, Florida. Her division handles child homicides, physical child abuse, sex crimes (including those with adult victims), and child pornography. She received her bachelor's degree in psychology from the University of Central Florida in 1979, and graduated from Florida State University College of Law in 1984. After graduation, she started work at the State Attorney's Office. She has been a prosecutor for more than 11 years, and has worked in the child abuse unit for more than 7 years. She has handled more than 400 cases in this area and been involved in the investigation and prosecution of approximately 10 Munchausen by proxy syndrome cases. She lectures in public schools and to law enforcement and other agencies on subjects related to child abuse. She is a member of the American Professional Society Against Child Abuse, the Florida Bar, the Orange County Bar, the Florida Sex Crimes Investigator's Association, and the Central Florida Association of Women Lawyers. She has served as a board member for the Response-Sexual Assault Resource Center, a nonprofit organization that aids victims in receiving counseling. She received an award for Outstanding Achievement in Government in 1994 from the Women's Executive Council of Orlando, Florida.